1813
Empire at Bay

1813
Empire at Bay

The Sixth Coalition and the Downfall of Napoleon

Jonathon Riley

PRAETORIAN PRESS

First published in Great Britain in 2013 by
The Praetorian Press
an imprint of
Pen & Sword Books Ltd
47 Church Street
Barnsley
South Yorkshire
S70 2AS

Copyright © Jonathon Riley 2013

ISBN 978-1-78303-397-3

Typeset in 11/13 Ehrhardt by Concept, Huddersfield, West Yorkshire
Printed and bound in India by Replika Press Pvt. Ltd.

Pen & Sword Books Ltd incorporates the Imprints of Pen & Sword Aviation,
Pen & Sword Family History, Pen & Sword Maritime, Pen & Sword Military,
Pen & Sword Discovery, Wharncliffe Local History, Wharncliffe True Crime,
Wharncliffe Transport, Pen & Sword Select, Pen & Sword Military Classics,
Leo Cooper, The Praetorian Press, Remember When, Seaforth Publishing and
Frontline Publishing.

For a complete list of Pen & Sword titles please contact
PEN & SWORD BOOKS LIMITED
47 Church Street, Barnsley, South Yorkshire, S70 2AS, England
E-mail: enquiries@pen-and-sword.co.uk
Website: www.pen-and-sword.co.uk

Contents

List of Maps vi

List of Line Drawings and Figures vii

List of Plates viii

Abbreviations ix

Foreword x

Acknowledgements xi

1. Europe Re-arms: the Aftermath of Napoleon's Crisis in Russia, December 1812–March 1813 1

2. Spain and Portugal, Winter 1812–Spring 1813 25

3. The Spring Campaign in Central Europe and the Battles of Lutzen and Bautzen, April–May 1813 41

4. The Austrian Mediation and the Congress of Prague, June–August 1813 64

5. The Campaign of Vitoria, May–July 1813 76

6. The Battles in the Pyrenees, 25 July–2 August 1813 100

7. The Battles on the Frontier, August–October 1813 130

8. The Battles of Dresden, Kulm, Dennewitz and the Katzbach, August–October 1813 143

9. The Battle of the Nations: Leipzig, 13–19 October 1813 165

10. The Strategic Flanks: North America and the Mediterranean, 1813 186

11. The Invasion of France, November–December 1813 201

Select Bibliography 212

Index of Persons 215

List of Maps

Map 1. The Central European Theatre of Operations   2

Map 2. The Spanish Theatre of Operations   25

Map 3. The Battle of Lutzen: fixing the Prussians, Noon–2.30 p.m.,
2 May 1813   44

Map 4. The Battle of Lutzen: the attack in the centre and the French
envelopment, 5.00 p.m.–7.00 p.m., 2 May 1813   46

Map 5. The Battle of Bautzen: actions up to 3.00 p.m., 21 May 1813 .   54

Map 6. The Battle of Bautzen: the allied withdrawal,
4.00 p.m.–7.00 p.m., 21 May 1813   60

Map 7. Wellington's March to Vitoria, 20 May–21 June 1813   80

Map 8. The Battle of Vitoria, 21 June 1813   86

Map 9. The Attack on San Sebastian, 25 July 1813 105

Map 10. The Battle of Maya, 25 July 1813 109

Map 11. The Battle of Roncevalles, 25 July 1813 111

Map 12. The Battle of Sorauren 27–30 July 1813 118

Map 13. The Pursuit after Sorauren, 30 July–2 August 1813 123

Map 14. Wellington's Attack across the Bidassoa, 5–7 October 1813 . . 139

Map 15. The Attack above Vera, 7 October 1813 141

Map 16. The Battle of Dresden: allied moves on 26 August 1813, and
the French counter-attack 147

Map 17. The Battle of Dresden: the French offensive, 27 August 151

Map 18. The Katzbach, 26 August 1813 155

Map 19. The Battle of Leipzig: the situation at dusk on 16 October 1813 177

Map 20. Valencia and Catalonia 187

Map 21. The Louisiana Purchase (*Muir's Historical Atlas*, 1974) 191

Map 22. The Continental System: Europe under Napoleon, 1806–1813   193

Map 23. Isaac Brock's contemporary map of British North America and
the northern United States, 1813 197

List of Line Drawings and Figures

1. Charles Minard's combination of data map and time-series which portrays the horrifying losses of Napoleon's campaign in Russia . .   3

2. The proclamation *An Mein Volk*   17

3. Wellington's March to Vitoria, 20 May–21 June 1813   78

4. Diagram showing a summary of Napoleon's moves between August and October 1813   161

5. The manoeuvre of the central position   163

6. The Battle of Leipzig: the allied attack plan, 18 October 1813   180

List of Plates

Black and white

Plate 1. The senior commanders of the sixth Coalition in Central Europe
Plate 2. Napoleon in 1813
Plate 3. King Ferdinand VII in prison at Valençay
Plate 4. British infantry at Vitoria, 21 June 1813
Plate 5. The Passage of the Bidassoa River
Plate 6. a and b. A Cossack and a Bashkir drawn from life in 1813 by William Schadow
Plate 7. The Battle of Castalla, 11–12 April 1813
Plate 8. The Battle of Dresden, 26–27 August 1813
Plate 9. 'Soldiers on the March to Buffalo'. American troops and their camp followers
Plate 10. Fort George, the British headquarters in Upper Canada

Colour

Plate 1. French conscripts
Plate 2. An English recruiting party
Plate 3. British soldiers of the 6th (Warwickshire) and the 23rd (Royal Welch Fusiliers) in the uniform of 1813
Plate 4. The British Royal Artillery in the uniform of 1813
Plate 5. The British Royal Wagon Train in the uniform of 1813
Plate 6. Line infantry soldiers and a light dragoon of the King's German Legion in the uniform of 1813
Plate 7. Infantry soldiers and a hussar of the Duke of Brunswick-Oels's Corps in the uniform of 1813
Plate 8. The Battle of Lutzen, 2 May 1813
Plate 9. Tsar Alexander I, the Emperor Francis I of Austria and King Frederick William III of Prussia meet at the opening of the Congress of Prague
Plate 10. Wellington at the Battle of Vitoria, 21 June 1813
Plate 11. 'Boney Receiving an Account of the Battle of Vittoria', by George Cruikshank
Plate 12. Austrian troops storming a redoubt at the Battle of Dresden, 26 August 1813
Plate 13. The Battle of Leipzig, 18 October 1813
Plate 14. Close-quarter fighting at Leipzig on 18 October 1813

Abbreviations

C.O.	Colonial Office
C.S.P.D.	Calendar of State Papers, Domestic Series
K.B.	Knight of the Most Honourable Order of the Bath
K.G.	Knight of the Most Noble Order of the Garter
MS, MSS	Manuscript(s)
S.P.	State Papers (followed by numeral denoting series)
T.N.A.	The National Archive (formerly the Public Record Office (P.R.O.)), Kew

Foreword

I first wrote about the campaigns of 1813 in my 1998 book *Napoleon and the World War of 1813: Lessons in Coalition Warfighting*. Since then I have learned more about those campaigns, especially through writing *Napoleon as a General* in 2007. Through my own experiences in Iraq and Afghanistan, I have also learned more about the nature of alliances and coalitions. Much of the basic research that I carried out remains, however, sound. Since I retain the copyright of this material I have not hesitated to use it, although considerably edited, in this book. Since this book is primarily about the downfall of Napoleon at the hands of the allies in Central Europe and Spain, I have not gone into any depth about the war in North America, merely setting out its place in the context of the global war against Napoleon; nor have I done more than sketch the supporting campaign in Valencia and Catalonia. I have, however, provided new maps to support the narrative and many new illustrations, some of which are published for the first time.

Acknowledgements

I would like to acknowledge with thanks for their help and patience the following people and organisations: Rupert Harding and the staff at Pen and Sword; Dr Malcolm Mercer and the staff of the Royal Armouries in H.M. Tower of London; Mr Philip Abbot, Mr Stuart Ivison and the library staff of the Royal Armouries in Leeds; the staff of the National Archives, Kew; the staff of the British Library; the staff of the Bodleian Library in Oxford; the staff of the Brotherton Library at the University of Leeds; Deutsche Fotothek SLUB for 'Napoleon in 1813', by Günter Rapp; the Stapleton Collection and the Bridgeman Art Library for 'The French Conscripts' and 'The Passage of the Bidassoa'; Science, Industry and Business Library, New York Public Library, Astor, Lennox and Tilden Foundations for 'The Recruiting Party'; Bildarchiv Preussicher Kulturbesitz/Kunstbibliothek, SMB/Knud Petersen for 'The Meeting of the Allied Sovereigns at the Congress of Prague'; the Trustees of the British Museum for 'Boney Receiving an Account of the Battle of Vittoria'; Sammlung Hecht Collection and the Bridgeman Art Library for 'The Battle of Dresden'; Bibliotheque Marmottan, Boulogne-Billancourt, Paris, France/Giraudon and the Bridgeman Art Library for 'The Battle of Leipzig'; William L. Clements Library, University of Michigan for 'Soldiers on the March to Buffalo' and 'Fort George'. Last but not least, my thanks go to Steve Waites, who drew all the maps to a high standard, as he has done with my last six books.

Chapter 1

'... we must conquer or be annihilated'

Europe Re-arms:
the Aftermath of Napoleon's Crisis in
Russia, December 1812–March 1813

The 29th Bulletin of the *Grande Armée*, issued from Molodetchno close to the Polish border on 3 December 1812, reached Paris on 16 December. In it Napoleon confessed that a disastrous calamity had all but destroyed the army in Russia, so that only his personal presence in Paris would forestall the consternation, perhaps even panic, that the Bulletin would cause. On 5 December 1812, therefore, the defeated French Emperor left his army at Smorgoni, appointing Marshal Joachim Murat, the King of Naples, to command the 60,000 or so men who represented all that was left of the *Grande Armée* after the debacle: perhaps one tenth of the total force of many nations that had set out the previous summer. Many have criticised his decision to leave the army but as Napoleon himself saw matters, it was the only thing to do. The Russians were in pursuit, albeit cautiously; Prussia and Austria – and therefore much of the rest of Germany – were showing signs of unreliability; and his implacable enemies the English continued their war against him both at sea and in Spain. Another army had to be raised, and quickly.

Although Napoleon's shattering defeat could not be hidden, it was by no means clear either that this defeat would prove decisive, or that a new European coalition was about to be formed. Napoleon's military potential was still huge: he controlled most of Germany, including the Confederation of the Rhine and parts of Prussia; Poland; Italy, Illyria and Naples; the Low Countries and Denmark; Switzerland; and half of Spain. His arch-enemies the English were now at war in America as well as Spain, and he controlled the mountain barriers of the Pyrenees and the Alps as well as the fortresses on most of Europe's major river lines. This great span of command certainly gave him the ability to raise new armies to replace the horrific losses of 1812 while his enemies were still far from united. The possibility that in early 1814 the armies of Austria, Prussia

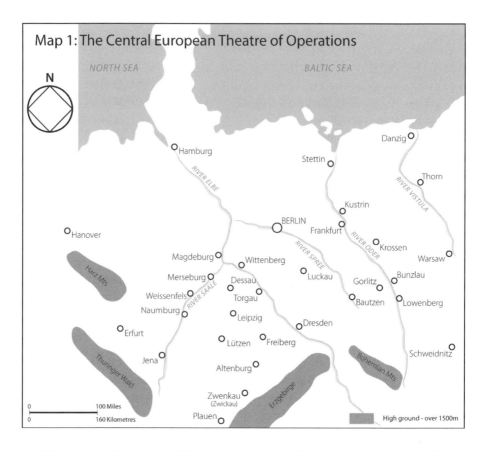

Map 1: The Central European Theatre of Operations

and Russia would cross the Rhine, while those of England, Portugal and Spain would march into Bordeaux, could scarcely have been imagined.

In 1806, when Napoleon had last conducted a campaign in Germany, he had been strategically and operationally on the offensive. Now, he was on the defensive, for it was not only his possessions in Germany that were under threat, but France herself. Almost as bad, Bonaparte's reputation had been seriously dented and it was this reputation – however undeserved – that was as important in keeping the empire in thrall as the numbers and capabilities of French and allied troops. Amazingly, in spite of such imminent danger of invasion, Napoleon's imperial ambitions remained and he had already resolved to recover both his prestige and the territory which he had lost. No thought of any compromise peace settlement entered his mind; complete victory was his aim. And indeed, there would be times during the forthcoming year when this would look distinctly possible. So a new army was to be raised from scratch, for the old army, which in its day had bludgeoned most of Europe into submission,

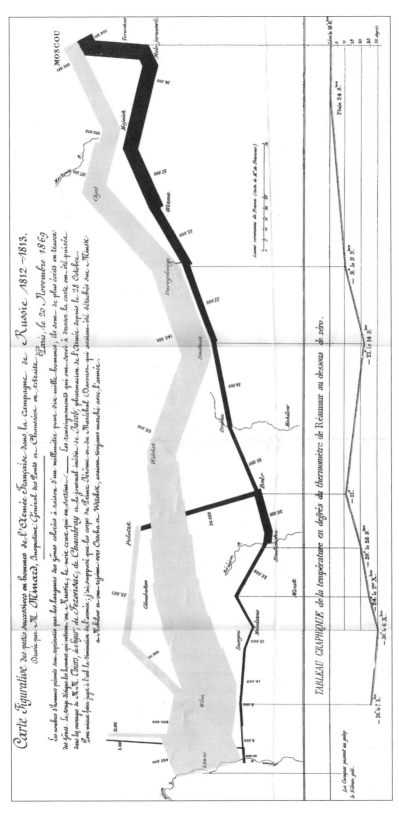

Figure 1: Charles Minard's combination of data map and time-series which portrays the horrifying losses of Napoleon's campaign in Russia. (*Author's Collection*)

had been to all intents and purposes destroyed in Russia. Little remained to form a nucleus – only 500 fit men were left of the 50,000-strong Imperial Guard Corps; I, II, III and IV Corps could muster a mere 6,400 men between them. But in any case, such troops that remained of the old army were required to keep the Russians at bay and thus buy time for the formation of the new army.

To restore the empire, therefore, Napoleon determined on a colossal force of 650,000 men to be distributed between Central Europe, Spain, Italy and the Low Countries. Of these, 200,000 – or to make him unbeatable, 300,000 – would be required for the Central European theatre, for it was here that the issue would be decided and here, therefore, that in terms of military strategy, Napoleon placed his main effort. Of course, a relatively well-trained and battle-hardened army of almost 200,000 men did exist – in Spain. But these men were needed on France's southern frontier to keep the English out. Other sources must therefore be tapped, although in the event, Napoleon was forced to weaken his Peninsular army, with serious consequences, by withdrawing the four remaining regiments of the Imperial Guard, as well as cadres of experienced NCOs, many of whom had to be commissioned to make good the serious shortage of regimental officers. To these cadres were added the first available fresh troops, some 137,000 conscripts drawn from all over the annexed territories, who had been called up during the Russian campaign and had now completed their training. In addition there were around 80,000 men of the National Guard, who were formed into eighty-eight new battalions; another twenty-four battalions were formed from 3,000 mobilised gendarmes and sailors from the blockaded fleet. Some 12,000 more sailors were formed into artillery batteries. These measures made good a large measure of the shortfall in the infantry and artillery; the reconstitution of the cavalry, however, appeared impossible and indeed the numbers and quality of the cavalry, both its horses and its men, were to remain a weakness for the rest of the war. The lack of mature, trained horses was chronic. Suitable draught horses for the artillery and commissariat were also in short supply, although the artillery was 'very good and numerous, though the draught horses were rather young'.

Still Napoleon looked for more. The conscription class of 1814 was therefore called forward early at the age of 16 – some were as young as 15 – and it was these youths whom the wagsters named 'Marie-Louises', after the Emperor's second wife. There was also a stiff combing-out of sick men and of those who had evaded conscription in earlier years. Last of all, the municipalities of France were required to produce 20,000 additional troops, along with 5,000 municipal guards, old soldiers retired on pension. Nor did the conquered territories, allies and client states escape. Napoleon is generally thought of as a general who, with a unified command, opposed a series of coalitions, rather than being himself an alliance or coalition commander. Because of his position at the centre of French power, he faced none of the difficulties that beset Wellington, or Prince Karl von Schwarzenberg. He was head of state and commander-in-chief; he called no councils of war but rather gave out demands for resources; he consulted no peers but rather issued decrees; and he had no need to placate any opinion – public or political. Not for him the difficult processes of compromise, consultation and subordination of separate interest to an over-riding common purpose faced by his opponents. However, it cannot be denied that from 1806 onwards, and certainly from 1812, Napoleon's armies were heavily reliant on manpower supplied by allies, client states or annexed territories. In doing this, Napoleon was, as in many other areas, not an innovator. From 1654 Richelieu and Mazarin had enrolled regiments and brigades of English, Irish, Scots, Spaniards, Italians, Corsicans, Walloons, Swedes, Danes, Poles, Hungarians and Croats into the armies of Louis XIV. By 1748 there were 52,000 foreign soldiers in the French army, to which were later added Turks, Wallachians, Tartars and black Africans.

Napoleon's wars began in order to guarantee the frontiers which the Revolution had won: essentially the Rhine, the Alps and the Pyrenees, the so-called 'natural frontiers' of France. It was soon apparent, however, that these frontiers did not in themselves guarantee security and so had to be extended through the creation of buffer states. These in turn had to be defended, especially against the enmity of the English and their coalition-forming activities, and thus was born the system of client states and allies. Clearly, neither France nor England was capable of defeating the other without the extensive help of allies, except perhaps by a long and ruinous war of attrition. Apart from the territories physically annexed to France, client states took two forms: first, satellite kingdoms and secondly, allies. The satellite kingdoms had usually begun as liberated territory under the Directory and were transformed into kingdoms by the imposition of members of Napoleon's own family as crowned heads. From these, Napoleon drew military manpower and obtained income. Italy, the most successful of the kingdoms, supplied a total of 142,000 conscripts and 44,000 volunteers over the years, and its contribution in 1813 was 36,000 conscripts for an army which numbered 90,000 men, of whom 10,000 were in Spain and 28,000 in Central Europe. Westphalia did even better: in 1813 the Westphalian army was 27,000 strong and the country also supported 30,000 French troops, making it the largest *per capita* supplier of manpower of all the satellite kingdoms and probably the most effective, as its troops served in every theatre of operations. Naples produced an army of only 11,000, of whom a mere 2,000 were Neapolitans and the rest Germans, Frenchmen, Corsicans, Italians and North Africans. Spain was poor ground: Spanish brigades served in the French Army of Spain and in the Baltic, but the French army in the Peninsula was never less than 190,000 strong and very French.

After the satellite kingdoms came the allies, of which the most numerous and militarily significant were in Germany. But there were others: Switzerland, after the creation of the Helvetic Republic in 1803, was more a satellite than an ally, providing 16,000 Swiss soldiers recruited directly into the French army. Napoleon's creation of the Confederation of the Rhine in 1806 united the small and medium-sized German states in an alliance which was protected by, and dependent on, France. Of its members, Bavaria contributed 20,000 troops, Baden 3,000 and Württemberg 8,000. Dahlberg, Berg, Hesse-Darmstadt and the rest of the smaller states, later joined by Wurzburg, Saxony and the Anhalt and Saxon Duchies, Oldenburg and the city of Frankfurt am Main, all had to find upwards of 4,000 men between them. Thus the confederation was partly a new security zone on the Rhine frontier, and partly a source of manpower – it made the *Befreiungskreig* of 1813 as much a German civil war as a war of liberation.

The creation of the Grand Duchy of Warsaw in 1807 marked the emergence of a greater Empire. It fired up Polish hopes for the re-creation of their country, but in reality it was merely a tool of Napoleon's diplomacy designed as a compromise with Russia – since its territory was formed mostly at the expense of Prussia – while at the same time drawing the Poles firmly into Napoleon's camp. But just as the creation of the Confederation of the Rhine guaranteed Prussian resistance, so the creation of the Grand Duchy of Warsaw was bound to offend Russia. In 1809 the Tsar had demanded a guarantee that Poland would never be revived as a kingdom. He never received any such assurance, but Napoleon never went further in the opposite direction, making vague statements to the Poles in 1812 which raised their expectations to the extent that they contributed 90,000 troops to the Russian expedition; the remnants of these were still fighting in Central Europe right up to the end of 1813. The total Polish contribution to the *Grande Armée* over a six-year period was some 200,000 out of a population of 2.5 million, and therefore no other satellite or ally gave its support so strongly to Napoleon.

The degree of Napoleon's reliance on his clients and allies becomes clear through an examination of the Central European army in 1813, which numbered between 230,000 and 280,000 at any one time, of whom between 75,000 and 125,000 were certainly French – but this included large numbers of Dutchmen, Catalonians, Illyrians, Belgians and northern Germans from the annexed territories. The remainder consisted of 8,000 Westphalians, 28,000 Italians, 12,000 Danes and 9,000 Bavarians, as well as a separate Bavarian army of over 20,000 under General Count Karl von Wrede, 13,000 Neapolitans, 15,000 Poles,

15,000 Saxons, 10,500 Württembergers, 7,000 from Baden, and 4,300 other Germans. Only one-third or less of the army can truly be said to have been French. These enormous figures make it impossible to believe that Napoleon could have fought either campaign with a truly French army. They also dispel any doubts about the importance of the Spanish war in keeping such large numbers of wholly French troops tied down. Not that all were completely trustworthy, for by 1813 only the Bavarian army under Wrede was allowed a truly independent role, as no doubt Napoleon was mindful of the defection of the Austrians and Prussians in Russia.

The method by which these vast armies were raised was conscription, which began as a one-off act of necessity in the *levée en masse* of August 1793. From its inception as an annual process in 1799 until April 1815 there were thirty-two levies on native-born Frenchmen, as a result of which around 2 million men passed through the ranks of the army. No other policy intruded the Napoleonic state so forcefully into the lives of people or the fabric of states, for it was imposed throughout the empire and the client states during the entire period of Napoleonic rule. Certainly, no other policy engendered so much hatred and it was without doubt a central issue of the Napoleonic strategic system and as such, a continuous problem for mayors and heads of departments who were obliged to enforce it – not to mention a devastating imposition for the millions of families touched by it. Not surprisingly, the scale of avoidance – either legally through buying substitutes or illegally through desertion – was massive, especially in the annexed territories and the policy was only maintained through heavy-handed enforcement. Napoleon himself had no interest in people's opinion or feelings: he was merely concerned to see that the system worked smoothly.

For Napoleon, coalition war was a vicious circle of necessity. The extension of the empire flowed from the nationalism unleashed by the Revolution, which he then tried to harness as a French-led pan-European super state. What Napoleon really aimed to create, however, was not a free association of nations, but an empire directed from Paris. The further the scheme was extended, fuelled by the need to make the Continental System watertight, the larger were the military forces required both to defend the existing territory and to extend it. This need, combined with the huge losses in Russia, Spain and Central Europe, wore down the ability of France herself to supply manpower for the armies to the extent that reliance on the annexed territories, clients and allies had to increase. The price of greater reliance was increased security guarantees, thus completing the circle. So if Napoleon had succeeded in sustaining his empire after 1813 it must be certain that, like his *Grande Armée*, it would before long have become an organisation two-thirds foreign.

To equip this host there was frenzied activity across France. The country became a vast workshop in which, as the Marquis de Caulaincourt, General and Grand Master of the Horse, wrote:

> ... the entire French nation overlooked [Bonaparte's] reverses and vied with each other in displaying zeal and devotion. It was as glorious an example of the French character as it was a personal triumph for the Emperor, who with amazing energy directed all the resources of which his genius was capable into organising and guiding the great national endeavour. Things seemed to come into existence as if by magic.

By dint of these means it began to look as if Napoleon might after all meet his target. But his new army had severe limitations: the troops were inexperienced, they were from an enormous variety of nationalities and the young boys and old men who now formed much of the army were less resilient than the veterans of previous campaigns, being especially unsuited to the sort of long-distance marching that a Napoleonic campaign usually entailed. Caulaincourt described the army as 'an organised mob'. But it was a more formidable force than it at first appeared and one whose morale was surprisingly good:

> Certainly, the new troops were not the equals in value of the bands destroyed in Russia, and, moreover, their constitution exposed them to a rapid exhaustion: nevertheless, they were good ... Anyhow, the army with which Napoleon opened the campaign was a good instrument of war; however, it had in itself serious germs of weakness.

It was not all bad news. Even as late as 1813, Napoleon enjoyed a considerable advantage over his enemies in the organisation of his army and of his staff. Again building on earlier foundations, in this case those of Marshal Maurice de Saxe, the French Army had instituted an all-arms divisional organisation in 1797, and in 1804, with his armies swollen by conscription, Napoleon created seven army corps each of up to five divisions. Each corps was in effect a miniature army organised for its task and the assessed abilities of its commander, normally a marshal. A corps would contain varying proportions of infantry, cavalry, artillery, engineers and bridging, with integral supply and medical units. The size of the corps could vary enormously, sometimes amounting to between one third and one half of the army. Because they were so well balanced, the corps were capable of fighting a superior enemy for some time and, as a basic principle, Napoleon would insist on corps being able to support each other. This meant moving a maximum of one day's march apart – about 35 kilometres. Thus a corps could survive on its own for some time until other help arrived, as Ney's corps at Lutzen would prove. This organisation allowed the French to move on several routes simultaneously, thereby easing the pressure on limited roads and providing each corps with a discrete area for foraging, a significant factor in the 1813 campaign where the commissariat was somewhat inadequate. General movement would also help confuse the enemy as to the exact location of the main effort. It thus enabled Napoleon to move his formations faster than his opponents, essentially enabling him to get inside their decision-making and implementing processes, even though, after nine years of campaigning, it might have been expected that his opponents would have learned something from their bitter previous experiences.

To achieve the concert of an army of ten corps or more, to direct and control it, to frame and transmit orders, to gather intelligence and provide supplies required an advanced apparatus of command and control. Orders were issued through the staff, which was fully organised and headed by Marshal Louis-Alexandre Berthier, the Army Chief of Staff. No document left the head-quarters nor was received by it unless it was properly logged and here the doings of the army were recorded scrupulously in war diaries and records of correspondence. Every corps had to submit a daily situation report, supple-mented by the reports of Napoleon's own aides. In June 1813, for example, Napoleon instructed General Charles-François Lebrun to report to him on Oudinot's corps: 'You will report to me on the status of his infantry, artillery, train, magazines and hospitals and also on his intelligence gathering in his corps area. In a word, you will report anything that could be of interest to me.' The problem, of course, was that the staff had no devolved responsibility, since everything was decided by Napoleon. He failed to develop his staff officers, just as he failed to develop his subordinate commanders. He was quite explicit about this, writing after Dresden, for example, that 'In my situation, no plan is acceptable in which I am not personally at the centre.'

The headquarters itself consisted of three principal branches. First, *le petit quartier général*, or Napoleon's personal headquarters. This can approximately be related to a modern tactical command centre, with the proviso that this one included many senior officers and was where Napoleon conducted his own planning. It contained three elements: the Statistical Bureau, responsible for strategic intelligence through agents, spies and missions abroad; the Secretariat or the Emperor's cabinet; and the Survey department, responsible for providing Napoleon with the best available maps. Next came *le quartier général du major-général* – the General Staff under Berthier, responsible for tactical intelligence, the issue of orders, the provision of information on the state of the army and all other matters of routine staff work. In many ways it was a larger replica of Napoleon's own personal headquarters. Berthier had three assistants: his own chief of staff who oversaw the processing of staff work and internal coordination; the Quartermaster of the Army, responsible for camps, cantonments and marches; and the director of the topographical department. Thirdly, there was *le quartier général de l'intendant*, the Administrative Bureau or headquarters of the Quartermaster General, responsible for all matters of supply, and the hospitals and medical services. In addition there were the staffs of the commanders of the Artillery, Engineers, Military Police and the Topographical Bureau. Below these came corps staffs which, although smaller, mirrored the functions of the army staff. This system of staff organisation is still the basis of most army staffs today, and indeed is still described as the Napoleonic model. However, there was then no staff college, nor any system of supplying trained officers for the staff.

In addition there were arrangements for Napoleon's travel in close proximity to the enemy for, like a modern commander, Napoleon needed the ability to separate himself and his tactical headquarters from the impedimenta of the main headquarters. With the Emperor were two aides, two duty officers, two interpreters, a page and a groom, Berthier or another senior staff officer, General Armand Caulincourt, General Claude-Etienne Guyot, commander of the horse-grenadiers of the Guard, and the duty marshal. About 400 metres behind came a group of staff officers and aides; and after another 400 metres, a group of Berthier's staff – all covered by an escort found by the horse-grenadiers. These arrangements were most necessary, for Napoleon insisted on personal reconnaissance at every opportunity. They gave him the flexibility that any general needs in order to move rapidly, with a reasonable degree of protection, in order to exercise command at wherever the decisive point of a battle might be – but for limited periods. In doing so he would reinforce his own intuitive powers of decision-making by ensuring that his own awareness of the situation was as current as it could be. Meanwhile the main headquarters, much larger, kept control of the army. Napoleon could use this main headquarters for planning, or could return to it to rest and recuperate under the umbrella of its life-support, or could base himself there to command the battle in, for example, a dispersed situation where the flow of information most naturally coalesced in the main headquarters through its communications network. This flexibility allowed Napoleon to do the three things that any general must be able to do in order to fulfil his command functions: to find out what is going on, to communicate his intentions to his subordinates, and to maintain contact with the staff so that problems can be solved.

Although the organisation was sound, the command and staff system was beginning to creak in early 1813. At lower levels the officer problem had been solved, at least in the short term – but the Marshalate was growing stale. Not that Napoleon intended delegating any responsibility to his marshals: he had never encouraged initiative, nor had he trained his senior commanders, just as he never instituted a staff college. He required only that his marshals should carry out his instructions. Baron Ernst von Odeleben, a Saxon officer, noted early in 1813 that: 'it appears that in this campaign the officers of Marshal Louis Berthier's headquarters staff were not so skilful nor so experienced as those who had formerly surrounded him ... As a whole, the army was too complex and imperfect a machine to permit true co-ordination during this campaign.'

In spite of all the imperfections of his armies, Napoleon retained one major advantage: his own self-confidence. By late April he would be in the field with the prospect of meeting the armies of three major powers: Russia, Prussia and England. Sweden, Spain, Portugal and Hanover were also against him, and the Austrians were far from friendly. This prospect would have crushed the spirit of other men and would have seemed hopeless to anyone who did not consider himself the mental superior to any combination of European monarchs. Furthermore he derived enormous advantage from two factors in the forth-coming struggle: first, his reputation, which as already discussed was, although dented, still formidable; and secondly, his habit of attending to all but the most trivial tasks personally. By contrast, the allies had to work as a coalition, not a situation which sat easily with autocrats. Napoleon alone, in spite of the presence of contingents from client states and conquered territories in his armies, was the sole co-ordinator of French policy and this to a great extent gave him the initiative.

*   *   *

Who then were the enemies who could thwart Napoleon's ambitions? First of course was England, his implacable foe, whose navy controlled the oceans of the world; who had seized every one of his overseas colonies; whose trade and subsidies continually raised new alliances against him; and whose armies had fought in alliance with those of Portugal, Spain, Sicily and Hanover, waging constant war against his southern flank in the Mediterranean. On 8 January 1812, while Napoleon was preparing to invade Russia, Wellington for the first time embarked on an offensive at the operational level into Spain. The fortress of Ciudad Rodrigo was captured on 19 January, followed, after a costly assault, by Badajoz on 6 April. Wellington's ability to push on eastwards in the face of an enemy that was numerically far superior was made possible by the increasingly competent Spanish regular forces fixing French troops elsewhere in Spain, while the simultaneous use of guerrillas – irregulars – against the French lines of communications posed French commanders with an insoluble problem: if they concentrated against Wellington, they exposed their flanks and rear to the guerrillas; but if they dispersed to fight the guerrillas, they opened opportunities for devastating attacks by conventional forces. On 17 June Wellington entered the city of Salamanca, knowing that General August Marmont's French army lay close by. The two armies shadowed each other for almost a month until Marmont attempted to out-flank Wellington on 22 July. Wellington seized the opportunity to attack and in the ensuing Battle of Salamanca won a crushing victory. Wellington entered Madrid on 6 August and even reached as far as Burgos before being forced to withdraw when threatened by combined French forces.

But to Napoleon, how did even the Battle of Salamanca compare to the enormity of the struggles on the Moskova or the Berezina? To both the French Emperor and Tsar Alexander I the 'Spanish ulcer' was still only an irritation. In the Central European theatre Napoleon's main – indeed only – opponent was Russia, but the Russian armies had suffered almost as severely as had the French during the terrible winter campaign. Russian troops were exhausted, supplies were low and the generals were unwilling to push on into the west. The Russians had learned hard lessons between 1807 and 1812: in their case the lessons of Austerlitz and the Polish campaign. In 1811, just prior to the French invasion, the army had undergone significant reorganisation, closely supervised by Tsar Alexander himself, who by his intervention (or interference) in military affairs often had direct results upon the tactical handling of troops. In the dying days of 1812, having seen the French off the sacred soil of Mother Russia, the Tsar saw himself as the liberator of Europe, or, as Chancellor Metternich called him, 'the conscience of Europe'. This desire to intervene in European affairs was greeted with nothing short of disgust by Field Marshal Prince Kutusov, who remained in overall command of the army, and it was probably just as well therefore that the structural reforms of the army were placed in the hands of General Prince Michail Barclay de Tolly. Barclay decided to abandon the existing concept of mixed divisions in favour of a corps structure similar to the French model. The Russian Army was an immense entity and it is by no means certain that Barclay's reforms had reached all areas by the time of the war of 1812. To give an idea of the scale of the Russian Army, its size in 1812 was 14 grenadier battalions; 92 infantry regiments, each of three or four battalions; 97 garrison battalions; 8 cuirassier regiments; 36 dragoon regiments; 56 Uhlan regiments; 11 hussar regiments; and an artillery train of 37 brigades.

In spite of the enormous losses of the 1812 campaign and a war in the southern provinces of the empire against the Turks, the Russian Army in 1813 had actually increased in size. In addition to the regular forces, one should not forget that the Russians made excellent use of irregular cavalry like the Bashkirs, Kalmachs and Cossacks, who gave the Allies valuable superiority in mobile, mounted troops. By no means all this enormous army was committed to pursuing the French in Germany. In February 1813, at the time of the conclusion of the Treaty of Kalisch, the Russian forces in the Central European theatre of operations numbered at most 70,000 infantry, 30,000 cavalry and Cossacks and 10,000 artillery and engineers – about 110,000 men in all. There was also a command problem within the army, precipitated by the increasing illness and frailty of Kutusov; by April he was so close to death that the Tsar was obliged to appoint a new Commander-in-Chief. The Tsar's choice was Lieutenant-General Prince Ludwig von Wittgenstein, son of a German general in the Russian service, to whose appointment the Prussians agreed. However, Lieutenant-General Count Alexander Tormassov, the commander of the Guard Corps, and Lieutenant-General Count Mikhail Miloradovich both stood on their seniority and refused to serve under Wittgenstein. A thoroughly unsatisfactory compromise was reached by which Wittgenstein was given command of all allied formations except those of Tormassov and Miloradovich, which were held under the Tsar's personal control.

These disagreements masked others, for the Tsar himself continued to interfere in matters of day-to-day command and surrounded himself with advisers whose counsel he seemed to prefer to that of Wittgenstein. These included Jean Moreau, the former French general and victor of Hohenlinden in 1800, who had lived in exile in America since being implicated in the royalist plot of 1804 in France. The Tsar had summoned him back to Europe and Moreau had agreed to serve. As well as Moreau there were also Major-General Count Karl von Toll, a German, and the British Major-General Sir Robert Wilson, who after the French invasion had managed to get himself sent on a mission to the Russian Army. He had reached Smolensk in August 1812 by way of Constantinople, where he tried to mediate in the Russo-Turkish War. As the British government was already pursuing this policy by diplomatic means, Wilson was told to confine his activities purely to the military mission; his Journal is a fascinating description of the campaigns of 1812 and 1813 from the Russian perspective. Given the lack of any distinctive Russian doctrine, the presence of so many advisers could only lead to confusion: and confusion was something that the allies, faced with an opponent of the calibre of Bonaparte and looking as they did to the Tsar for inspiration, could ill afford.

Then there was Prussia. In 1806 the army, which twenty years before under the great Frederick had been the embodiment of European military virtue, had been comprehensively thrashed by Frederick's greatest pupil – Napoleon. The terms of the subsequent Treaty of Tilsit were designed by Bonaparte permanently to emasculate Prussian military power and to consolidate French ascendency in Germany. It had the opposite effect. Led covertly by the redoubtable Queen Louise until her death, and then by Baron Karl von und zum Stein; fuelled by the influence of the poets Arndt and Körner; and permeated by the secret society of the *Tugenbund* – the League of Virtue – led by Stein, Prussian society had been regenerated. This is not to say that liberal ideas gained the ascendency, for this rejuvenation, led by the *junkers*, was not entirely what Stein had in mind. Political rejuvenation was mirrored in the clandestine military reforms introduced by Major-Generals Gerhardt von Scharnhorst and August Gneisenau. The Treaty of Tilsit had limited the army to a m iximum strength of 42,000 men, but by February 1813 Scharnhorst's *Krumpersystem*, begun in 1810, had produced a total available force of around 79,000 trained men by the simple expedient of compelling a proportion of trained regulars to retire each year and replacing them with recruits. This was the nucleus around which the new Prussian army would be built. Some 60,000 of the trained men were mustered into the infantry; the cavalry accounted for some 12,000 of the total and although the general shortage of horses after twenty years of war was felt here as in France, enough animals were available to ensure the efficiency of the cavalry, artillery and supply services. The artillery had in fact required a major rebuilding programme, having lost over 800 guns in 1806. By 1813, 236 guns were available. In terms of organisation, almost all the existing regiments and battalions had been disbanded and new ones formed; brigade, divisional and corps structures also rose from the chaos of 1806. Ironically, the rebuilding of the army had been assisted by Napoleon himself. In 1812 he had demanded a contingent for the campaign in Russia and had authorised the raising of an additional 33,000 men, over and above the limits imposed at Tilsit. The contingent for Russia had been formed into a corps under the command of Major-General Johann Graf Yorck von Wartenburg; the regiments themselves had been based on companies of other regiments, which had then been replaced by recruits, so that the whole regiment would not be mobilised and perhaps lost.

In parallel with the re-formation of the structures in the army, the old rigid discipline was replaced by 'a more enlightened attitude which stressed civic responsibilities rather than the former demand for feudal obedience; the lash had almost disappeared.' By 1813 the military had risen as high in popular esteem as it had been low in 1806. Moreover, a fair standard of expertise was now available among the senior commanders at division and corps level. Below Scharnhorst there were Karl von Clausewitz, at this time in the Russian service; General of Cavalry Gebhardt von Blücher, fired with hatred for Bonaparte; Yorck and Lieutenant-General Friedrich von Bülow, who, although less inspiring than Blücher, were at least competent as corps commanders and had benefited from serving under French command.

In 1812 the opinion-forming class of Prussia was seething with anti-French resentment and nationalist fervour: it was ripe for revolt. But there had been tension between King Frederick William III and his people since 1809, when the King had refused to join Austria in the war which ended at Wagram. Tension turned to rage when Frederick William had given in to Napoleon's demands for troops in 1811 – Gneisenau wrote in disgust that 'The King stands ever by the throne on which he never sat.' The example of the Spanish guerrillas had filled Prussian youth with hope and shame; now the spectacle of the invincible French army limping back in rags from Russia was enough, in a single night, to bring underground resistance into open rebellion. Although terror of the Emperor's name was enough to keep Saxony, Westphalia, Baden, Württemberg and Bavaria outwardly submissive, the flame of *Befreiungskrieg* – War of Liberation – was well and truly alight in Prussia. The flame was fanned by the unlikely figure of Yorck, whom Clausewitz described as having:

> a fiery and passionate will, hidden by apparent coldness; a powerful ambition, suppressed by constant resignation. He was distinguished by strength and boldness of character. But he was gloomy, choleric and reserved, a bad subordinate. He did not make friends easily. He was motivated by desire for fame and his natural abilities supplied the means for it. He was unquestionably one of the most distinguished men in our army.

Although the devastation of the French centre in Russia had been concealed from French commanders further afield, the Austrian corps under General of Cavalry Prince Karl von Schwarzenberg, and the Prussians, forming part of the right and left wings respectively, had been secretly supplied with information by the Russians, who used Clausewitz as their medium for talking to Yorck. In December 1812 Yorck, acting on this information, managed to separate his corps from Marshal Macdonald – the commander of the left wing of the army – and on 30 December he concluded the famous Convention of Tauroggen with the Russians. By this convention the Prussian corps became nominally neutral but in reality, although it took no part in operations against the French, it effectively changed sides. By taking such a course, Yorck was walking a tight-rope: the French would certainly have executed him for treason if they had laid hold of him, while King Frederick William, in dread of Napoleon and conscious that French troops were still garrisoned throughout Prussia, at first publicly disowned Yorck's action. At Tsar Alexander's headquarters during the winter of 1812/13 Count Karl Nesselrode had pushed forward the view that Russia alone would never force a settlement with France on any basis but the status quo. Such a settlement would not provide stability, for it would leave Napoleon's power base intact. Thus the objective must be to restrict Napoleon to at least the so-called 'natural frontiers' of France and the means to achieve that would have to be a coalition. The Convention of Tauroggen provided the opportunity to move from a truce into a treaty which would be the basis of that coalition. In private, Frederick William had already sent General Karl von Knesebeck to the Tsar's headquarters with a draft treaty of alliance, suggesting that Prussia would join the Russians in return not only for the restoration of Prussian territories lost in 1806 – which included much of western Poland and indeed Warsaw itself – but also territorial acquisitions in north Germany. The Tsar reacted unexpectedly to this proposal, knowing that, since opinion in Prussia was with Yorck, Frederick William was in no position to bargain. Stein was dispatched at once by the Tsar to Prussia, where he so frightened the King with the spectre of losing his throne to the French on one hand or his own people on the other that Frederick William was compelled to follow Yorck's lead. Thus Yorck, although by no means a major European military figure of the period, occupies a place of honour in the history of German nationalism as the initiator of overt revolt against Napoleon. It was his Convention that lit a fire which would, in time, make two wars – one Franco-Russian and the other in the Peninsula – into a European, coalition war.

While French forces had remained in Prussia, Frederick William had feared Bonaparte more than Russia, but by early February 1813 Russian pressure and the rising spirit of revolt had compelled the French to evacuate much of Prussia. On 3 and 4 February royal decrees augmented the regular forces by calling up 110,000 *Landwehr*, or militia, a figure which was later increased by the addition of volunteers, *Freikorps,* garrison and depot battalions to 156,000 infantry and 18,500 cavalry: altogether, just over 6 per cent of the Prussian population was under arms, an astonishingly high figure by modern standards. On 27 February Frederick William secretly joined the Tsar at his headquarters on the Polish frontier: the Treaty of Kalisch was signed and ratified the following day and on 16 March Prussia openly declared war; on 17 March Frederick William issued his proclamation *An Mein Volk* ('To My People'). Even so, the cautious Frederick William still had doubts, perhaps fearing another Jena. 'Well, gentlemen,' he remarked to his ministers, 'You force me to this course but remember that we must conquer or be annihilated.' He was perhaps right to be cautious, for although the nucleus of the Prussian Army was in the field by February, it would clearly be some time before Prussian strength reached its peak. During the interval, therefore, the brunt of any fighting would be borne by the Russians.

Figure 2: The proclamation *An Mein Volk.*

While Prussia and Russia prepared for open war, the Austrians were still obliged to opt for guile. After the disastrous campaign of 1809, the strength of the Austrian Army had been fixed at 150,000 men, for such had been the demands of war against France that the empire was practically bankrupt and the necessary economies had been chiefly made at the expense of the army. However, when Napoleon invaded Russia, Chancellor Metternich made an uncharacteristic miscalculation: he did not believe that Napoleon would secure an overwhelming victory, still less did he believe that Tsar Alexander would emerge victorious. His estimate was that Napoleon would score a partial success and, with this in mind, he set out to insure himself and his country with both sides. With Napoleon he made a limited treaty, by which Austria would supply a contingent of 30,000 troops under Schwarzenberg for the *Grande Armée*; but at the same time he assured the Tsar privately that 'Russia would find an active friend in the French camp without having to meet an enemy in war'. Indeed, the participation of the Austrian force in Russia can at best be described as half-hearted. This Austrian corps, 23,000 infantry and 7,000 cavalry, represented almost the total effective force of the Austrian Army. Lorraine Petrie says that: 'The corps of 1812 ... appears to have been excellent, whilst reserves and recruits were perhaps not far behind the corresponding elements of the Prussian Army. The cavalry was generally good, the artillery less so ...' Like Yorck, Schwarzenberg had reached an agreement with the Russians, although as his Emperor was Napoleon's father-in-law and was bound to him in formal military alliance, Schwarzenberg would put nothing in writing. Under the terms of this agreement, the armistice of Zeyes, Schwarzenberg retired on Krakow in late 1812 and from there into Bohemia, leaving the Franco-Saxon corps of General Jean Reynier to shift for itself, while the Polish division of General Prince Josef Poniatowski was left in Polish Galicia. This division became so isolated from the retiring French army that, although it escaped the worst of the destruction, it was unable to take part in the opening phase of the campaign of 1813.

Austria itself, even with the return of Schwarzenberg, was in a similar position. Unable to put an army of any size into the field in Central Europe and still maintain the security of her borders with Bavaria and in Italy, the Habsburg Empire had to assume a position of armed neutrality, posing as mediator between Bonaparte and the allies: for the French disaster in Russia which filled Tsar Alexander with hope filled Metternich with alarm. Metternich was in favour of a European settlement that would restore the *status quo ante bellum*. He was deeply concerned with the dangers unleashed by revolutionary sentiment following Napoleon's interventions in Italy and Germany; and Stein's vision of a united Germany under Prussian leadership was a further threat to Austrian dominance. In addition, Polish national feeling, which Napoleon had awakened by the creation of the Grand Duchy of Warsaw, threatened instability in the east. In a multi-ethnic entity like the Habsburg Empire, nationalist sentiment was a truly dangerous thing.

In late 1812 there was therefore a sense of danger in the possibility of Napoleon and Alexander making a separate peace on terms favourable to Russia, ignoring Austria, which was still, on paper, in alliance with France. Metternich responded with characteristic skill. He sent General Baron Ferdinand von Bubna to Napoleon, warning the Emperor not to take the Austrian alliance for granted, nor to assume that rivalry between Prussia and Austria was irreversible. At the same time he sent his foreign minister Count Johann Stadion to the Tsar, warning him that Napoleon was still dangerous and likely to raise a new army. His third emissary was the diplomat Baron Johann von Wessenberg, who was sent to London to suggest that a continental peace was now possible – a suggestion which was firmly rebuffed by a British government with no interest in making any peace with Napoleon which did not address maritime rights, the independence of the Low Countries and the British pledges to Sweden, Sicily, Portugal and Spain. At the same time, however, furious covert moves were in hand to rebuild the army and to subvert Bavaria and Saxony from the French cause. But for all these reasons it was not until after the ten weeks' truce in August 1813 that Austria joined the allies, thereby adding a field army which had grown to 270,000 men and 290 guns, tipping the balance fatally against Napoleon.

The last prospective partner in the coalition of 1813 was Napoleon's former Marshal, Charles Bernadotte – now Crown Prince and Regent of Sweden. Bernadotte's conduct as a Marshal of the Empire had, especially at Auerstadt, been marked by crooked dealing. Having failed to gain French backing for his attempts to annexe Norway to the Swedish crown at the expense of France's ally Denmark, and having lost Swedish Pomerania to French occupation in January 1812, Bernadotte was out for revenge. Between April 1812 and March 1813 he had concluded treaties with the Tsar and with England, giving him substantial territorial gains in northern Europe and the West Indies, as well as financial subsidies. Shortly afterwards he landed in Swedish Pomerania at the head of an army of 12,000 Swedes. To these he added 15,000 Germans recruited in Pomerania and the island of Rügen, and a contingent of 6,000 Mecklenburgers. The Swedish Army was, at the time, generally reckoned to be first class, but Bernadotte clearly had no intention of risking it in battle unless absolutely necessary. For him, membership of the coalition was purely a means by which he would gain more territory and a seat at the councils of the mighty. To do this, it was enough merely to be present in the theatre of war. Small wonder, then, that the Swedish contingent took no part in active operations until after the ten weeks' truce and even then did very little actual fighting.

Thus as the campaigning season approached, both France and the allies needed time to complete their reorganisation and rearmament. Strategically, time would usually be on the side of the allies, for the longer the war lasted, the more their strength would increase. For Napoleon, on the other hand, an early tactical success might be enough to shake coalition unity to an extent that would bring peace on his terms and guarantee his survival. His own dictum, that the essence of war consists of a careful and circumspect defence, followed by a rapid and audacious attack, seemed tailor-made for the occasion.

* * *

Napoleon's intuition was quite right, for the allies were, even as early as February 1813, suffering the difficulties of prosecuting coalition warfare: and this with only two allied armies in the field. The Russians, not unnaturally, were anxious to preserve their lines of communication through Poland. The Prussians, equally, were anxious to cover Berlin. Disagreements like this increased once Austria and Sweden joined the coalition and although the Tsar generally took the lead, perpetual councils of war continued to be a characteristic of allied operations. One practical method of achieving unity of purpose was agreed, the creation of mixed formations: Bernadotte, Lieutenant-General Count Friedrich von Kleist, Blücher and Schwarzenberg would all command corps or armies composed of troops of two or three nations. It was hoped that by mixing the troops in this way, the temptation for any one nation to act on its own account would be removed.

Allied moves in the early months were understandably cautious. After leaving forces to watch the isolated French garrisons on the Vistula and Oder, and in Danzig, the allies began to develop two distinct axes of advance. In the north Wittgenstein, reinforced by the Prussian corps of Blücher and Yorck to a strength of 50,000 men, moved through northern Prussia. Further south the main Prussian line of advance lay from Warsaw to Kalisch and on into Saxony. Here the advance was led by the Russian corps of Lieutenant-General Baron Ferdinand von Winzingerode. It was fortunate indeed for the allies that Napoleon himself was not yet in the field, for their forces were so far separated as to be beyond mutual support. In the event of a major engagement, Napoleon would have punished them by adopting the strategy of the central position and destroying the allied armies piecemeal. As it was, a planned junction of the allied forces was forestalled by a much inferior force under General Eugène de Beauharnais, which gained the time Napoleon needed to prepare for what he believed would be his masterstroke.

When Napoleon had left Smorgoni, he had entrusted command of the remnant of his old army to Murat. This rump force was to delay the Russians for as long as possible, and as far to the east as possible, in order to gain time for the rebuilding of the *Grande Armée*. A glance at the map shows that this would be no easy task: there was little or no ground which seemed suitable for delaying operations between the Bohemian mountains and the Baltic, and although the area is crossed by a series of defensible river lines – the Vistula, Oder, Spree, Elbe and Saale – there were plenty of crossing places and too few French troops to cover the ground. Murat hoped at first to defend the Vistula, but the news of Yorck's defection warned him to withdraw west of the river. Garrisoning the fortresses of Thorn and Danzig with the remnants of Marshal Jacques Macdonald's corps and a few fresh troops from East Prussia tied up his best men; he then fell back in early January 1813 towards Posen. There Murat handed over his command to Prince Eugène de Beauharnais and returned to Naples. Why Napoleon allowed the command to pass to his stepson, the inexperienced Eugène, is not clear, as older and wiser heads were available in the shape of Marshals Laurent St Cyr and Louis Davout.

Eugène took up his command on 16 January 1813. After only two weeks Russian pressure from Cossack troops, which Eugène, with only 2,000 cavalry, found impossible to counter effectively, forced him to withdraw to the Oder with about 30,000 men all told, including the remnants of the Guard Corps. He concentrated his force around Frankfurt-Oder, where he was joined by St Cyr with two weak infantry divisions. Another 13,000 men were tied down in the fortresses of Stettin, Krossen, Kustrin and Glogau – where there were also 9,000 men commanded by General Jean Reynier. Behind Eugène's force, forming an operational second echelon, lay the garrisons of Berlin, about 6,000 men under Marshal Jean-Pierre Augereau, and Spandau, about 3,000 strong. Further back still in a third echelon at Magdeburg on the River Elbe was General Jaques-Alexandre Lauriston's V Corps. Last of all, there were around 2,000 Saxon troops still in Swedish Pomerania, as well as Poniatowski's Polish division in Galicia, but these formations were so far away that they were unusable in the short term.

Napoleon laid out his views on the delaying operation in his correspondence, telling Eugène that he should defend the Oder from the eastern side in order to gain time for the move-up of V Corps from Magdeburg. But Eugène's inexperience led him to retire west of the Oder, encouraged by Augereau, who feared an insurrection in Berlin. Napoleon was furious when this news reached Paris but, even as new instructions were being sent to Eugène, word of the Convention of Kalisch decided Eugène on a further withdrawal, west of Berlin. This encouraged the allies and further enraged Napoleon, who wrote that 'if ... you had taken up a position in front [to the east] of Berlin the enemy would have had to believe you wished to fight a battle. You could have gained twenty days which would have been very advantageous from a political, as well as military point of view.' Allied reaction was to send out a forward detachment of 7,000 cavalry and Cossacks and about 5,000 infantry, hoping to rattle the French and keep them moving. Sure enough, Eugène gave way before this weak force, abandoning the garrisons of Frankfurt-Oder and Krossen; this time he did not stop until 10 March, by which time his whole force was behind the Elbe.

From north to south, Eugene had about 82,000 men under his command, but they were well dispersed over a frontage of 360 kilometres and in various stages of readiness. Much of his combat power was dissipated in isolated garrisons and he had no designated reserve available. On hearing of these dispositions, which showed how little Eugène understood Napoleon's intention, Napoleon himself condemned them absolutely. Although he still underestimated the strength of the enemy, he spelled out what was required in a series of letters on 9 March. Eugène must establish a blocking position east of Magdeburg; to his rear, Marshal Claude Victor's reinforced division would guard the Elbe as far south as Torgau; from Torgau to the Bohemian mountains Reynier's two divisions would screen the river, but were not to attempt to hold the city of Dresden if the enemy advanced against it in strength; last, behind Victor, Davout's VII Corps would concentrate around the junction of the Elbe with the Plauen canal. These dispositions had two purposes. First, and most immediately, both Victor and Davout, while denying the passage of the Elbe to the enemy, would also maintain bridgeheads at Torgau, Wittenberg and Dessau so as to be able to cross the river in support of Eugène if necessary. Secondly, the enemy would be forced by Eugène's position to cross well above or well below Magdeburg, thus opening up a flank for Victor or Reynier to attack. In the longer term, although Eugène's task was still to delay the allies, his remit did not include fighting a major battle. If the allies came on in strength and forced him from the Elbe, he was to withdraw towards the lower Rhine, drawing the enemy after him. The last thing Napoleon wanted was for Eugène to fall back towards Erfurt, where his own developing plans required the concentration of the revitalised *Grande Armée*.

It was not until 18 March that Eugène put these arrangements in motion and it was no easy task to re-concentrate his scattered army. More importantly, it was not until 31 March that he himself moved east of the Elbe. By this time the allies, who for a week had been squabbling among themselves, had also begun to move. Disagreeing with the ailing Kutusov, Wittgenstein decided to march south-east of Magdeburg in order to fix Eugène's main body. Simultaneously, he would throw a bridge across the Elbe at Rosslau so that, once he and Blücher had joined forces, he could cross the river in strength. As Wittgenstein's troops moved forward, they met Eugène's force of about 50,000 men, now including 4,000 cavalry and 180 guns. The result was the action around Möckern on 3, 4 and 5 April. This confused series of battles ended at nightfall on 5 April with Eugène's withdrawal back over the Elbe, precipitated by a false report that Wittgenstein was crossing the river at Rosslau. Eugène took up a new, strong, position on the lower Saale, but St Cyr's troops had been forced out of Hamburg and Blücher had occupied Dresden. Eugène had certainly gained some time for his master, but had still not produced the Emperor's desired conditions, for he had drawn only a part of the allied forces against him rather than the main body. The allies, because they had still not concentrated, were as much responsible for their own salvation here as was Eugène; and they could claim a victory at Möckern with the resulting moral effect in Germany. It was not until 19 March that the assembly of the allied armies began in earnest and by that time Napoleon's own plans were already laid.

*   *   *

As early as 11 March, in a letter to Eugène, Napoleon had outlined a grand scheme for the reconquest of Germany and Poland. Circumstances, however, forced him to modify this design, not least because the strength of his army was still insufficient. However, by early April the new Army of the Main consisted of four corps: Marshal Michel Ney's III Corps, 45,000 strong; Marshal Auguste Marmont's VI, 25,000; General Henri-Gratien Bertrand's IV, 30,000; and Marshal Nicolas Oudinot's XII, also 25,000. In addition there was the Guards Corps at a strength of only 15,000 and two weak cavalry corps. There were also the troops on the Elbe: I Corps under St Cyr, with a strength of 20,000, along with General Horace Sébastiani's II Cavalry Corps on the lower Elbe. With Eugène's army there remained General François Rouget's division of the Guard with a strength of 3,500 men, General Michel Latour-Maubourg's I Cavalry Corps of 4,000 men, the V and XI Corps each 22,000 strong, and parts of II and VII Corps.

This entire force totalled around 200,000 men and although it outnumbered the allies, who were still strung out on the line of march, it had several inherent problems: it was itself dispersed; it was 100,000 men short of the strength that Bonaparte himself had envisaged as being necessary; and it was chronically short of cavalry. Napoleon had already, in his correspondence with Eugène, shown that he lacked the detailed knowledge of the enemy which only cavalry reconnaissance could bring him; moreover he was less and less able to keep the raiding Cossacks away from his lines of communication. General Antoine Marbot recorded a letter on this subject to his ally King Frederick of Württemberg, in which Napoleon said that 'I would find myself in a position to finish matters very quickly if only I had 15,000 more cavalry; but I am rather weak in this arm.' Even so, by 13 April Napoleon had enough information from Eugène to indicate that a major allied advance was in progress across the Elbe towards Jena, and it gave him the opportunity he sought. His orders called for an immediate concentration of the army west of the Saale. From there he intended to detach the corps of Bertrand and Oudinot southwards in the direction of Bayreuth to distract the allies. He himself would then advance on Leipzig and Dresden with the main body of the army, seize the crossings over the Elbe in the allied rear and cut their lines of communication. This would force one of two things: either an immediate allied retreat over the Elbe with such a resulting loss of cohesion as might lead to the breakup of the coalition amid mutual acrimony and mistrust; or a major battle on terms favourable to the French: 'My intention is to refuse my right and allow the enemy to penetrate towards Bayreuth,' he wrote. 'The result will be my arrival at Dresden ahead of him, and his severance from Prussia.'

From the destruction of the enemy army, either in battle or in retreat, at least five important operational and strategic consequences would follow. First, it would allow Napoleon to advance initially on Berlin and then on the Vistula, thus recovering his territory and the 50,000 or so experienced troops who still held out in the isolated garrisons. Secondly, a quick victory would blood his new army and give it confidence. Thirdly, his own wavering allies – Saxony, Bavaria and the rest – would be brought into line, while the designs of Austria and Sweden would be thwarted. Fourthly, the treachery of Frederick William and of Bernadotte would be punished – a lesson that would not be lost on others. Last, but by no means least, his own reputation and prestige would be restored.

Chapter 2

'... in Fortune's Way'

Spain and Portugal,
Winter 1812–Spring 1813

The 29th Bulletin did not reach King Joseph Bonaparte in Madrid until 6 January 1813 and news of the Emperor's return to Paris did not get through until 14 February. Joseph had, therefore, no idea of the ruin which had overtaken his brother's armies in Russia. Even if he had, it is doubtful that events

Map 2: The Spanish Theatre of Operations

would have fallen out differently, for if 1812 had been a disastrous year for French arms in Eastern Europe, it had not exactly been a startling success in Spain. Napoleon's involvement in Spain dated from the series of treaties in 1800 under which Spain subsidised French military operations and which effectively transformed the Spanish armies, and more particularly the navy, into adjuncts of the French. The treaty of San Ildefonso ceded the Spanish territories in Louisiana to France on condition that they would not be disposed of to any other party. This arrangement ended in humiliation for Spain, for the Louisiana purchase in 1803 was a direct violation of the San Ildefonso treaty, which Spain was powerless to prevent. Worse followed, for naval co-operation ended with the destruction of the fleet at Trafalgar and the loss of colonies in the West Indies. These losses stirred up anti-French feeling in Spain, but in 1806 Napoleon was at the height of his power and was in no mood to be defied. Anti-French sentiment gave him just the excuse he needed to consolidate his power over the whole of the Iberian Peninsula, complete his Continental System, exclude the English and dominate the Mediterranean. He achieved these ends through the Franco-Spanish expedition against Portugal. With French troops in the Peninsula, it was only a step to the agreement of 5 May 1808 by which Charles IV abdicated in favour of Joseph Bonaparte, and then another step to the imprisonment of the rightful heir, Ferdinand VII, at Valençay. Thus Napoleon overran first Portugal and then Spain by treachery.

The consequences of Napoleon's actions were the reverse of what he had intended. He managed to trigger first a popular revolt in Spain, and then the English intervention in Portugal. The events of early 1808, culminating in the convention of Cintra, had freed Portugal from the French and allowed the country to be used as a base for operations against the French in Spain itself. This had begun with Sir John Moore's autumn campaign of 1808. Moore's intention had been to sever the French communications through Burgos, forcing them back towards Bayonne, but the plan had been allocated inadequate forces and ended in the evacuation of the English from Coruna in January 1809 and the death of Moore. Having driven the English off, the French, commanded by Marshal Nicolas Soult, had once more invaded Portugal, only to be pushed out by Sir Arthur Wellesley (hereafter referred to as Wellington), who had then himself invaded Spain. His move seemed successful when he fought and won the battle of Talavera, but a further advance on his flank by Soult's forces forced Wellington to retire back into Portugal. During 1810 the French attempted to consolidate their position in the Peninsula but the following year, after emerging from the lines of Torres Vedras, Wellington succeeded in clearing Portugal of the French for good.

Looking back, 1812 had proved as much a turning point in Spain as elsewhere. As we have already seen in Chapter 1, Wellington had not been able to exploit the success of Salamanca and, as a result, at the end of the year the French military command still felt relatively in control as far as the English were concerned – at least on land. But after four years of hard campaigning, what had they really to show for their pains? The fortresses on the Portuguese frontier were in allied hands; Spain south of the Tagus had been lost; and 20,000 prisoners had been shipped off to England in the last year alone, men desperately needed in Europe. General Maximilien Foy wrote that 'Lord Wellington has retired unconquered ... having restored the Spaniards the country south of the Tagus, and made us destroy our magazines, our fortifications – in a word all that we have gained by our conquest, and all that could assure the maintenance of it.' Looking forward, things did not seem any brighter. The French army in Spain had already been heavily milked of manpower for the Russian campaign, and as the campaigning season of 1813 approached, the army was again plundered both of formed units and cadres of veterans as Napoleon desperately strove to rebuild his army in Central Europe. Secondly, the English exercised absolute control over the seas, so that all communications had to be across land. This laid them open to the third difficulty: the Spanish guerrilla war.

During 1810 and 1811 there had been signs that French control was gaining ground in Spain, especially in Catalonia, where there was a long-cherished ambition of independence from Castille, and that the establishment of order and normal government was supported by people weary of war. However, anti-French sentiment and support for the guerrilla war remained strong and French retaliation against the civil population as well as organised plunder by the commissariat did nothing but increase Spanish hostility: in December 1808 the Spanish Council of Regency had given legal existence to the guerrillas and after the allied victory at Salamanca in 1812 – a blow from which French prestige never recovered – the guerrillas were filled with new confidence. Certain that Wellington would return, virtually the whole country came out in arms against the French. The guerrillas were able to surround and destroy isolated French garrisons, throw down bridges, ambush marching troops, prey on supply convoys and depots, loot and burn whenever a weak spot was exposed. Many guerrilla bands were actually regular troops acting as irregulars; conversely, over time the most successful guerrilla bands – or more accurately *partidas* – became competent enough to act as regular troops. So bad was the menace that in order to keep the communications open, every village along the main roads had to be garrisoned, every road regularly patrolled, every convoy – even despatch riders – escorted in force. When, in 1812, Marmont tried to institute a regular commissariat and supply system, the internal security situation had deteriorated to such a degree that this too, with its reliance on supply routes, was an easy target for the Spanish irregulars. The guerrillas probably maintained a force of around 50,000 men under arms at any one time, and their activities cost the French around 145,000 casualties over the five years from 1808 to 1813; they were probably also responsible for the deaths of at least 30,000 *Afrancescados* – collaborators – which should be borne in mind when considering the Spanish civilian casualties at Ciudad Rodrigo and San Sebastian. The greatest contribution of the guerrillas was in helping to present the French with a tactical dilemma which they could not solve – what modern terminology calls simultaneity – through the interaction of Allied regular and irregular forces. This was a technique that the native warriors also demonstrated in North America: if the French concentrated to fight the allied main armies, their communications and rear areas were vulnerable to the guerrillas; if they dispersed to contain the guerrillas, they became vulnerable to destruction by a strike from Wellington's main force. Wellington's great achievement in this respect was to induce the guerrillas to take part in a concerted plan and then, during the course of 1813, to bring them gradually into the regular army.

It was because of this domination by the guerrillas that Napoleon's dispatches to his brother in early January did not reach Madrid until the middle of February. These dispatches were of considerable importance to Napoleon, for they carried his instructions for the reorganisation of the French army in Spain and its role in supporting his campaign in Central Europe. First were details of the troops which Joseph was to send back to France: all the remaining Young Guard units; two or three complete infantry battalions and between thirty and forty cadre battalions; fifteen cavalry squadrons and a complete division of dragoons; six batteries of horse artillery; the majority of the German and Polish auxiliary units serving in Spain; and finally twenty-five picked men from every battalion of infantry and regiment of cavalry, and ten from every artillery battery, for the Imperial Guard. Next, Napoleon ordered his brother to concentrate the armies and to place the main headquarters at Valladolid, only holding Madrid as an extremity of his line. He was also to divert large numbers of troops into the Basque regions to put down the guerrillas and thus secure the lines of communication.

By March 1813 the French army in the Peninsula consisted of five formations. First, the Army of Portugal, under General Honoré Reille with his headquarters in Salamanca, numbered between 35,000 and 40,000 men divided into eight infantry divisions, a cavalry division and a division of dragoons. This army was deployed behind the Tormes and Esla rivers in order to watch the allied forces in northern Portugal and Spanish Galicia, but four of Reille's divisions had been diverted to support the Army of the North in anti-guerrilla operations. Next came the Army of the South, which was now commanded by General Théodore Gazan, since its former commander Marshal Soult, along with Marmont, had been recalled to Central Europe. This army was around 37,000 strong, and deployed behind the Tagus and Tietar rivers to observe the allied armies in central and southern Portugal and southern Spain. Thirdly, the Army of the North under Marshal Count Bertrand Clausel secured the line of communications back from Burgos to Bayonne. This army was around 40,000 strong, but most of the men were tied down in fortresses and garrisons along the main routes and in the fortresses of Biscay and Navarre. Clausel was able, however, to maintain a reserve of 6,000 men at Bayonne. Fourthly, the Army of the Centre under General Drouet D'Erlon numbered 16,000 men and was well spread out covering Madrid, connecting the other armies with mobile columns and operating against the guerrillas in central Spain. Finally there was the Army of Aragon and Catalonia under Marshal Louis Suchet, tasked with holding the line of communications through Perpignan. Suchet had about 64,000 men in all, but most were tied down in garrisons and in anti-guerrilla duties, leaving him only 18,000 men available for field force operations. All these armies were predominantly French, but there were still significant numbers of foreign troops present. There were several Spanish regiments (not all Spaniards hated Bonaparte and what he stood for); there were also two Italian divisions under Generals Giuseppe Palombini and Filippo Severoli; and in spite of the withdrawal of many German units, there were still Baden infantry and artillery regiments, Nassau infantry and cavalry and a battalion of Frankfurt troops, all with the Army of the Centre. There were also infantry regiments from Würzburg, Nassau, Berg and Westphalia with Suchet's Army in Catalonia.

Napoleon's continued insistence on trying to command the Spanish theatre by remote control along guerrilla-infested communications did little to help King Joseph. Moreover Napoleon consistently under-estimated the powers of both the guerrillas and Wellington. With the departure of Soult, Souham and Marmont for the Central European theatre, there were few generals on the French side capable of manoeuvring a corps, let alone an army, and thus Napoleon probably felt he had no choice but to give precise directions. Suchet could manoeuvre a corps, and Clausel had also proved his ability in 1812, but such a task was far beyond the capacity of Joseph Bonaparte, as Napoleon well knew. However, the Emperor insisted that Joseph should make a demonstration towards Portugal in order to tie down the allies, a proposal which Joseph greeted with some heat:

How am I to make a demonstration towards Portugal? To do so I must in the first instance concentrate the troops which is impossible owing to want of victuals. And what is the use of it, if I make such a demonstration? Wellington will not be deceived, for he knows that the whole Army is engaged in the north and that I have had to send large drafts to the Emperor ... I hope Clausel may succeed, but I doubt it, and I am afraid that his divisions will be exhausted when they have to meet Wellington.

Thus as the campaigning season drew on, the French army of 198,000 men was dispersed throughout Spain and Joseph could assemble at most 32,000 infantry, 9,000 cavalry and 100 guns without depleting his anti-guerrilla operations. This at a time when he knew that the allies had been reinforced and could be expected to move at any moment. Nor, given the impossibility of scouting in guerrilla-infested country, could he determine Wellington's intentions – so what should he do? Defend the Douro with his available striking force and risk destruction? Stop his anti-guerrilla operations and concentrate the army? Or retire behind Burgos, wait until the guerrillas had been smashed and then advance? These questions were not answered until those very answers had become irrelevant.

* * *

French military operations had also to contend with the factors of climate, weather and terrain – factors that bore equally, of course, on their opponents. Portugal and northern Spain are mountainous, arid, poor, thinly populated and difficult to cross. In the northeast of Portugal the highlands of Beira Alta and Tras-os-Montes, which rise above 2,000 metres (6,000 feet), are a continuation of the Castilian Plateau, while further south the Beira Baixa and Alentejo regions are part of the same geographical area as the Estremadura region of Spain. The central mountain range that slices Portugal diagonally in two, the Sierra da Estrela, is a westward continuation of the Gata, Gredos and Guadarrama ranges of Spain. Similarly the two principal rivers – the Tagus and the Douro – are also Spain's. Thus the strategic and operational geography of the peninsula cannot be divided. The political border between Spain and Portugal is one based on language rather than geography but it is dominated by high, rough and dry terrain for most of its length. Roads are few, and in the nineteenth century they were poor even by the standards of the rest of Europe at that time. Rivers and streams, usually deeply incised, ran in torrents that obstructed movement for a few months of the year and then, perversely, dried up during the heat of summer, leaving deep channels that had to be traversed without the benefit of anything to drink for the parched soldiers and animals who had to struggle over them. It could take a whole day for even a moderate army to cross a river obstacle, even if the river was low.

The area of Portugal and north-western Spain in which the action of 1813 unfolded has two climatic zones. The northern zone is Atlantic, characterized by an average annual rainfall of 991 mm (39 inches), with temperatures influenced by the ocean air currents and the Spanish Meseta. The smaller, southern zone, which has a Mediterranean climate with hot, dry summers and mild, wet winters, has weather conditions influenced by high pressure systems that develop over the Azores. Average temperature ranges in Lisbon are from 8 to 14° C (46 to 57° F) in January, to 17 to 28° C (60 to 82° F) in August. From mid November, rain, cold and sometimes snow restricted the ability to move on the roads, as well as being outside the growing seasons; it was because of this that the rivers and streams became torrents impossible to cross except on the very few bridges at this time of year, so that campaigning often stopped. Traversing the country only became possible from mid-April, but even in spring, heavy rain could turn roads into bogs. In summer, high temperatures and the lack of food and water could make armies cease campaigning again: these conditions of climate combined with geomorphology had historically produced two short campaigning seasons of spring (mid April–mid June) and autumn (mid September–late November) unless the armies could move into better-watered and better-supplied areas. Unless this could be done, or supplies could be brought from elsewhere, the campaigning seasons were restricted by the insatiable demands for food – of which more will be said at the end of this chapter.

*   *   *

The French had many problems, but they retained one considerable advantage: that of a unified command. As already outlined, there were foreign contingents in the armies, but they formed part of a single force with one chain of command, even though the armies in Catalonia and Aragon remained largely autonomous because of geography. This level of integration was not the case for the opposing coalition forces, which included British, King's German Legion, Brunswick, Portuguese, Sicilian and Spanish formations. In theory, Wellington exercised supreme command over all allied forces, but such were the differing political aims of the partners that this was at times more a command in name than in fact – certainly as far as the Spanish were concerned. For them, the war was a struggle against foreign occupation in which allied contingents were minor players. For the Portuguese it was similarly a struggle against occupation – by either France or Spain – but as time went on the war receded from their borders and its immediacy diminished. For the British, it was the only land theatre in which they could make a significant contribution to the defeat of Napoleon. Although France and Spain had been at war at various times since the early seventeenth century, for ten of the twelve years before 1808 Spain had actually been allied to France and at war with England. Religious difficulties underscored national rivalries and above all the overweening pride of the Spanish nation made close co-operation with England difficult in the extreme. It must be ranked as a considerable French achievement that their policy and behaviour were so humiliating that they brought this coalition together against them. As General Count Francisco Castaños had remarked to his French prisoners after the battle of Baylen, 'Let not Napoleon persevere in aiming at a conquest which is unattainable. Let him not force us into the arms of the English. They are hateful to us ...' Almost equally hateful to the Spanish were their partners against the French, the Portuguese, with whom a series of wars had been fought since the sixteenth century and which twice before had involved English intervention against Spain.

The revolt of the Spanish people against occupation had been given political expression and a voice in the councils of the allies by the assembly of a *Cortés* or parliament at Cadiz, representing the free parts of Spain and the colonies. This *Cortés* swore to uphold the Catholic religion, restore national territorial integrity, and remain loyal to the exiled King Ferdinand. The *Cortés* promulgated a new constitution in 1812 which was a statement of uncompromising resistance to Joseph Bonaparte, who, although hated as a foreign usurper, represented, by a supreme irony, a system that stood for many of the ideals of liberty which the constitution of 1812 embraced. The same could hardly be said for the exiled Bourbons, whose first act on regaining the throne was to suspend this constitution.

The Spanish regular army, as opposed to the guerrillas, has generally received a bad press from the early years of the Peninsular War. Wellington had tried to co-operate with Spanish field armies but had given up at the end of 1809 after a series of frustrations, let-downs, outright cowardice and major defeats of Spanish arms by the French. At Talavera, he had reported how: 'Two thousand of them ran off – not one hundred yards from where I was standing, who were neither attacked, nor threatened with an attack, and who were only frightened by the noise of their own fire.' However, as time went on, both the Spanish armies and the guerrillas improved and gradually became highly effective in keeping large numbers of French troops tied up, thus helping to create more favourable force ratios for pitched battle. The field armies were, at least on paper, numerous: the 1st Army under General Francisco Copons in Catalonia numbered 10,000; the 2nd Army in Murcia under General Francisco del Elio was around 20,000 strong; General Diego Del Parque's 3rd Army in Morena had 12,000 men; General Francisco Castaños's 4th Army, the largest with a strength of 40,000, was deployed with one division in Estremadura and seven divisions in Spanish Galicia; finally the Spanish reserve corps of about 8,000 men remained in Andalusia. There were many defects: the organisation was overstaffed and highly bureaucratic and although Spanish formations were subordinated to Wellington, true integration like that of the British, Portuguese and German formations was rarely achieved, with the exception of artillery batteries.

Salamanca had brought a major change in the allied relationship. On 22 September 1812 the Council of Regency had created Wellington Generalissimo of the Spanish armies. This for the first time in four years gave him – in theory – real authority, at least to co-ordinate the activities of all the allied forces, but still he had no great confidence in the ability of his major partner in terms of political will or military high command in spite of the growing fighting prowess at grass roots level. 'I do not', he wrote,

> expect much from the exertions of the Spaniards. They cry *viva* and are very fond of us, and hate the French; but they are, in general, the most incapable of useful exertion of all the nations I have known; the most vain, and at the same time the most ignorant, particularly of military affairs, and above all of military affairs in their own country.

He later added: 'The Spanish armies are neither disciplined nor provided nor equipped in such a manner as that they can perform any operation even of the most trifling nature if there should be any opposition on the part of the enemy.' How far this view changed during the course of the year will be seen as the campaigns of 1813 are examined.

Wellington had accepted the post of Generalissimo, pending the approval of the Prince Regent, with reluctance, but having accepted, he was determined that his power over the Spanish armies must be made real and for this he intended to turn the financial screw – all future subsidies from Britain to Spain would be used only to support Spanish troops actually fighting alongside the Anglo-Portuguese army. He was also determined to control personally all senior appointments and promotions and to have the power of dismissal over Spanish commanders. To help him in this he determined on having a Spanish chief of staff appointed to his own headquarters. Finally he was absolutely set on having the large numbers of senior Spanish commanders and staffs reduced and the armies organised into proper fighting formations. He put these unpalatable demands in person to the *Cortés* in December 1812, which accepted them with some variations. But there was one significant problem: the Council of Regency which had created Wellington Generalissimo had been replaced in March 1813 by the *Cortés*, which appointed a puppet council while itself retaining all real authority. Effectively, therefore, when the allied armies took the field in 1813, Wellington was able to exercise command over only two Spanish divisions in his own army and three more of the Army of Galicia. The reserve corps in Andalusia in particular did not join him until late June, so that only 90,000 out of 160,000 Spanish troops under arms were actually available.

* * *

The English relationship with Portugal and the Portuguese army was entirely different. England and Portugal had been allies since the Treaty of Windsor in 1386; English troops had made a decisive contribution to the Portuguese War of Independence between 1662 and 1668, and again during the War of the Spanish Succession. The Portuguese economy relied heavily on English subsidy, and English prestige was high after the expulsion of the French. People were generally well aware that freedom from French rule depended absolutely on the alliance, and the English policy of paying for all forage made the army generally popular, in contrast to the French. The Portuguese army had been re-formed and re-trained by an English Generalissimo, Lord Beresford, who was also Viceroy. Wellington's authority over it was absolute, since being given overall command by the Portuguese government in 1809 – a rare state of affairs indeed in coalition warfare. The Portuguese government remained responsible for all aspects of supply, pay and equipment of their own national troops, but these troops were equipped and trained entirely to British standards and, formed into brigades, they were fully integrated into British divisions to the extent that, as Wellington said, '. . . it is nearly indifferent what the Portuguese government does; and I never give myself the trouble of writing to them, or of consulting their opinion on any subject whatsoever.'

The relationship was not without difficulties. Under Beresford as Viceroy, Portugal was almost completely militarised and the effort drained the nation: the population, for example, fell from 3.2 million in 1807 to 2.9 million in 1814. At local level, the daily movements of troops and the inevitable lapses of discipline caused friction with the populace. The want of money to pay and supply the army was also a source of difficulty, for in spite of its responsibilities the Portuguese government frequently could not pay its troops: Wellington was forced to threaten appeal to the Regent of Portugal in Brazil unless action was taken. This threat achieved the desired result, but one has to sympathise with the Portuguese: all available money went to the army, leaving the civil administration starved. Even so, large subsidies and loans were required from England just to maintain the *status quo*. This was made more galling to Portuguese pride by the fact that British officers filled nearly all senior command positions to the exclusion of the Portuguese themselves. It is hardly surprising that as the campaign of 1813 progressed and Portuguese troops fought further and further from home, enthusiasm for the alliance and for the coalition war, especially on behalf of Spain, began to diminish.

By 1812 the Portuguese element of the allied army was significant. It consisted of over 18,000 men formed into a Portuguese infantry division; a cavalry brigade of three regiments; an artillery battery; two battalions of *caçadores*, or light troops; two independent infantry brigades; and seven infantry brigades, each of two line battalions and a light infantry battalion, one brigade in each of the British 2nd, 3rd, 4th, 5th, 6th, 7th and Light Divisions. These troops formed therefore around 35 per cent of the main army. This level of integration had taken five years and much shared hardship to achieve.

* * *

In January 1813, after almost twenty years of fighting against the French, the total strength of the British Army was 255,000 men; it rose to 260,000 by the end of the year. Of these, 65,000, or a quarter of the total, were in Spain and Portugal. Another 29,000 were in the East Indies; 23,000 in the valuable colonies of the West Indies; and 37,000 in the Mediterranean forming garrisons in Gibraltar, Malta, Sicily and the Ionian Islands, of whom 7,000 had been detached to Spain. Some 80,000 men remained in Britain, including Ireland, of whom 55,000 were regulars and the rest embodied militia, but this total included not only the troops required for home defence, internal security and police duties, but also depots, recruits under training and convalescents. The remaining 21,000 were distributed between British North America, the Cape, Madeira, New South Wales, West Africa, Heligoland and the garrison of the city of Stralsund in Swedish Pomerania.

The army in Spain was, after five seasons' campaigning, an experienced and highly capable force of eight infantry divisions, a light division and a cavalry corps. As already noted, it contained significant numbers of Portuguese troops, as well as one brigade each of infantry and cavalry, with supporting artillery and significant numbers of light infantry, found by the King's German Legion and the Brunswick-Oels Corps. The retreat from Burgos in the autumn of 1812 had caused great disruption and losses in the army, to which Wellington had turned his full attention during the winter. The normal turnover of manpower across the whole army was around 24,000 per year, an enormous problem to overcome even when after 1811 militiamen could be used for foreign service. Within the theatre, James McGrigor, Wellington's chief of medical staff, had cleared the hospitals in spite of losses of 400–500 men per week during

December 1812 and January 1813; the returns for 1 January 1813 indicated a sickness rate of 30 per cent, reducing to 16 per cent by June after the decentralisation of the hospitals, which some authorities attribute to the continuing high incidence of Walcheren fever, a form of malaria contracted by many soldiers during the expedition to the Low Countries. At the same time, the newly appointed Judge-Advocate, Francis Larpent, had cracked down on discipline, hanging and flogging deserters and plunderers, assisted by the creation of a new staff corps of 200 officers and men to take on military police duties. Between them, McGrigor and Larpent had managed to ensure that as many veterans as possible were returned to the Colours. This was highly necessary in view of the large numbers of new recruits coming into the theatre. Enlistment for the army had done exceedingly well in 1812 and for the first time in the course of the war a surplus of 2,000 men had been produced over and above the recruits needed just to replace battle and sickness losses. In the West Indies the scourge of diseases like malaria and yellow-jack were horrifying: 13,000 out of the original 20,000 British soldiers sent to San Domingo between 1793 and 1798 are estimated to have died from these diseases. A total of 45,000 British soldiers are believed to have died there between 1793 and 1803 – half of those sent to the island. This figure rose to a total of 75,000 by 1815. This was a staggering drain on the military manpower of Britain during the period and must at least in part explain the difficulties in raising the strength of the peninsular army above 50,000 until 1813.

Allowing for the needs of the navy, even normal wastage could barely be met from recruiting and impressment, so that any increases in the army could usually only be made by enlisting colonials and foreigners. In 1804 there had been 17,000 of these, or 11 per cent of the army; by 1813 this figure had risen to 53,000, or 20 per cent, and included not only 8,000 KGL and Brunswickers, but also 8,000 blacks in the West India Regiments, fencible and regular regiments in British North America, West Africans, French exiles, Italians, Dutchmen, Greeks and even Albanians. Better recruiting had been accompanied by adjustments to the Militia Laws in England, which governed the employment of the 69,700 militiamen, with the result that many more regular units were being released from home service. By March 1813 only 25,000 regulars were retained for home defence. All these measures resulted in a substantial reinforcement to Spain, especially of cavalry, so that the British and KGL troops with the main army now numbered 65,000. Other improvements had been set in train to accompany the reinforcement. A proper pontoon train had been organised for river crossing; a train of heavy artillery and a small corps of sappers and miners had been formed for siege operations; the commissariat system had been improved by the Commissary General, Sir Robert Kennedy, and the

Chief of Staff, Major General George Murray, who had been reinstated after a period of absence in Ireland. For the first time, for example, the troops were issued with tents. But the supply system depended absolutely on command of the seas and in 1813 this was being disrupted by American privateers.

As well as difficulties in the relationships among the allies, there also remained problems in the relationship between Wellington as field commander and the Duke of York as Commander-in-Chief of the Army in Whitehall. Even though Wellington had a staunch ally in the Military Secretary, Colonel Henry Torrens, one of the chief difficulties lay in the appointment of senior commanders. 1813 was the first year in which Wellington was able to send unsatisfactory generals home and thus cut out some of the dead wood in his organisation. There also remained difficulties over regimental organisation, but in general terms this issue was also resolved to Wellington's satisfaction. Finally, in addition to the main army, Wellington commanded an Anglo-Sicilian army at Alicante of 7,000 British, 2,000 KGL, about 1,000 Sicilians – including Croat and Swiss mercenaries and French deserters – and 8,000 Spanish troops under the immediate command of Lieutenant-General Sir John Murray. All these except the Spanish were troops which Lord William Bentinck had despatched from the British garrison in Sicily; Wellington had received authority in August 1812 to take them under his own command. Bentinck, as commander of the British Army in Italy, was not keen to see them go as he had great plans for a descent on the Italian mainland during 1813, which the news from Russia only served to encourage. Wellington, however, was quite clear that the army in Alicante would have a vital role to play in tying down French troops that might otherwise be sent against him; he made the case successfully against their withdrawal in the strongest terms to Lord Bathurst, the Secretary of State for War and Colonies.

With the reinforcements he received during the winter of 1812/13, Wellington's force, although just enough to do what he wanted of it, was close to the limit of what he could support logistically. Much of southern Spain produced large amounts of food and fodder, in spite of years of French occupation; the north was more barren and less productive, and could barely support a large force and feed the civilian population. Agricultural surpluses – such as they were – could be bought by the military commissariat but a static military force, for example one engaged in a siege as opposed to an army moving through the territory, would rapidly consume these. The extra food required would have to be brought in along the tenuous line of communication across the mountains, or better still by sea.

While Wellington had carefully and correctly determined where and when his combat forces should be positioned, it was quite another matter for him to get them there and then sustain them. The risks involved in his logistic calculations were huge, and logistic supply had therefore to be a major factor in his operational planning and execution, just as it was for his opponents. In Joseph's case things were further complicated by expeditionary warfare on hostile territory dominated by guerrillas. Both commanders had to ask themselves a series of questions, therefore, concerning what supplies were available or could be expected; the available transport by land and water; the length, security and nature of the line of communication; the available manpower and the time needed to bring up replacements; and the medical arrangements for dealing with wounds, non-combat injuries and diseases. The organisation of the force and its general administration mattered as much then as now.

Before he could launch any operation, Wellington and his quartermaster-general had to determine how the army was to be fed, clothed, armed, ammunitioned, resupplied, reinforced and cared for. Had they not done this, his force would rapidly have ceased to be effective. Modern doctrine summarises the factors governing the development of any logistic plans and systems as demand, distance, duration and destination. Wellington would not have thought of things in those terms, but he was clearly aware of the principles, as his correspondence with the Horse Guards shows. Above all, by planning carefully according to these factors, operations had to be kept within reach of adequate sustainment. Beyond this reach, the troops would receive inadequate supply and operations would culminate rapidly. Relying solely on supplies carried along the bad roads of early nineteenth-century Iberia made any army vulnerable and this to a large degree explains Wellington's push northwards in his campaign of 1813, in order to open up supply directly from home through the Basque ports.

Given the numbers of people and animals in a field army of the time, the most bulky logistic problem was food and fodder. Most professional soldiers agreed that a satisfactory ration for a soldier consisted of about 1 kg or 2 lbs of bread, ½ kg or 1 lb of meat and 4½ litres or 1 gallon of water per day – of which the most important ration item was bread: wheat, barley or rye, in loaves of 1, 1½ or 2 lb. The daily ration had to be supplemented by meat or other protein, and beer or wine since water was seldom safe to drink unless sterilised by alcohol. Based on eighteenth-century French figures for requisition, an army of around 20,000 people and 9,000 animals could consume 40,000 lbs of bread, 10,000 lbs of meat, 50,000 bushels of oats, 70,000 lbs of hay and 100 barrels of wine or small beer *per day*. When advancing through friendly territory, the army could buy or requisition from the local area, or draw on the stocks held in depots and fortresses. In enemy territory, organised plunder was the general rule, but this was an orderly process in which units were allocated an area. Random plundering not only caused indiscipline and problems with the population, but was inefficient. Because of the quantities needed, local supplies of animal fodder were the most important resource: a horse required a daily ration of about 20 kg (50 lbs) of green forage, or 4 kg (10 lbs) of hay, plus 2.5 kg (6 lbs) of oats and 1.75 kg (4 lbs) of wheat or barley in its stead in winter – and three bundles of straw every week. Horses could graze on the march but in camp, foraging was required every third or fourth day. Armies foraged to the front and flanks, leaving the rear intact to support a retreat. It was therefore every army's insatiable appetite for green forage that restricted the campaigning season to the growing season – and in parts of Iberia this was confined to the months between the cold of winter and the hot drought of high summer – the two short campaigning seasons in the spring and the autumn.

To supplement requisition, the armies of both Wellington and Joseph needed a system of depots and units to transport logistic stocks and distribute them to the point of use. Inseparable from this was the need to understand the environment in which any campaign would take place. This informed, for example, route selection, security and maintenance; the effects of terrain, obstacles, climate, weather, and altitude all had to be taken into account. In Iberia at that date this was a huge challenge. Not only were roads of poor quality and few in number, but for the French, they were subject to frequent attack. The guerrillas who interdicted the French supply routes would no doubt have appreciated and understood the tactics used by the Taliban in Afghanistan, or Iranian-backed insurgents in southern Iraq in 2006. The problem of feeding the army has probably undergone the biggest change in the intervening years, for with the technology to can, dry, condense and freeze food, the field ration requirements for the combat elements of a modern infantry brigade of around 3,000 men for one day will be a mere ten pallets, and thus can be carried on a single 8-tonne supply vehicle. This was far from the case in 1813, when only drying, pickling and salting of meat or fish were feasible. Therefore even with a system of depots, living off the land was an absolute necessity. A force of even 5,000 men in the Basque countryside of 1812 could not possibly carry all its food for men and horses, without ceasing to do everything else. Secondly, for an army in the field, a standing crop (other than grass) was not the same thing as food: the men had to spend time gathering raw materials, grinding corn, baking bread, slaughtering animals, salting meat and so on.

Finally there was the problem of medical support, the task of which was to maintain the fighting strength of the armies both by preventing and curing sickness, and by returning the wounded to duty. Good medical services thus contributed not only to the physical strength of the army, but also to its moral strength, by reassuring the soldiers that they would be well cared for in the event of sickness or wounds. This is one area in which modern practice has changed the face of war: in Wellington's day a badly wounded man would expect to die – of blood-loss, shock, thirst or subsequent infection. Nowadays, these factors only apply to irregular combatants in remote parts of the world, such as the Taliban in Afghanistan or the Revolutionary United Front in Sierra Leone. Soldiers in regular armies can expect treatment at every stage from the point of wounding to a fully equipped hospital, with systems in place for rapid evacuation. Provided he is identified, and put into the medical system, the odds are that he will live. In 1813 a soldier who entered the medical system would generally die slightly later than he would otherwise have done, unless his wounds were relatively light.

In all, Wellington could count on an effective striking force of 113,000 allied troops for the campaign of 1813 – more if all the Spanish armies could be brought into the field. The Royal Navy enjoyed command of the seas, and he had the almost total support of the Portuguese and Spanish people and, with that, the ability to harry the French communications and gather intelligence on their movements while concealing his own intentions from his enemies. The force levels were relatively small beer when compared with those in Central Europe, but even so, these were advantages which he fully intended to use. 'I propose', he wrote, 'to take the field as early as I can and at least place myself in Fortune's way.'

Chapter 3

'After such a slaughter, no trophies?'

The Spring Campaign in Central Europe and the Battles of Lutzen and Bautzen, April–May 1813

On 1 May 1813 Napoleon issued orders to the Army of the Elbe to complete its passage over the River Saale and, led by a strong advanced guard, to move on Leipzig in three columns. In the north, the first column was to be composed of General Jacques-Alexandre Lauriston's V Corps, Marshal Jacques Macdonald's XI Corps and the Imperial Guard. These formations would all cross the river at Merseburg and move directly on Leipzig. In the centre, the second column was to be made up of Marshal Michel Ney's III Corps followed by Marshal August Marmont's I Corps, which would cross at Weissenfels and head initially for Lutzen. Further south, the third column was to be formed by General Henri-Gratien Bertrand's IV Corps and Marshal Nicolas Oudinot's XII. These two corps would cross near Naumberg and head north-east. Napoleon was aware of some kind of allied presence near Zwenkau, but incomplete intelligence, probably due to the inexperience of his cavalry and their faulty reconnaissance, failed to reveal that at Zwenkau lay Field Marshal Prince Ludwig von Wittgenstein's powerful allied army of four Prussian corps, 75,000 strong, supported by a further Russian corps in reserve. Napoleon therefore determined to maintain his momentum and push on to occupy Leipzig, relying on Ney to protect his southern flank against this undefined threat.

The advance was contested strongly in several places by the allies, especially at Poserna, just to the east of Weissenfels. Here 45-year-old Marshal Jean-Baptiste Bessières, commander of the Imperial Guard Corps, who had soldiered with Napoleon since 1796, was killed. Napoleon felt his loss sorely and 'regretted him more than [did] the army, which', as Baron Marbot remarked, 'had never forgotten that it was the advice of this Marshal on the evening of the Battle of the Moskova, that had prevented Napoleon from completing his victory by sending in the Guard.' In spite of this fierce opposition, the French successfully crossed the river, but Napoleon began to have second thoughts about his right flank. He therefore issued new orders for 2 May. While Lauriston and Macdonald pressed on to Leipzig, Ney was to pause at Lutzen in order to allow Marmont to close up with him. Ney was further ordered to occupy the villages of Kaja, Rahna, Gross Gorschen and Klein Gorschen. Later, in a subsequent order, Ney was also instructed to send a strong force to reconnoitre towards Zwenkau and Pegau. This Ney failed to do – possibly he did not receive the order. Even so, Napoleon had little real expectation of a major enemy attack from Zwenkau, but should this happen, Ney was to pin the enemy frontally with his own and Marmont's corps, while Napoleon manoeuvred the other corps from the north and south to attack the enemy in both flanks.

Meanwhile, patrols of allied cavalry were busy probing the Lutzen area. In due course they reported to Wittgenstein that the main body of the French was pressing on towards Leipzig and that a weak flank guard was positioned in the area of Kaja. Another strong force was detected even further south, near Teuchern, which in fact was Bertrand's corps. The allied assessment was substantially correct, for not only had Ney failed to push out the reconnaissance screen as he had been ordered, but also he had retained three of his five divisions in Lutzen itself, sending two out into the villages. Wittgenstein decided therefore to annihilate this flank guard, being unaware of Ney's three rearmost divisions. His orders were for General Count Friederich Kleist's Prussian corps to hold Leipzig in the north, while General Count Mikhail Miloradovich's Russian corps was to move forward towards Zeitz to block Bertrand. The rest of the allied army, around 48,000 infantry, 24,000 cavalry and nearly 500 guns, was to press on towards Kaja, clear the French from the area, then cut the main Lutzen–Weissenfels road before turning northwards to attack the flank and rear of the French main army.

Thus, after a sequence of events which provide a salutary lesson in the necessity for high quality reconnaissance forces, the scene was set for a classic meeting engagement. A meeting engagement occurs when two forces moving forward on the line of march, each with incomplete information on the enemy, collide. Victory goes to the side which is quickest to react to the situation and exploit the opportunity thus created to pin the enemy and destroy him. It was the sort of battle in which Napoleon, who welcomed the chaos of war as an ally, showed his genius.

On 2 May 1813 the allied army had been due to begin its move very early, at 1.00 a.m. The army was to have completed its assembly around the village of Kaja at 7.00 a.m. that same morning. It proved a highly over-optimistic time-table, for in the manner of these things the move in darkness became very confused. It was not until 11.00 a.m. that the leading corps reached their forward assembly areas south-east of Lutzen. The area around Lutzen had changed little since Gustavus Adolphus had fought his last, fatal, battle there in 1632; it has probably changed little today in spite of the impact of forty years of socialist collective agriculture followed by rapid modernisation since 1991. The open, arable land slopes gently from north-west to south-east; the few villages are of stone houses with narrow, cobbled lanes and stone-walled gardens. A few hedges cross the area, notably along the Flossgraben stream, which winds sluggishly past Klein and Gross Gorschen. This stream would have been a hindrance to wheeled vehicles and guns and would have disrupted infantry and cavalry formations, but it in no way constituted an obstacle. Some authorities speak of an escarpment to the east, and contemporary illustrations of the battle do depict a range of hills to the north. In reality there is neither escarpment nor hills, only a low crest about 2 kilometres south and east of Gross Gorschen, which marks the course of the Flossgraben.

It was this low crest that Wittgenstein's scouts climbed just before midday. All that could be seen were around 2,000 French infantrymen busy cooking their dinners. There were no signs of sentries or supporting units, nor had the French placed piquets on the crest. Confident of a speedy victory, Wittgenstein ordered General of Cavalry Gebhard von Blücher to send in his horsemen and sweep this paltry force aside. But as it moved forward into the attack, the Prussian cavalry suffered a severe shock. Instead of a bunch of frightened con-scripts, the cavalrymen found themselves facing two complete French infantry divisions – which were themselves every bit as surprised as the Prussians. Just as at Auerstadt in 1806, Blücher had sent in his cavalry unsupported. To his credit, however, Blücher quickly realised that the tactical situation had changed, so he halted the cavalry and sent for his artillery. This delay gave just enough time for General Joseph Souham's French division to occupy Gross Gorschen while General Jean-Baptiste Girard's division occupied Starsiedel. Messengers were sent at once to bring up the rest of Ney's corps and the whole of Marmont's corps.

By mid-day the action opened afresh. Allied cavalry moved in a wide arc to attack Starsiedel, where Girard's men easily held their ground until at around 12.30 p.m. they were joined by the leading regiments of Marmont's corps. In Gross Gorschen, however, Souham's soldiers were forced out of the village by heavy Russian artillery fire. As Souham was evacuating the village, Ney arrived on the scene, leading up the three reserve divisions in time to check the retreat. With his usual impetuosity, Ney at once ordered his whole corps to counter-attack: soon a desperate hand-to-hand battle was raging in the villages of Gross Gorschen, Klein Gorschen and Rahna.

Napoleon, en route for Leipzig, was undoubtedly surprised by the volume
of cannon fire he could hear from the south. When he reached Markranstadt,
some 5.5 kilometres north-east of Lutzen, on the heels of Lauriston's V Corps,
news reached him from Ney of the unexpected developments on his right flank.
After a few moments' thought, he issued his orders. Ney and Marmont must at
all costs continue to fix the enemy. The Guard was to march at once to Kaja.
At the same time Macdonald would swing his corps south from the Leipzig
road to attack the allied right flank, while Bertrand moved up from the south to
take the allied left. Finally, Lauriston would detach a single division to screen

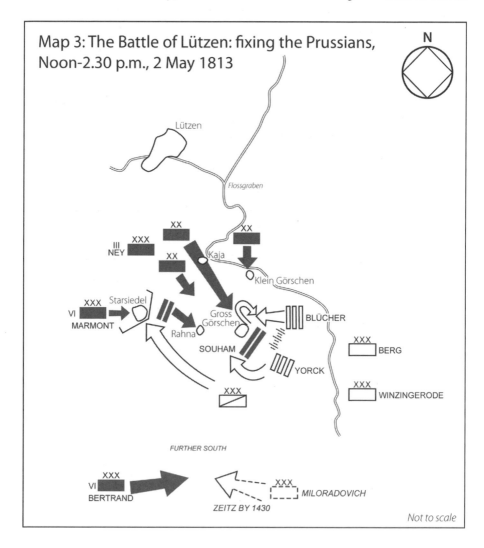

Map 3: The Battle of Lützen: fixing the Prussians,
Noon-2.30 p.m., 2 May 1813

Kleist's corps in Leipzig before marching the rest of his corps to Markranstadt. Having issued his orders, the Emperor at once set out for the scene of battle.

Napoleon reached the battlefield at 2.30 p.m. and found the situation critical. Ney's corps, weary and badly mauled, was on the point of collapse and had been forced back from every village including Kaja. Moreover Bertrand had halted his advance from the south on discovering the approach of the corps of Miloradovich near Zeitz. It was a moment when personal, very physical, leadership was required – and Napoleon showed it. Riding among the wavering conscripts, he exhorted them to stand firm, then himself repeatedly led them up towards the enemy. His presence had a magical effect: confidence and resolution flooded back into his troops. From all sides the cry of '*Vive L'Empereur*' rose from wounded and unwounded alike. Marmont later recorded that 'This was probably the day, of his whole career, on which Napoleon incurred the greatest personal danger on the field of battle. He exposed himself constantly, leading the defeated men of the Third Corps back to the charge.'

In the fighting which followed, Blücher's Chief of Staff, Major-General Gerhard von Scharnhorst, was mortally wounded. The situation was grave: a desperate struggle raged around the villages, from where Ney and Marmont both appealed repeatedly for help. Napoleon refused to budge, even though the Guard Corps, now commanded by Marshal Nicolas Soult, reached Kaja at 3.00 p.m., for he knew that he could not commit his reserve until he could be sure of smashing the enemy. 'Tell your Marshal', he replied to Marmont's messenger, 'that he is mistaken; he has nothing against him; the battle turns about Kaja.' But even as the struggle raged to and fro, every minute brought closer the approach of Macdonald and of Bertrand, who had now resumed his march.

A series of mistakes and mishaps on the part of the allies now came to Napoleon's aid. Blücher was wounded and his command devolved on Yorck, a much less inspiring leader. Worse still, Wittgenstein's reserves had not yet appeared. Wittgenstein had sent orders back for the III Reserve Corps of General Count Alexander Tormassov's Russian Guards and Grenadiers to move up to join the battle. Until they arrived, Wittgenstein was unwilling to risk a general attack. The delay seems to have been due to the personal intervention of Tsar Alexander, who wished, apparently, to lead personally the final *coup de grâce*. So while Napoleon's strength grew and he husbanded his reserve for the right moment, the allies let their moment slip away, for Wittgenstein was by now finding it increasingly difficult to control the battle: his leading corps were tiring and he was aware of the growing threat to his flanks – but he was too deeply embroiled to break off the action.

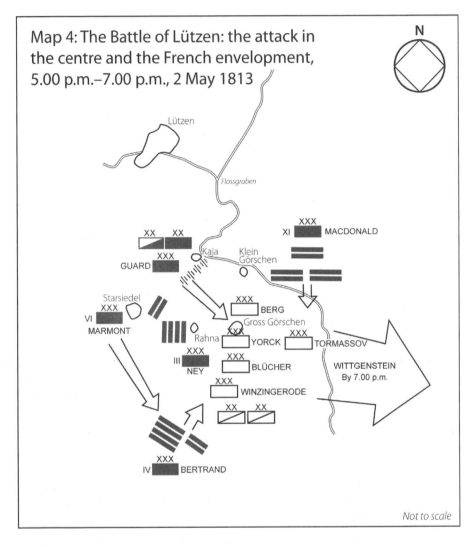

Map 4: The Battle of Lützen: the attack in the centre and the French envelopment, 5.00 p.m.–7.00 p.m., 2 May 1813

Lützen

Flossgraben

N

XXX
XI   MACDONALD

XX   XX
GUARD   XXX

Kaja   Klein
Görschen

XXX
BERG

Starsiedel
XXX
VI   MARMONT

Rahna

Gross Görschen
XXX   XXX
YORCK   TORMASSOV

XXX
III   NEY

XXX
BLÜCHER

WITTGENSTEIN
By 7.00 p.m.

XXX
WINZINGERODE

XX   XX

XXX
IV   BERTRAND

Not to scale

At last, at 4.00 p.m., Tormassov's corps came up and Wittgenstein ordered a general attack. This almost succeeded: the French were driven out of Klein and Gross Gorschen and the Prussians almost reached Kaja. Napoleon, knowing that he could not permit this degree of penetration at this time, unleashed the Young Guard, who, in a spirited charge, drove the enemy back. The struggle for control of the village line once more raged on, but the allies were well and truly fixed, and by 5.30 p.m. the French outflanking forces were almost in position. Macdonald was just north of the village of Eisdorf on Ney's left, and Bertrand had made contact with Marmont's right. But although the French had succeeded in re-occupying the villages after the Young Guard's charge, they now changed hands once again as a violent attack by the allies seized Klein and Gross Gorschen and Rahna. It was all too late, however, for Napoleon's concentration was complete and his forces, although weary, outnumbered the enemy by 110,000 to 80,000. At 6.00 p.m. Napoleon judged that the time had come to settle the matter. General Antoine Drouot was ordered to mass the seventy guns of the Guard artillery into a great battery, protected by the Old Guard, to the south-west of Kaja. This he did, so that very soon a devastating cannonade was raking the weary allied formations at close range. The losses, on both sides, were horrific. Von Caemmerer in his account said that 'The field between Klein and Gross Gorschen resembled a bivouac where whole battalions had lain down.'

As the battery continued its work, the Young Guard formed up in four columns each of four battalions and moved forward to the attack, followed by the Old Guard, the Guard Cavalry and the remnants of Ney's III Corps. Within a short time, the allied centre was smashed, the villages retaken and the entire Prussian and Russian line fell back. Simultaneously, the French enveloping forces made their move. From the south came Bertrand, followed by Marmont from Starsiedel. Macdonald's corps formed up behind Eisdorf and crashed into the flank of the enemy. This was enough to settle the outcome, and the whole allied army began to retreat – but it did so in reasonable order. Two more hours of daylight would have clinched a shattering French victory, but the approach of night brought the battle to an end. The crippling shortage of French cavalry made pursuit almost impossible and the allied rearguard remained in good enough order to beat off Marmont's infantry. The action at Lutzen undoubtedly ended in a victory for Napoleon, who had showed his old flair and skill of improvisation which had been absent for some time. Lutzen not only gave Napoleon the initiative in 1813, but also, perhaps more importantly, it repaired at least some of the damage to his reputation which he had suffered in Russia. It had been dearly bought. The French lost 20,000 casualties, the allies 18,000. Battles of manoeuvre, no less than battles of attrition, can be bloody affairs and the ferocity of the struggle at Lutzen had shaken even Napoleon's famous disregard for blood, for it had been almost as dense a battlefield and as fierce a struggle as Borodino. 'These animals have been taught a lesson,' he remarked in his correspondence. True, the allies had caught Napoleon by surprise but the customary flexibility of his dispositions, in three columns, had enabled him to react to the unexpected energetically and successfully; by applying the principles of concentration of force, speed and offensive action he had rapidly turned the tables on his enemies to seize back operational and tactical surprise. Speed had been a key element, for here as elsewhere, Napoleon's insistence on rapid movement was closely connected to the concentration of force: the assembly of the greatest number of men at the correct time and place to achieve a favourable battle situation. Assembly is probably a better word than concentration, for in Napoleonic terms it usually meant, as here at Lutzen, the placing of his major formations within marching distance of the place of battle. This he had achieved, after an approach march in which dispersion was the rule, since dispersion made use of more routes and was therefore quicker, increased security and eased the ever-present problem of finding enough green forage for his animals.

At Lutzen, just as at Jena, Napoleon achieved a phased concentration after a period of dispersion and thus managed to reconcile the principle of concentration of force with the sometimes contradictory requirements of security and deception. This is no easy matter, as Edward Luttwak points out in his description of the conscious use of paradox in war:

> As for secrecy and deception, the two classic agencies of surprise that often set the stage for manoeuvre, they too exact some cost of their own. Secrecy is often recommended to those who practise war as if it were costless, but an enemy can rarely be denied all knowledge of an impending action without some sacrifice of valuable preparations ... every limit on the assembly and preliminary approach of the combat forces will leave them less well arrayed and less well positioned than they might have been.

Therefore this reconciliation of the advantages and disadvantages of mass and dispersal, and the fusing of these two contradictory elements into a single operation of war, was, as David Chandler has pointed out, Napoleon's greatest contribution to the art of war, marking him as a true military genius. While his eighteenth-century forebears – with the notable exception of Frederick the Great – distinguished rigidly between manoeuvring and giving battle, Napoleon, with his sights always fixed on the opportunity for a decisive battle, combined marching, fighting and pursuing into one process. Although the inadequacies of the pursuit robbed him of a complete success, Napoleon at Lutzen had demonstrated the ability to achieve, even in 1813, the goal of manoeuvre – that is, he placed just enough forces to fix the enemy and, having fixed him, manoeuvred the rest of the army to destroy him.

Finally, the Napoleonic command system and his staff, weakened by losses as they were, were still clearly more than a match for the divided allies. Napoleon himself exercised undisputed command without any possibility of interference; Wittgenstein, on the other hand, faced the practical problems of a coalition commander at the tactical level: the need for consultation with the Prussians

and the associated difficulties of language, different staff procedures and interference from the Tsar all affected his ability to conduct battle with the speed
and flexibility of his opponent. On top of all that, Napoleon had once again
shown that he could judge better than the allies the moment to launch reserves,
and he still understood better than they the vital necessity of supporting
manoeuvre with firepower. His plan for battle, as worked out in the saddle and
executed on the field, remains a classic blueprint for the conduct of a meeting
engagement even today.

*   *   *

Very soon after the battle of Lutzen, Napoleon was hard at work on plans to
retain the initiative he had gained. Ney was allowed a day's rest and then with
his own and Marmont's corps he was to move north to relieve the besieged
French garrison in Wittenberg-Elbe. By 4 May it was becoming clear that the
allied main body was retiring on Dresden, although the corps of Kleist and of
General Friedrich von Bülow remained undetected. Equally clearly, the allies
were retiring in good order. One observer, Rudolf Friederich, noted that 'The
Prussian troops have covered themselves with glory, they have become once
more the Prussians of Frederick.' Stretching a point, perhaps, but certainly the
allies remained a formidable force. Napoleon's limited cavalry was now fully
occupied in trying to identify the exact locations of the allies. He himself felt
it most likely that they would retire towards the city of Bautzen in order to
preserve their line of communications through Warsaw, while detaching part
of their force to screen Berlin. His plan therefore called for a large detached
force to be formed under Ney's command, consisting of II, III and VII Corps,
reinforced by part of I Corps and II Cavalry Corps. This force was to cross the
Elbe at Torgau and Wittenberg, take the Saxon Army into the VII Corps, and
threaten Berlin. While Ney moved north, Napoleon himself would follow the
allies through Dresden, and Lauriston's V Corps would move towards Grimma
on the River Mulde to act as a link between the two forces. By threatening the
Prussian capital, Napoleon hoped to detach the Prussians from the Russians
and then destroy the two armies piecemeal. The focus on Berlin also reflects
Napoleon's continuing preoccupation with his original intention of advancing
to Danzig on the Prussian coast. Even allowing for Napoleon having a clear
grasp of the difficulties of preserving allied unity, it is difficult to see why he was
so obsessed with Berlin, unless it was to repay Frederick William's treachery.
For it was one of Napoleon's cardinal principles to focus first on the destruction
of the enemy army in battle rather than the acquisition of territory. Either he
had a very strong belief in the capture of Berlin as a decisive point in his attack

on allied unity, or else he had put aside his own belief, disregarding the probability that by beating the allied army in battle, he would inevitably capture Berlin.

The allied withdrawal, meanwhile, was not unduly hasty and in fact Napoleon's estimate had been quite correct. After some initial disagreements, it had been decided to leave Bülow's corps covering Berlin while the main army withdrew to Bautzen, where a strong new defensive position was to be surveyed and prepared by the Russian engineers. As the allies withdrew, there was a sharp action at Colditz on 5 May when the French rearguard caught up with Miloradovich's Russians, who were acting as rearguard. In spite of this, the allies made good their withdrawal through Dresden on 7 and 8 May. Napoleon followed up, throwing a bridge across the Elbe at Briesnitz just south of Dresden covered by his artillery. Determined action in Dresden itself also succeeded in driving the allied rearguard from the city bridge before it could be demolished. Thus by the evening of 11 May Napoleon had 70,000 troops across the Elbe at Dresden and another 45,000 at Torgau, while the allies offered no serious opposition at all to his crossing operations.

A short operational pause then followed, during which Napoleon decided to simplify his command arrangements to conform with his concept for Ney's force. The Army of the Elbe under Eugène and the Army of the Main, Napoleon's own command, were merged. Eugène was removed from the scene and ordered to Italy, where a strong corps of observation was being formed in order to tie down the Austrians, hindering any potential involvement in the Central European theatre. Napoleon also used the pause to convert Dresden into his new centre of operations and to complete the assimilation of the Saxon Army into the VII Corps. He then formalised the division of the army into two wings under Ney and himself, and reinforced Ney with Lauriston's V Corps: Ney's strength stood at 79,500 infantry and 4,800 cavalry, while Napoleon himself retained command of 110,000 infantry and 12,000 cavalry.

On 12 May the IV, VI and XI Corps under Napoleon began a reconnaissance in force towards Bautzen in order to fix the allies, while Ney's army moved forward to concentrate at Luckau ready for a drive on Berlin. By 16 May Macdonald, commanding the reconnaissance, had run the allies to ground at Bautzen. Napoleon therefore ordered the three corps concerned to fix the enemy while Oudinot's XII Corps worked around to the south of the allied position. Napoleon also sent word to Ney to be ready to turn round, march south with his own corps and Lauriston's V Corps, while detaching II and VII Corps to continue the march on Berlin. Ney, however, failed completely to understand what was required of him and in the end he marched south with his entire command. This was in many ways a sensible tactical course – and had he gathered his full strength, the outcome of Bautzen would have been substantially different – but it ignored the operational and strategic imperatives that Napoleon had identified. As it was, Ney's two leading corps became separated by a full twenty-four hours' march from the remainder. On 18 May Napoleon sent further orders to clarify Ney's tasks and instructed him in particular to cut the enemy's communications back through Lobau and Gorlitz, so that the allies would be forced onto the mountains along the Austrian frontier. There, they would have to accept surrender or destruction, unless they violated Austrian neutrality. But still Ney did not grasp the Emperor's intention and it must be said that Napoleon's instructions were far from clear. What the Emperor actually intended in terms of tactical effect was very simple: to fix the allies frontally and then roll up their position from the north and rear. Ney's slowness and Napoleon's divergence from his own principles were, however, to rob him of a decisive victory and ruin this brilliantly simple plan.

The allies, meanwhile, had reached Bautzen, where Wittgenstein found a welcome reinforcement in the form of General Barclay de Tolly with 13,000 more Russian troops. Napoleon was not far behind them. By 10.00 a.m. on 19 May he was close to Bautzen and he spent the day in a detailed observation and reconnaissance of the allied position. He saw that the allies had drawn up their forces in two lines along a series of shallow ridges, which they had fortified, with the River Spree to their front. The lines were some 11 kilometres long, with the city of Bautzen as an occupied outwork slightly in advance of their centre. He also appreciated that the village of Hochkirch, where Frederick the Great had fought a bloody battle during the Seven Years' War, was the key to the rear area since it commanded the main road eastwards towards Gorlitz. Thus the battle of Bautzen provided a strong contrast with Lutzen in three ways. First, Lutzen was fought on a confined battlefield, while Bautzen took place on an extended frontage of 11 kilometres. Secondly, Lutzen was a meeting engagement where ground was nothing; Bautzen was a set piece battle fought on a selected position where ground was everything. Thirdly, Lutzen was won by manoeuvre, while Bautzen was – deliberately – to contain a strong element of attrition.

*   *   *

The area in which the Battle of Bautzen was fought is dominated by a series of rivers and intervening low ridges. The most significant of these rivers is the Spree. From the area below Bautzen the river flows in a steep-sided valley some 50 metres deep, which is practically a gorge in places and is certainly a considerable obstacle. However, it is of some significance that the command of the river valley varies from bank to bank. Also of significance is the number of large ponds in the river valley higher up, where the Spree becomes in-considerable and is fordable in many places. Unlike the large reservoir which now exists just north of the city, many of these ponds were of great antiquity and were used for fish farming. These ponds, although not deep, and the marshy ground between them, were a serious obstacle to infantry, guns and wheeled vehicles. Roughly parallel with the Spree and approximately 3 kilo-metres to the east of it is the Blossauer Wasser. In itself this was relatively unimportant, but its valley was also marshy and this afforded protection to any formation placing a position to the east of it. No doubt the allies first favoured holding the line of the Spree, but the varying command of the stream, the fordable nature of much of the river and the natural protection afforded by the Blossauer Wasser swung the argument in favour of a rear line with only an advanced guard action being fought in Bautzen and along the Spree. As well as the rivers, there is some higher ground of significance. In the extreme south are the densely wooded hills and the villages of Drohmberg and the Schmortzberg, which provided a strong flank. Just north of Bautzen and north-west of Kreckwitz is a confused mass of low, lumpy hills generally known as the Kreckwitz heights. On these heights the villages were fortified by the allies and obstacles were set up in the woods. North of this area the ground is again generally flat with a few knolls, the most notable being between Malschwitz and Gleina and known as the Windmill Hill. All over this area the ground is still dotted with carp ponds. Bautzen town in 1813 had between 7,000 and 8,000 inhabitants living within the medieval defences, much of which remained intact. The deep, narrow gorge of the Spree to the west of the city was difficult for a frontal assault but the position could be turned via a stone bridge higher up or by fording the river lower down. The old walls had been modified by the construction of artillery platforms, which produced interlocking fields of fire covering the Spree crossing and the main approach road to the city. There is no mention in any account of the battle of earthworks being constructed on the western bank of the river. This could have been due to the fact that the allies assumed that Bautzen itself was so naturally strong that it needed little improve-ment and any more work would detract from the main effort of construction behind the Blossauer Wasser. To that end it was relatively lightly held by only one regiment of Russian troops from the corps of Miloradovich.

Having determined on the Blossauer Wasser as their main effort, the allies carried out numerous fortification works along the line, which generally afforded them excellent fields of fire. On the left, the line rested on the wooded hills of the Drohmberg and Schmortzberg. The centre ran from these hills to Kreckwitz, where the heights projected like a bastion on the allied right, and was covered by artillery redoubts whose fire swept the exposed slope. From here the line extended north and east towards Klix and Guttau. The scale of the effort expended on this position can be judged from the fact that the French engineers who later dismantled the position found seventy-eight redoubts, batteries and emplacements throughout the allied defensive system. There were, however, two problems with the position. Although naturally very strong, it was probably over extended; also its right, or northern, flank was not fixed on any particular feature and was vulnerable to an enveloping movement from the north.

*   *   *

Bautzen was a two-day battle of very great severity. It will be recalled that Napoleon's plan called for his leading corps to pin the enemy frontally, a deliberately attritional attack designed to wear the allies down, which would be undertaken by the corps of Marmont, Oudinot and Macdonald. Ney and his own III Corps would then advance on the northern flank, forcing the allies to weaken the centre and then commit their reserves in order to block this move. Concurrent with Ney's move, the corps of Lauriston would move from the north deep into the allied rear, seize the village of Hochkirch and block the allied withdrawal route. Then, at the critical moment, the Guard and the corps of Bertrand, both under Soult's command, would smash the allied centre north of Bautzen. Although the allies were well entrenched, and Napoleon's formations were tired, the French were at a numerical advantage throughout and Napoleon was confident that, if all went well, Bautzen would be a second Jena.

Throughout the day of 19 May the various French corps made their appearance and took their places. The allies, aware of the approach of forces from the north, believed this to be a reinforcement to the frontal attack and tried to launch a spoiling attack using the corps of Barclay de Tolly and Yorck. This rash expedition achieved nothing but the loss of 2,000 men, and by the early hours of 20 May Barclay had returned to the main position, followed at noon by Yorck. By the evening of that same day Ney and Lauriston were both within striking distance of the allied right, although the I Corps of Marshal Claude Victor and the VII Corps of General Jean Reynier were spread out some distance behind. The enveloping manoeuvre was thus proceeding to plan – or so it seemed. The Emperor therefore decided, to ensure that Ney and Lauriston would be in position, the whole of 20 May should be given over to the battle of attrition. The actual envelopment and final attack would be held over until 21 May.

For their part, the allies had also been making contingency plans. The orders for the battle which were issued on 19 May were extremely detailed and tried to provide for all contingencies, although they failed, notably, to produce any

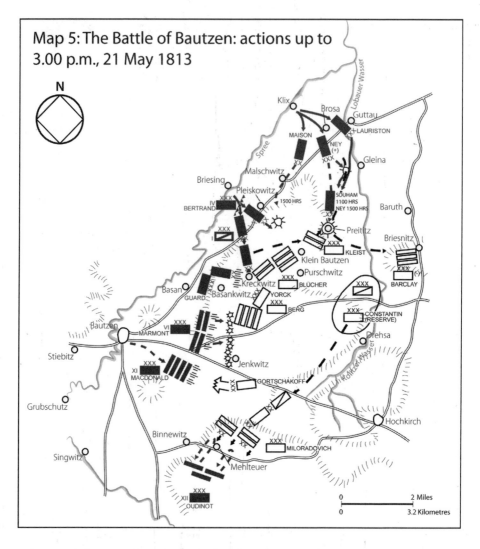

Map 5: The Battle of Bautzen: actions up to 3.00 p.m., 21 May 1813

coherent defence against the very situation that Napoleon envisaged and which later occurred. In essence, the allies planned to contain and exhaust any French attack, before launching a counter-attack around the French left – northern – flank with the idea of rolling the French up onto the mountains to the south. No provision was made for what was to happen if Napoleon did not attempt to seize the position immediately, nor for the likelihood of attack from the north. This approach could, to a large degree, be attributed to the Tsar, who had misread Napoleon's operational and tactical plan. Alexander was convinced that it was Napoleon's aim to separate the allied armies from the Austrians and therefore the main effort of his attack would come against the allied left. Napoleon had, of course, the opposite view, as, to his credit, did Wittgenstein, for by forcing the defeated allied army into Bohemia, Austria being neutral would either have to disarm the allies or declare for them. Being still unready for war, Austria would face the possibility of a French follow-up operation to Vienna which she could not prevent, and thus the collapse of the Sixth Coalition would be the inevitable result. With the idea firmly in the Tsar's mind that the only real danger could come from the south and west, the main effort was formed there by placing the bulk of the allied forces, including the reserve corps of the Grand Duke Constantin. Thus the inherent weakness of the position if attacked from the north was being reinforced by the dispositions of the defenders.

From early morning until noon on 20 May the French held back, but shortly after this the bombardment of the allied line began. The first attacks began three hours later as Oudinot's troops crossed the Spree at the village of Singwitz. The river was very low at the time and the corps crossed easily by a mixture of fording by the infantry and pontoon bridging for the guns. Having crossed, Oudinot re-formed his corps and was able to outflank the positions occupied by Miloradovich. He therefore came up against the southern flank of the corps of General Prince Andrei Gortschakoff in the area of the village of Mehlteuer. By 6.00 p.m. Oudinot's artillery was pulverising the allied southern flank, fuelling the Tsar's *idée fixe*, so that although the allies were by now well aware of Ney's approach in the north, they miscalculated his strength and intentions – this after twenty years of war, during which the workings of the Napoleonic battle system must have become well known to them. Oudinot continued his attack early on 21 May but by this time Gortschakoff and Miloradovich had pulled back to oppose his advance directly. Oudinot's corps remained in action, under great pressure, all day and its commander not unnaturally appealed to the Emperor for assistance. He should have known better. His first appeal received no answer at all. The second received the response 'Tell your Marshal that the battle will be won at 3 o'clock and that until then he must do the best he can!'

In Bautzen town it was Macdonald's XI Corps which forced the passage of the Spree under heavy fire from the defenders. Four crossings were established around the town – two at the southern end around the existing stone bridge, one at the northern end near the schloss and the fourth about half a kilometre further north. By 6.00 p.m. on 20 May Macdonald had taken the town and his regiments had pushed out up to a kilometre beyond it, forcing back Miloradovich's troops. He renewed the attack on the morning of 21 May but fared little better than Oudinot – however, both formations were achieving the Emperor's desired effect. Further north still, Marmont's VI Corps, the final element in the pinning action, crossed the Spree at the same time as Macdonald and Oudinot, using two bridging sites which are now obliterated by the modern reservoir, and by fording. The division of General Jean Compans managed to assist Macdonald by getting into the north-western suburbs of Bautzen soon after 3.00 p.m., thus forcing the Russians to evacuate before they were enveloped. The remainder of Marmont's corps assaulted the Prussian lines on the east bank of the Spree held by the corps of Kleist and, after a hard fight, Marmont was able to secure the high ground between Burk (then called Basan) and Basankwitz. By 6.00 p.m. on 20 May, therefore, much of the allied advanced position in the south was in French hands. Napoleon was content to continue the attritional action of 21 May in this area, while the main effort shifted to the envelopment and main attack in the centre and north.

*   *   *

At 4.00 a.m. on 21 May new orders reached Marshal Ney. These instructed him to drive the allies from the area of Drehsa and then march on Weissenberg in the allied rear in order to complete the enveloping movement. These orders were, however, confusing in two respects. First, Ney believed that he should march not directly on Weissenberg but rather first on Hochkirch, since this was what Lauriston had originally been ordered to do. Secondly, and more importantly, there were two villages called Drehsa. The first is now called Brosa and is near Klix. The second is north of Hochkirch. Napoleon's order did not specify which he meant and there has been controversy ever since. Ney at once sent for further guidance and Napoleon explained the allied dispositions to the messenger. He also stated that Ney should be at Preititz by 11.00 a.m. and that once he, Napoleon, had word of Ney's arrival there, and provided that the enemy reserves had been drawn off, then the final attack would be pressed home in the centre. Ney was further exhorted that the corps of Lauriston should move on his left so as to block the enemy withdrawal route. This direction should have clarified matters.

Ney's movement began soon after 5.00 a.m. with Lauriston's corps leading. This corps had only two divisions under its command, as Ney had detached the third division, and Lauriston was soon heavily involved with Yorck's advanced guard around Brosa. The 18,000-strong III Corps followed, led by Ney, who decided that to comply with the Emperor's instructions he should attack the corps of Barclay de Tolly and the Gleina redoubt, a feature which can still be traced on the ground. As Barclay had only 5,000 men available, he was rapidly pushed back from Gleina onto the fortified village of Preititz, from where he called on Blücher for reinforcements. On arrival in Preititz, Barclay soon became aware of the advance of Lauriston on Ney's left and became seriously alarmed at the prospect of the allied army's right flank being completely turned. He therefore left only two battalions to help garrison Preititz and moved the main body of his corps to the south-east of some high ground around Baruth. There he faced his corps to the north to cover the vital withdrawal route from Bautzen towards Würschen.

By 10.00 a.m. Ney's men had stormed and taken Gleina redoubt, and the division of General Nicolas Maison, which Ney had detached from Lauriston's corps, was preparing to storm Malschwitz. Instead of pressing on to Preititz, Ney stuck rigidly to the Emperor's instruction to arrive at 11.00 a.m., even though his strength had risen to 23,000 with the arrival of straggling divisions and he could have secured Preititz with ease. Worse still, at this point Ney had a new idea. He had become aware of the Kreckwitz heights, which although not high, certainly dominate the area and draw the eye, and he became completely carried away with the idea that here lay the key to the allied position. At 11.00 a.m., therefore, he sent only one division to take Preititz, while the rest of the corps moved against Blücher. Ney had done what the Emperor insisted no one ever should: he had focused on the ground first and the enemy second. Had he continued against Preititz with his whole force then he would have manoeuvred Blücher's force off the heights anyway and at the same time removed pressure from Soult, who was having a decidedly difficult time. In fairness to Ney, when one sees the ground today it is easy to understand how, in spite of the prominence of Hochkirch church spire as a landmark for navigation in the distance, his attention would have been drawn by the heights – especially as his grasp of the essentials of Napoleon's plan was incomplete.

In spite of all the warning signs and all the activity thus far, Tsar Alexander remained convinced that the danger still lay on the southern flank. Wittgenstein was, however, only too well aware of the danger in the north. 'I will wager my head', he said, 'that this is only a demonstration; Napoleon's idea is to outflank our right and drive us into Bohemia.' In that one sentence he had correctly summed up Napoleon's intention, but the Tsar refused to listen. Blücher meanwhile had received Barclay's request for assistance. Ney's delay before Preititz gave him just enough time to act. He sent four battalions to the area above Klein Bautzen and three more into Preititz. As these latter were advancing they met the leading elements of the French, who had brushed Barclay's two battalions aside. The French leading elements were just leaving Preititz when the three Prussian battalions counter-attacked so fiercely that the French were pushed right back to Gleina. It was bitter hand-to-hand fighting, but it gained time for the allies on this flank.

Ney could now see the majority of the allied centre and knew that Napoleon had not yet attacked it. He sent word to Lauriston to break off the action and join him. Lauriston was clearly unhappy, but he could not disobey. Leaving one division and half his cavalry to contain Barclay at Baruth, he moved with his remaining troops – about 10,000 all told – to Preititz. His third division was still moving up and his fourth, detached by Ney, was still fighting in the villages of Malschutz and Pleiskowitz, where it remained fully occupied until 3.00 p.m. The attack on Preititz was renewed at 2.00 p.m. and for an hour the fighting swayed this way and that until Ney's men gained the village; they had done so at great cost in casualties and in time. Urged now by General Antoine-Henri Jomini, his chief of staff, to push on to Hochkirch, Ney still hesitated, drawn to the Kreckwitz heights. The outcome of this hesitation was that the allied line of retreat remained unclosed, with significant consequences. Worse still for Napoleon's plans, Ney had failed either to draw off the allied reserves or to weaken the centre, making Soult's task a great deal harder.

Soult, it will be remembered, was in command of the Guard and Bertrand's IV Corps and it was he who was to effect the master stroke that would win the battle in the centre. On 20 May Soult's troops had made an unopposed crossing of the Spree by a mixture of fording and pontoon bridging in an area where the river is a minor obstacle. Having secured the crossings, Soult moved up 20,000 infantry, 1,000 cavalry and thirty guns of IV Corps. His intention, while the allies were focused on Ney, was to capture the area of Kreckwitz and Pleisskowitz, including the Pleisskowitz redoubt. At the same time the Emperor ordered part of the Guard forward into the gap between the corps of Marmont and Bertrand, along with a sizeable proportion of the artillery of the Guard Corps. This, with the artillery of IV Corps, formed the favoured Napoleonic grand battery: from 1.30 p.m. onwards these guns began to fire on the allied centre. At 2.30 p.m. Napoleon, who had spent much of the morning sleeping, heard the sounds of Ney's attack and ordered Bertrand to attack. Under a murderous fire from the allied positions, the divisions of IV Corps began to advance and, although the losses were cruel, by 3.00 p.m. they had forced the corps of Blücher and Yorck to retire to the eastern edge of the high ground.

After 3.00 p.m. most of the action in the north centred around Blücher's position on the Kreckwitz heights. His position was becoming more and more perilous in that he was in great danger of being encircled, for Bertrand's attack had penetrated as far as the villages of Doberschutz, Weinberg and Kreckwitz. At the same time Maison's division was advancing from Pleisskowitz and Lauriston was still moving from the north-east. Worse still, Blücher could see Napoleon's Guard apparently advancing from Basankwitz towards Litten. His first reaction was to call for assistance from Yorck and indeed he had good reason for alarm, for the high ground from which he had just retired, and on which the Imperial Guard was now developing its attack, was vital to the cohesion of the defence. In short, Blücher realised that his position was untenable and he therefore ordered a further withdrawal – just in time: General Karl Müffling estimated that he had had only fifteen minutes to spare before being completely surrounded. Fifteen minutes, though, was enough. The Prussian retirement was carried out in perfect order, covered by the cavalry. On reaching Kreckwitz, Blücher's troops conducted a successful rearward passage of lines through part of Yorck's command, then continued the withdrawal for almost a kilometre to a new position south of Purschwitz. This limited movement was absolutely crucial for the allies' salvation, for as the Prussians left the high ground, the French rose to the attack. Ney's men from the north and Bertrand's from the west and south rushed onto the plateau – to find the enemy gone. These two corps became hopelessly intermingled and it was an hour before they could be re-formed and realigned. Ney, realising to his disgust that the allies had given him the slip, realised also that it was his diversion towards the heights and his drawing in of Lauriston which had created the gap through which they had slipped. He at once sent orders to Lauriston to block the allied retirement, but it was too late – the allies had been forced to withdraw, but the attacks which should have destroyed them had missed their mark.

Wittgenstein, meanwhile, had not been idle. He had redeployed Yorck's corps to cover Blücher's movement and had committed part of the Russian Guards Division in support. Even so, it was not until Ney took Preititz that the Tsar finally realised the danger to the allied northern flank. He agreed at once that the only course of action was an immediate general withdrawal, for which orders were given at 4.00 p.m. The retirement would be conducted in three columns: in the north, Barclay was to hold his position until the Prussian and Russian Guards had withdrawn to Wörschen, after which he was to follow, covered by his cavalry.

In the centre, the two Prussian corps would retire through the Russian reserve corps, which would act as rearguard to the army. In the south, Gortschakoff and Miloradovich were to retire on Lobau.

In the centre, Napoleon still hoped that Marmont, the Guard and the cavalry reserve would be able to push the Russian formations on the allied left onto Bohemia. However, the rearguards retired in such steadfast order that the whole allied army got away: the inferior French cavalry in particular could do nothing against the vastly superior numbers of the allies. Napoleon watched in fury as the allies marched off the field. 'What!' he cried, 'after such a slaughter, no trophies? These people will leave me no claws!' And so indeed the battle of Bautzen ended. Like Lutzen, it was a bloody affair: the allies lost 11,000 killed and wounded, but few prisoners, and no trophies other than several spiked and

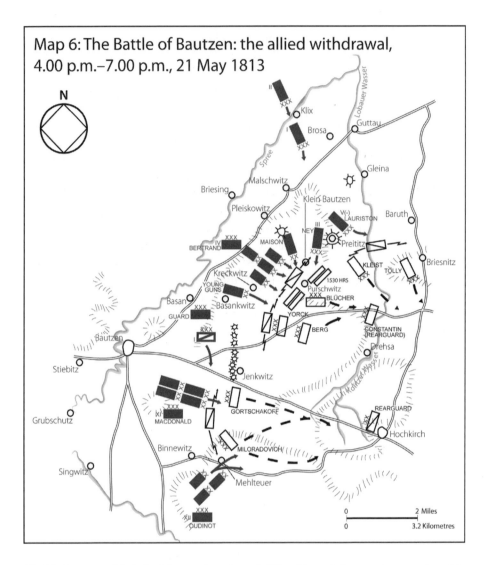

Map 6: The Battle of Bautzen: the allied withdrawal, 4.00 p.m.–7.00 p.m., 21 May 1813

disabled guns which had been abandoned. The French lost at least twice this figure, so although Napoleon was left in possession of the field, it was a Pyrrhic victory.

Bautzen should have been the perfect Napoleonic battle – why was it not? Its failings have as much to say on this as did the success of Lutzen. First, the declining quality of the *Grande Armée*, the result of repeated mass casualties, was becoming obvious. At both Lutzen and Bautzen Napoleon had been forced to commit the Guard, something he had rarely done in the past, for on the allied side the Russians and Prussians had shown discipline, determination and a desire for revenge – and their troops were gaining in experience all the time. Secondly, Napoleon's command and staff system was still good, but it, like the army, had also declined through losses and fatigue. Napoleon had aimed to concentrate actually on the battlefield rather than short of it, and the event showed that his system was no longer capable of carrying through this sort of high-risk operation. Ney is often held responsible for the failure of the plan, but part of the failure must lie in Napoleon's highly centralised command system which did nothing to educate subordinates, bring on new men, produce a trained staff or allow initiative. The choice of Ney for such an important independent command reveals just how little choice Napoleon had in selecting a key lieutenant, as with a man so impetuous and so little given to analytical thought, there was every chance of a disaster. Possibly Napoleon hoped that Jomini would keep things on the rails, but, as von Caemmerer remarked, the cases in which a chief of staff can make up for the deficiencies of his commander are few. Thirdly, the shortage of cavalry made it very difficult to form a reserve or strike force capable of conducting a pursuit. By contrast, the allied superiority in quality and numbers of mobile troops allowed them to form an effective rearguard capable of holding off the French pursuit for long enough to allow the main body to escape.

* * *

It was as well for the allies that when Napoleon was able to pick up the pursuit eastwards on 22 May, he could do so only slowly. In the immediate aftermath of Bautzen, allied morale at all levels was far from high and there were more disagreements within the high command as to the future conduct of the war, in particular between Wittgenstein and the Tsar. After Bautzen, Wittgenstein resigned in protest over the Tsar's interference and was replaced by Barclay de Tolly. There were other differences: both Blücher and General August von Gneisenau were prepared to offer battle again, but Barclay proposed a retreat into Poland. Eventually a compromise was offered by the Tsar and accepted, whereby the allies prepared to fall back in two columns on Schweidnitz in Silesia. From here, communications could be maintained both with Poland and with Austria, while at least some defence of Prussian territory could be undertaken.

Napoleon, meanwhile, had given orders to follow up the retreating allies. Reynier's VII Corps, with General Michel Latour-Maubourg's I Cavalry Corps, set off for Reichenbach, followed by the Guard Corps and Marmont's VI Corps. To the north Lauriston's V Corps, and further north again Macdonald's XII and Bertrand's IV Corps, marched towards Lobau. The left flank was protected by Ney's III Corps at Weissenberg. Finally Oudinot's shattered XI Corps was left to rest at Bautzen and recover its strength. By 10.00 a.m. on 22 May VII Corps had reached Reichenbach, where a stiff little battle was fought against the allied rearguard under Prince Eugen of Württemberg. By 3.00 p.m. Reynier had forced Eugen to withdraw to a position short of Gorlitz, but Eugen had achieved his mission of delaying the French advance. Reynier asked the Emperor, who was close by, for permission to break off the action as his troops were close to exhaustion, for VII Corps had marched 27 kilometres and fought a five-hour action only a short time after the battle at Bautzen: the reply was a peremptory order to press on. As VII Corps began to move once more, a cannon shot passed close to the Emperor and killed Grand Marshal Christophe Duroc. Napoleon had a great affection for Duroc and he took his death, following close on that of Bessières, very badly. At Reichenbach, Duroc was joined in death by General of Engineers François Kirgener and General Jean-Pierre-Josef Bruyère. The result was that, most uncharacteristically, Napoleon ordered the action to be broken off.

Throughout the next three days the allied withdrawal continued, followed up by the French. In spite of their ordeal at Bautzen and the process of retreat, the fighting spirit of the allied rearguard held up remarkably well, so that, what with bad roads, frequent river crossings and delaying actions, the French advance began to slow. XI Corps in particular fought a bitter twelve-hour battle with the Russians on 25 May and on the following day the leading division of V Corps was heavily attacked by 3,000 Prussian cavalry supported by artillery near the village of Michelsdorf. The surprised French lost 1,000 men, a quarter of their strength, in less than fifteen minutes. The remainder were only saved by the prompt arrival of the second division of the corps.

By 26 May the allied main body had passed over the Katzbach stream and on the following day swung south-east towards Schweidnitz, which was reached on 29 May. On arrival, the allied commanders found that the fortifications of the place, demolished in 1807, had not been repaired so that its potential as a defensive position was nowhere near what had been hoped. Napoleon's main body was about two days' march behind the allies and on 1 June he occupied Breslau on the Oder. Here he was well situated west and north of the allies, able to cut off their withdrawal and in an excellent position to inflict another, this time fatal, Bautzen. News from elsewhere was also good, for only three days earlier Marshal Louis Davout's forces had succeeded in re-taking Hamburg. Only Oudinot had suffered a reverse. Sent northwards to threaten Berlin once his troops had recovered, he had been caught and defeated by Blücher at Luckau on 28 May. But all was not what it seemed: there were as many disagreements between the Marshals as there were between the allied commanders; the lines of communication were being constantly harassed by Cossacks, who had even attacked Leipzig itself and indeed entered the city in strength. And last, the conscript army was showing signs of exhaustion as battle, sickness and straggling took their toll.

Both sides seemed to have lost the chance of a quick, decisive victory. When the Austrians proposed a ceasefire and the possibility, with their mediation, of a negotiated settlement, both sides were very willing to accept. On 2 June a 36-hour truce began, extended on 4 June after a short conference to 20 July. This was again later extended to 10 August, with six days' notice to be given before hostilities recommenced. A strip of neutral territory was designated between the armies in which neither side would position troops. Beyond this strip, the French accepted a ceasefire line roughly along the Katzbach to its confluence with the Oder. Their northern limit would be the frontier of Saxony from the Oder to Wittenberg on the Elbe. From Wittenberg southwards they were confined to the west of the Elbe, inclusive of the islands in the river, and as much of the territory of the 32nd Military Division as they held on 8 June – in the event, most of it. The garrisons of Danzig, Mödlin, Zamosc, Stettin, Kustrin and Hamburg, if besieged, were to be supplied every five days. Thus the spring campaign came to an abrupt and somewhat unexpected close.

Chapter 4

'Sire, you are a lost man'

The Austrian Mediation and the Congress of Prague, June–August 1813

Secret negotiations between Napoleon and the allies for an armistice, or even a settlement, had actually been in progress even before the battle of Bautzen, both with and without the mediation of Austria. The Austrian 'good offices' had been offered by General Ferdinand von Bubna on behalf of the Emperor of Austria as early as 20 December 1812. Napoleon had accepted the principle out of necessity – his armies were in no shape to go on the offensive at that stage – although he had no desire for an armed mediation. In the immediate aftermath of Bautzen, Chancellor Metternich, Napoleon's Minister of Foreign Affairs Hughes Maret and Foreign Minister of the Empire Armand de Caulaincourt all urged Napoleon to make a settlement while favourable terms could still be had, but to no avail. By late May it seems with the benefit of hindsight that Napoleon had the possibility of peace on even better terms within his grasp: he had inflicted two sharp reverses on his enemies and was now poised to deliver at least another Bautzen – and maybe another Jena. Jomini later spoke of Napoleon's hesitation as the greatest mistake of his career, so why did he not finish the war at Schweidnitz? The answer is clear both from Napoleon's correspondence and from his situation. In two letters dated 29 May and 2 June he wrote that 'Two considerations have made up my mind: my shortage of cavalry, which prevents me from striking great blows, and the hostile attitude of Austria.'

The weakness of the cavalry had been a recurring theme thus far both in reconnaissance and pursuit, but what of Austria? True, there were now close to 150,000 Austrian and Hungarian troops concentrating around Prague, from where they could certainly threaten Napoleon's southern flank. However, on 1 June, with the allies at Schweidnitz, Napoleon was positioned in such a way that within thirty-six hours he could have interposed his army between the allies and their communications, forcing them either to accept battle with their backs to the Bohemian mountains or else to make a forced march to the south-east.

The Ornamental Embellishments Engraved by Topham the Portraits by Freeman.

From Portraits taken at Berlin, Vienna, Stockholm, S? Petersburg & Paris.

te 1. A contemporary engraving of some of the senior commanders of the Sixth Coalition in
itral Europe 'from portraits taken at Berlin, Vienna, Stockholm, St Petersburg and Paris.' The
d Moreau has pride of place; also included is the Cossack General Platov. (*Author's collection*)

Plate 3. A contemporary engraving of King Ferdinand VII in prison at Valençay. (*Author's collection*)

Plate 4. A contemporary illustration of British infantry advancing at the Battle of Vittoria, published by Thomas Kelly in London in January 1814. (*Author's collection*)

Plate 5. 'The Passage of the Bidassoa River', illustration from *Hutchinson's History of the Nations* (litho), Beadle, James Prinsep (1863–1947) (after). (*Private Collection/The Bridgeman Art Library, IL 370617*)

Plate 6. A Cossack (top) and a Bashkir (bottom) drawn from life in 1813 by William Schadow. The sight of these half-savage troops from Central Asia must have been terrifying to friend and foe alike in Central and Western Europe. (*Author's collection*)

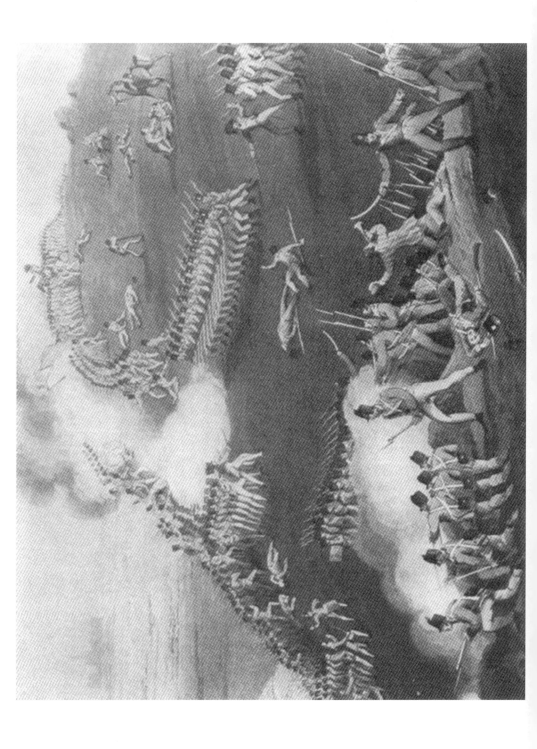

Plate 8. A confused and confusing picture of the Battle of Dresden, 26–27 August 1813. Although showing the town and the bridge very accurately, it portrays the action of the battle as happening on the north bank of the river rather than the south bank. (*Author's collection*)

Plate 9. 'Soldiers on the March to Buffalo.' A rather cynical contemporary cartoon of American troops and their camp followers based on Thomas Rowlandson's 'Women and Children on the March. Old Buffs 1808.' (*William L. Clements Library, University of Michigan*)

Plate 10. Fort George, the British headquarters in Upper Canada, fell to the Americans in the early summer of 1813 but was recaptured before the end of the year. The troops drilling in front of the distinctive wooden buildings are probably the 41st Regiment of Foot. (*Painting by Edward Walsh. William Clements Library, University of Michigan*)

For the allies, the first course risked being driven into Austria as Wittgenstein had foreseen, in which case it is hard to imagine Austria taking up the allied cause in the wake of a third defeat; the second would certainly separate the Russians and Prussians, perhaps permanently. At best, the allies would have been forced to a humiliating peace; at worst, their military power would have been destroyed.

But by 4 June the allies had moved out of the trap and the chance had passed; that Napoleon allowed it to pass without acting with the merciless drive that characterised his earlier campaigns points to other factors influencing his decision. These factors were significant and had to do with the condition of his army. By 1 June, counting battle casualties, sick and stragglers, the *Grande Armée* had almost halved in size since April. James Dunnigan in his work on Leipzig has calculated that a Napoleonic corps could lose 80 per cent of its strength over a period of six to eight months through sickness, disease, desertion and straggling, without firing a shot. Some troops in both armies had now been marching and fighting steadily for five months. Reinforcements were on the way from France, but time was needed for their arrival. Moreover there was a shortage of ammunition and food: partly the result of the lengthy lines of communication; partly due to an imperfect commissariat system; partly because there was not much to be gained from forage in a part of Europe that had been fought over by large armies for years; and partly because of Cossack raiding. Last, the army was very close to exhaustion. The campaign had therefore reached a culminating point, in that the present level of operations could just about be maintained, but could not be developed any further. An operational pause was therefore an absolute necessity.

The allies too were in dire need of a pause for their situation was still extremely dangerous. They had suffered two defeats and were, like Napoleon, losing men rapidly. Again, reinforcements were on their way from Prussia, Russia and Sweden, but time was needed to allow them to come up. There was also a requirement to rethink allied strategic and operational plans, given the disagreements within the high command. Austria was also in need of more time. The general direction of Austrian foreign policy had been clear since Prince Karl von Schwarzenberg's defection from the French armies in Russia; moreover there was a score going back many years to be settled with Napoleon – but the army was not yet ready for war.

The truce, which is known to history as the armistice of Pleiswitz, was therefore a matter of convenience rather than a genuine attempt to reach a negotiated peace. The Tsar had accepted the earlier offer of mediation by Austria only because Metternich had assured him that it would fail. This reluctance to treat with Napoleon had not changed and the allies were more concerned to gain the time needed to persuade Austria to join the coalition. For his part, Metternich thought that in the wake of the spring campaign it might be possible to reach a continental peace, but not a maritime peace that would include English demands. Nor did he especially wish to see the total downfall of the Napoleonic system, which stood for the order and discipline he so much admired. All this led him to the conclusion that a compromise peace in Europe, which would force the English to a separate settlement, was most desirable. He therefore aimed to exclude England from the negotiations and thereby isolate her from the coalition.

However, the English ambassadors, Lord Cathcart and Sir Charles Stewart – Castlereagh's half-brother – were already ahead of Metternich. On 14 and 15 June they signed treaties with Russia and Prussia at Reichenbach and had already concluded an agreement with Sweden. The terms of the agreements provided financial subsidies in return for the promise that no separate peace would be made with Napoleon. This *fait accompli* was a powerful lever in persuading Austria to accede to the Treaty of Reichenbach twelve days later on 24 June and to concede that as England was a full party to the treaty, her interests must also be recognised. By the terms of the Reichenbach treaty, Metternich agreed to present the allied demands to Napoleon as the basis for a settlement, which would be negotiated at a Congress in Prague; but if the Austrian mediation failed, the treaty would come into effect and Austria would join the allies. It can of course be argued that once England had compelled all the allies to fight for her war aims as well as their own, Napoleon was bound to refuse the mediation and thus force Austria into England's arms. The treaties signed at Reichenbach were, therefore, a masterpiece of diplomatic skill and were the most important step towards uniting all the allies in one unbreakable block – which was achieved on 12 August 1813, the date on which the Central European alliance of England, Russia, Prussia, Austria and Sweden was confirmed at Teplitz.

At this stage London's grand design can be seen. England had, throughout the development of the Central European alliance, continued to follow the precepts which had been laid down by Pitt: that any expansion of Russia should be balanced by strengthening Austria and Prussia; that Prussian influence should be extended in northern and western Germany; that Austrian interests should be diverted away from confrontation with Prussia by extending her interests in Italy and Illyria; and that the colonial territories of France and her allies which England had seized should be used as bargaining chips to achieve the balance of power described by the first three precepts. To implement this policy, Pitt's successor, Lord Liverpool, used chiefly the weapon which Napoleon sought to destroy through his Continental System: money. Britain had, by means of its commercial wealth, been the paymaster of coalition war in Europe since 1793. In 1813 she again embarked on a programme of subsidies in money and equipment amounting to £10.4 million. Total government spending at this time was £87 million, of which £53.8 million, or 62 per cent, went on defence. These subsidies accounted for a fifth of that amount – £530 billion at 2013 rates – and thus the vast financial resources of the British Empire underpinned the allied will to continue the struggle. The power of subsidy cannot be overstated: without it the allies, even Austria, had almost no chance of continuing the war. These subsidies, in money, weapons and munitions, amounted to £7 million to Austria; £0.66 million to Prussia; £2.46 million to Portugal; £1 million to Russia; £0.87 million to Spain; £0.44 million to Sicily; and £1.33 million to Sweden. England may have been a minor contributor to the coalition war effort on land, but without her financial power no armies could have kept the field for long. As an illustration of their effect, Russia generated about £40 million in revenue in 1812 and spent £15 million of it on defence. Since a large amount of normal spending was eaten up with fixed costs like pay, food for troops and horses, clothing, general administration, the maintenance of fortifications and so on, the margins available for launching an expeditionary campaign were tight and it was the English subsidy of £1 million that provided the elastic.

In keeping with his undertakings, Metternich met Napoleon on 26 June in the Marcolini Palace in Dresden, the capital of Napoleon's ally the King of Saxony. After a stormy meeting, Napoleon had agreed to the mediation and to the Congress, which would commence on 5 July. Only four days later came news that would have a profound bearing on the position of both Napoleon and the allies. This news was that of Wellington's decisive victory at Vitoria, which had a marked effect on flagging allied morale while British prestige rose to new heights in Prussia and Hanover. In Russia the one and only *Te Deum* of gratitude for a foreign victory was sung. In Prague, Count Stadion rushed into Prince Metternich's bedroom to break the news, news which certainly undid Metternich's early intentions in regard to England and prodded Austria towards open membership of the coalition. For Napoleon it was evil news indeed. Having milked Spain of its best troops in the spring he now faced the prospect of having the English at his back, a war on two fronts that he could ill afford. His agreement to the prolongation of the armistice was given on the day following the arrival of the news of Vitoria, but he also needed time to influence the Spanish theatre more directly and it was an indication of the gravity of the situation that Soult, who had only left Spain in the spring, and who was Napoleon's ablest available lieutenant, was despatched to take up the command. The victory of the Anglo-Portuguese army in Spain also reinforced the convictions of Caulaincourt and Maret that peace must be secured now before all was lost. When Caulaincourt arrived at the Congress of Prague on 28 July Metternich warned him that unless Napoleon signed a peace treaty on 10 August, Austria would declare war on 11 August. Caulaincourt in answer gave the first hint of a rift in the French government and nation, which must have encouraged Metternich:

> You do not see in me the representative of the whims of the Emperor, but of his true interest and that of France. I am quite as European in these present questions as you can be. Bring us back to France by peace or war, and you will be blessed by thirty million Frenchmen and by all the clear-sighted servants and friends of the Emperor.

Not that Napoleon was in any way taken in by Metternich. He regarded the position which the Austrians had adopted as mediator between himself and the allies, to say nothing of England and Sweden, as an act of barely concealed hostility, especially in the light of Schwarzenberg's defection in 1812. This he had made absolutely clear to Metternich at the Dresden meeting, storming up and down, kicking his hat to and fro across the room in his rage as he did so. Napoelon's rages were famous and must have been terrifying for subordinates faced with a man who held – literally – the power of life and death. But Metternich was a man every inch as powerful and he was unmoved by Napoleon's tantrum. What made Napoleon angrier still was the knowledge that the allies – and as far as he was concerned, probably Austria too – were receiving financial subsidy from England. Napoleon was still confident of final victory but was prepared, if the terms were right – that is, if they restored him and his empire to their full extent and glory – to settle. Compromise was not on the cards, he saw no reason to do so: he had not been defeated; his prestige at home would certainly suffer badly if he gave in now; and who could say what future demands the allies might make? The whole direction of his foreign policy over the years had been geared to the acquisition of territory and he was not about to change this without a fight. He therefore saw the allied proposals as a trap and although militarily he gained much from the truce, diplomatically his failure to compromise was an error which drove Austria and England together.

The conditions demanded by the allies at Prague were certainly more than Napoleon was prepared to concede after his relatively successful spring campaign, in spite of Caulaincourt's words, which were underlined by Berthier, as Metternich had noted during the negotiations on 26 June: 'The Prince of Neuchâtel [Berthier] said to me in a whisper "Do not forget that Europe needs peace – France above all else wants nothing but peace."' The allies' demands were also rather more than Metternich himself wished to fight for. The allies were demanding no less than the restoration of Austria to her pre-1805 boundaries and of Prussia to her pre-1806 boundaries; the dissolution of the Confederation of the Rhine and the end of French influence in Germany; freedom for the Hanseatic ports; the dissolution of the Grand Duchy of Warsaw, including the evacuation of the Pomeranian garrisons; independence for the Netherlands; and the complete removal of French rule in Italy. The influence of England was also apparent in the demand for the restoration of the ancient dynasty in Spain – Portugal was already free. No wonder, then, that although he had agreed to the prolongation of the armistice, Napoleon eventually rejected the terms. No wonder too that Metternich, having been forced by Napoleon's intransigence into a position he did not much relish, is reported to have told Napoleon at their final meeting, 'Sire, you are a lost man.'

Diplomatically then, the prolongation of the armistice had worked to the benefit of the allies. Militarily too it had allowed them some much needed time in two respects. First, the Russians and Prussians had brought up their reinforcements; secondly, Austria had completed her mobilisation. By the middle of August the allied field armies numbered over half a million men, including 572 squadrons of cavalry, sixty-eight regiments of Cossacks and around 1,400 guns. Another 250,000 men were dispersed in garrisons, sieges of isolated French fortresses and in the reserves. For the Russians, the field army was supplemented by large numbers of reinforcements to make good its losses and by the new Third Reserve Army, 60,000 strong, which had formed in Poland under General Count Levin Bennigsen. Prussia, in addition to making good her losses with drafts of recruits, was raising a new force of *Landwehr*, ill equipped and trained it is true, but 160,000 strong and capable of relieving other troops by taking over static guards, garrisons and escorts. Bernadotte's Swedish corps, concentrated north-east of Berlin, numbered 40,000, although only 18,000 were actually committed to fighting a campaign in the field. Finally, the Austrians had about 123,000 men available for operations in the Central European theatre after taking account of the need to guard Italy and watch Napoleon's ally Bavaria. With time, these forces had the potential to grow even larger. Seen in this light, is not surprising that the eventual allied plan relied heavily on attrition. For this reason it was deprecated by German theorists until Delbrück's interpretation of Clausewitz, on the assumption that attrition was an inferior form of war, rather than a necessary strategy whose aim, having worn Napoleon down, was 'to strike the final blow with assurance.' And had not Napoleon too frequently proved better at manoeuvre than his opponents? But the plan took much effort to form for the simple reason that as the coalition expanded, so did the consultation processes which coalition warfare demands. In outline, the allied plan was hammered out by the Tsar, King Frederick William, Prince Bernadotte and their advisers at Trachenberg while the Congress of Prague was in session. It was subsequently modified by Austria at Reichenbach on 19 July after her formal accession to the coalition. Scharnhorst's view of the future direction of the war before his death in June had been that the allies should opt for a dispersed advance followed by a vigorous concentration when the opportunity arose for a decisive battle. Austrian doctrine on the other hand was based on the writings of the Archduke Charles – the much-respected soldier who had been the first to defeat Napoleon, at Aspern-Essling. This doctrine advocated cautious manoeuvre and security of the base of operations, much after the manner of eighteenth-century military thought. It was a philosophy based on the prudence which had so far effectively maintained the Hapsburg Empire rather than risking it on a single battle. Thus Field Marshal Count Josef Radetzky's operational memoranda of May and June, although claiming the destruction of the enemy army as the proper object of the allies, in fact relied entirely on the attrition of Napoleon's strength through wastage, rather than large-scale fighting. It was Schwarzenberg who proposed that the Army of Bohemia should advance on the French communications and that 'battle with a superior enemy force should be avoided until the Allied armies have united with us.'

General Karl von Toll, the Tsar's adviser, proposed several audacious plans but it was he who, by proposing a compromise between the Prussian and Austrian ideas, was father to the plan eventually developed. In this he was helped by Bernadotte who, although thwarted in his plans to secure the overall command for himself, proposed that 'the centre of the Austrian Monarchy will become the grave of the great Napoleon.' The Trachenberg-Reichenbach plan therefore laid down allied operational objectives. First, it would be an offensive campaign, with Napoleon's base of operations, Dresden, as the first objective. A most important qualification was that a general action against Napoleon himself was to be avoided unless under highly advantageous circumstances. French forces were only to be attacked when divided and when the allies were superior in numbers. If any allied army was itself attacked by strong French formations, it would retire, while other allied corps fell on the French flanks and rear. Any fortresses found to be defended would be masked, but troops would not be tied up in sieges. These actions would be accompanied by attacks on the French lines of communication by Cossacks, in the absence of any widespread partisan movement like that in Spain. Such attacks would, it was believed, tie down numbers of French troops in rear area security, who could be destroyed piecemeal but whose removal from Napoleon's field army would further increase favourable force ratios for the allies. This process of attrition would, it was felt, be a safer road to eventual victory than risking another large-scale battle just yet.

To put these plans into effect, the allies formed four armies, all multinational in composition, as a demonstration of solidarity. The main effort was placed with the Army of Bohemia under the command of Prince Karl von Schwarzenberg, since the allies believed that Napoleon was most likely to attack southwards towards Prague. This army consisted of 220,000 Austrian and Prussian troops, the latter from Silesia. Schwarzenberg was to move, according to circumstances, towards either Hof, or Eger, or Silesia, or if necessary to retire on the Danube if Napoleon attacked. In the last case, Bernadotte's army would then attack the exposed French left flank and rear. To make this possible, Bernadotte's Army of the North was reinforced by Russian formations to a strength of 100,000. He was to leave 20,000 Swedes to mask Davout in Hamburg and then be prepared to advance either in support of Schwarzenberg, or preferably towards Leipzig. If he was attacked he was to retire, while the remaining allied armies closed in on the French from the flanks and rear as before. The third army, the Army of Silesia under Blücher, was 95,000 strong and composed of Russian and Prussian formations. Blücher was ordered to follow any French retirement towards the Elbe, cross the river and unite with Bernadotte – but not to risk a general engagement unless he was sure of success. Last, the Russian Reserve Army in Poland under General Count Bennigsen was to advance towards Glogau ready either to attack the French main army in co-operation with the other allied armies, or to block a French advance into Poland.

Although no written Trachenberg plan survives, it was a concept which suited the Austrian ends very well. In their eyes it left little to chance, would probably ensure success and should preserve the Austrian army. The plan also clearly showed signs that Napoleon's opponents had at last learned something from him, in particular the need to focus on beating Napoleon himself and his army, rather than on taking territory. But their deliberate avoidance of Napoleon's favourite device, the decisive battle, gave the plan – as originally conceived – little chance of achieving a quick victory. It can best be summarised as a strategy to avoid any unequal battle and so wear down the enemy, in order to fall on his weakened elements with superior forces and defeat them in detail.

Supreme command was vested in Schwarzenberg, who in the absence of the Archduke Charles was Austria's senior commander and who enjoyed Metternich's confidence. In the strategic and operational direction of the campaign, his chief lieutenants were Field Marshal Count Josef Radetzky, the Austrian chief of staff; and Freiherr Friedrich von Langenau, a defector from the Saxon army. Once Austria had joined the allies, Metternich was determined that her preponderance in terms of troops should be recognised and that an Austrian should have the supreme command: 'The important thing', he wrote, 'is to have the decisive voice in the determination of the military dispositions, and to maintain . . . the principle that the power that puts 300,000 men into the field is the first power . . .' The Tsar conceded the point, but still wanted to influence the choice. The logical man in his view was the Archduke Charles, with Jomini as his chief of staff. Jomini had recently defected from the French army after a quarrel with his former commander, Ney, and had joined the allies. This was an interesting proposal, although both men were devotees of the methods of the *ancien régime* in warfare – and both were mistrusted by the Prussians, who were scornful of Bernadotte, Jean Moreau and Jomini, whom they regarded as French renegades. Not that Metternich considered such a combination as desirable, since he was aware of the personal connections between Charles and the Tsar; in any case, Charles was out of favour with the Emperor of Austria and his ministers and most unlikely to be approved. Metternich expected enough difficulties with his allies, let alone with Napoleon, without adding to them from within his own camp: 'We want a *Feldherr* who will make war, not one who wants to be a politician. The Archduke wants to be minister for foreign affairs too . . .'

Schwarzenberg may have held the command, but the allied sovereigns all surrounded themselves with their own advisers: the Emperor Francis with General Duka von Kadar; Frederick William with Karl von der Knesebeck; the Tsar with Jomini, Moreau, Prince Pyotr Wolkonsky, War Minister Count Alexei Arakchaiev, and General Karl Diebitsch. The turmoil which this crowd produced soon drove Schwarzenberg to complain bitterly that 'It really is inhuman what I must tolerate, surrounded as I am by feeble-minded people, fools of every description, eccentric project makers, intriguers, asses, babblers . . .' Commanders in modern operations complain of the effects that instant, real-time communications have on the ability of capitals to interfere with decision-making on the ground in theatres of operations. There is, it seems, little new in this, for Schwarzenburg had the allied sovereigns literally at his back throughout the coming campaign. Orders were often transmitted from headquarters to the armies by the monarchs, who were also prone to issuing threats to withdraw or redirect their contingents when it suited them. Everyone, too, was suspicious of Bernadotte, accusing him of secret negotiations with the French, and (with some justice), of saving his own troops while sacrificing theirs. But with all that said, the presence of the Emperors of Russia and Austria and the King of Prussia at allied headquarters did help to maintain allied unity and mitigate the independent spirit of Prussian, Russian and Austrian generals.

* * *

While the allies consulted, Napoleon had been making good his losses as fast as only he could. By August he had expanded Eugène's army in Italy, along with General Count Karl von Wrede's Bavarian corps, to a strength of almost 200,000 men. This force would, he hoped, tie down the bulk of the Austrian armies if and when she entered the war. In addition, the Elbe fortresses and isolated garrisons accounted for another 50,000 men. In the Central European theatre his main field army was reinforced to almost 400,000 men, with an excellent artillery arm of 1,300 guns, but only 40,000 cavalry. This army, like that of the allies, was becoming more and more multinational and now included formations of Danes, Poles, Italians, Saxons and other Germans, as well as a host of individuals from all corners of the empire. The difference was that Napoleon remained in complete command. He was therefore able to leave the completion of his plans to a relatively late date – it was 12 August before he had settled matters. He then took, for him, the highly unusual step of asking the opinions of his Marshals. This may have been inspired by the loss of Ney's chief of staff, Jomini, but more likely it was due to the circumstances, which were like no others Napoleon had ever faced.

Clearly, Napoleon had no intention of retiring behind the Rhine and waiting for the attack of a united Europe. Nor could he, given the force ratios, launch an all-out offensive campaign. Then there was still the treachery of Sweden and Prussia, which remained unpunished. It seems from his correspondence that Napoleon expected the allied main effort to be with the Army of Silesia, possibly reinforced from Austria. Alternatively, he felt that the Austrian army might move generally north or north-west to unite with the Army of Silesia. What he did not expect was what the allies actually did: reinforce the Army of Bohemia from that of Silesia. His intentions, in the light of these expectations, were set out in letters to Oudinot, Ney and Marmont on 12 August in which he wrote that:

> It seems to me that the present campaign can only lead us to a good result if, to begin upon, there is a great battle . . . However, it appears to me that, in order to have a decisive and brilliant affair, there are more favourable chances in holding ourselves in a more concentrated position and awaiting the arrival of the enemy.

For the first time in his career, therefore, Napoleon was contemplating an operational, if not a tactical, defensive – but as the precursor to further offensive action: 'I need not say that, whilst disposing yourself in echelons, it is indispensable to threaten to take the offensive.'

Napoleon's plan required a division of his forces – again this was most unusual for one who generally sought concentration – and given the strength of the allies it was a high-risk course. In the north Oudinot was given an independent command consisting of IV, VII and XII Corps, General François-Etienne Kellermann's III Cavalry Corps, Girard's division of III Corps and General Jan Dombrowski's Polish division from V Corps. Also joining him from Hamburg would be Davout's XIII Corps – in all, a total of 120,000 men. Oudinot's task was offensive: his forces were to advance on Berlin, destroy Bernadotte's army and then to advance on Stettin. In this can be seen not only Napoleon's wish to punish Frederick William and Bernadotte, but also traces of his original plan to recover the forces and territories in the east. The choice of Oudinot was a strange one. Soult would have been the obvious choice, but Soult had left for Spain. Even so, there remained Marmont and Davout, or Marshal Laurent St Cyr, or Marshal Jean-Pierre Augereau, or Marshal Adolphe Mortier, whom Napoleon had left behind in Moscow in 1812. All were proven combined-arms commanders and Mortier knew Germany as well as any French general. Napoleon owed Oudinot a debt after the crossing of the Beresina, but his choice for this command was ultimately to prove disastrous. What the plan seems to show is that by 1813 – and probably since the Danube campaign against Austria in 1809 – Napoleonic armies had become too large and unwieldy for even Napoleon's genius to command alone. The staff work involved in controlling so many subordinate formations and the systems for issuing orders in a timely manner stretched the technology of the time to an unsustainable degree.

While Oudinot carried out this offensive movement, Napoleon's main effort would be placed in an operational defensive between Görlitz and Dresden. With his left flank and his rear firmly anchored on the mighty River Elbe, on which he held every crossing and every fortress, Napoleon felt secure. From this line, he could exploit any allied mistakes with an army composed of the 300,000 men of I, II, III, V, VI, XI and XIV Corps; the Guard; and I, II, IV and V Cavalry Corps – this without taking into account the garrisons of his fortresses. Thus the Elbe was not to be just a line of defence: it was, with the city of Dresden, which was fortified and developed as the centre of operations, a base for subsequent offensive movements as well as an artery for the logistic supply of the army: 'What is important to me', Napoleon wrote, 'is not to be cut off from Dresden and the Elbe; I care little for being cut off from France.'

The plan had much to recommend it. The position of Austria remained uncertain until 12 August, and had Napoleon ordered an offensive straight away in the south he would probably have had to deal with an allied withdrawal deep into Poland, which he would have had to follow while the other allied armies closed in behind him. Given his already stretched communications, the state of his army and the threat to his southern flank, this was not a prospect to be relished. Even so, St Cyr was worried that Napoleon had divided his forces and had underestimated the power of the reinforced allied Army of the North. In answer to Napoleon's request for advice he wrote some prophetic words: 'I greatly fear lest on the day on which Your Majesty gains a great victory, and believes you have won a decisive battle, you may learn that you have lost two.'

On 7 August, in accordance with their agreed plan, Russian troops began marching from Silesia to join the Army of Bohemia. Five days later bonfires on the hills around Prague proclaimed that the Congress was disbanded without agreement, for Napoleon had rejected the terms proposed; and that the armies of Austria would march with their Russian and Prussian allies. That same day Blücher, with the Prussian corps of Kleist and the Russian corps of General Fabien Sacken von der Osten, General Count Guillaume St Priest and General Count Louis Langeron, moved into the strip of neutral territory. By 15 August he was in contact with the French piquets.

Chapter 5

'*Come on, you fighting villains!*'

The Campaign of Vitoria, May–July 1813

King Joseph may not have received the 29th Bulletin until mid–February 1813, but Lord Liverpool had it by the smugglers' route on 21 December 1812, just five days after its arrival in Paris. He sent it on straight away to Wellington, to consult him on possible future courses of action, since no one could yet be certain whether, faced by the threat to his empire in Central Europe, Napoleon would leave an army in Spain at all. If the French did withdraw, Lord Liverpool and the allied governments would have to decide quickly what to do with the armies in the peninsula. Although a number of schemes were discussed, this dilemma had, by March 1813, resolved itself when it became clear that Spain would not be abandoned by the French but that their force levels would be reduced. There was, however, pressure from Hanover and Brunswick to send the KGL and Brunswick contingents back to Germany to support the war there. Wellington consulted the senior Hanoverian general, Karl Alten, whose view was simple: the 7,000 or so German troops now in Spain made a considerable difference on any peninsular battlefield, but they would be lost among the great hosts assembling on the Elbe. 'The best thing for England, for Germany, and for the world', he said, 'is to make the greatest possible effort *here*.'

Once Wellington became aware of the extent of the French commitment to anti-guerrilla operations and of the scale of the thinning-out, he knew that the time was right to use his reinforced and experienced army to strike a decisive blow. This would entail a change in the 'cautious system', the waiting game which he had been forced to play since 1809. This caution resulted partly from the need to build up Portugal and its army, and partly because England could not replace the one-quarter of its entire army that Wellington commanded, if he lost it. Wellington knew this well: 'I could lick those fellows any day, but it would cost me 10,000 men and, as this is the last army England has, we must take care of it.' Thus the army could undertake defensive operations based on strong positions, but there would be no gambles. Salamanca had modified this view: it was an offensive battle which recalled Wellington's triumphs in India and brought home to the allies that they *could* fight offensive battles against the French and win.

Although he never wrote it down formally, Wellington's plan for 1813 is clear from his correspondence. The campaign's aim was no less than the complete liberation of Spain, which would follow as the natural consequence of the destruction of Joseph Bonaparte's armies in a decisive battle: 'I cannot', he wrote, 'have a better opportunity for trying the fate of a battle which, if the end should be successful, must oblige him to retire altogether.' The campaign thus conceived would be an offensive at the operational and tactical levels of war, a deliberate and well-planned seizure of the initiative brought about by a series of enveloping moves on the French northern flank, by which they would be pushed back to the plain of Vitoria, attacked frontally, enveloped from the north-east, and destroyed. To carry out this bold plan, two subsidiary, diversionary, operations were required. First, the Anglo-Sicilian army at Alicante would tie down Suchet's army, preventing it from joining Joseph, and thus create favourable force ratios for the main army. It was for this task that Wellington had held back this army against Bentinck's proposed expedition to Italy. Secondly, Lieutenant-General Sir Rowland Hill's 2nd Division at Coria would carry out a deception by threatening to advance up the Tagus, link up with Murray and turn the French left. To reinforce this deception, the Spanish armies would make demonstrations in La Mancha and Estremadura to confuse the French and prevent a concentration against the main allied army.

While these diversions unfolded, the main allied army was to concentrate in northern Portugal, divided into two wings. The main effort would be placed with the left wing under Lieutenant-General Sir Thomas Graham, who would command a corps of six infantry divisions and one cavalry division. Graham's tasks were to outflank the French positions on the Douro by crossing the river inside Portugal, then to move north and east across the Tras-os-Montes mountains and link up with the Spanish Army of Galicia. At the same time the right wing, commanded by Wellington himself, with the remaining British and Portuguese, and two Spanish, divisions would march on the River Tormes, link up with Hill at Moralaja and force a passage over the river. Once communications had been established between the two wings, the whole army would then advance, with the main effort always on the left, so as to envelop the French from the north. The army would cross the Esla river at its headwaters and traverse, with guns and wagons, one of the wildest and most trackless regions of Spain, until after a march of nearly 500 kilometres the allies would appear behind the French at Vitoria. If all went well, the French would be caught dispersed – and destroyed in detail.

This bold and simple plan was worthy of Napoleon himself at the height of his powers and it shows Wellington in his true light as a commander of genius at the operational level of war. It was, moreover, a plan that depended on surprise and on sea power. To ensure surprise, Wellington relied on the intimate knowledge of French movements and dispositions, and corresponding ignorance of their own by the other side, which the guerrillas gave them. Surprise depended too on the success of their deception operations and on detailed reconnaissance by their engineers and commissariat officers of the proposed route. This would help ensure a fast move to which the French, even if they realised what was afoot, would be unable to react in time. Sea power was

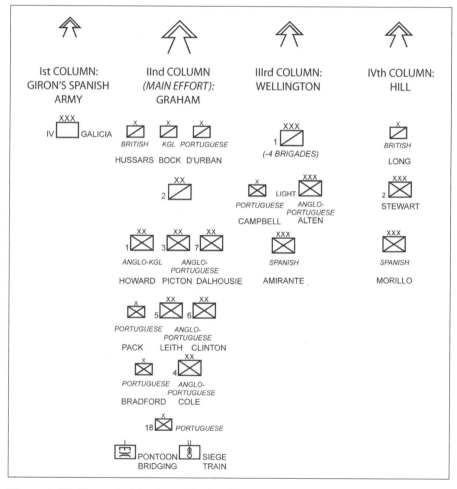

Figure 3: Wellington's March to Vitoria, 20 May–21 June 1813.

vital to cover the move of supplies, ammunition and heavy artillery by ship to Santander on the northern coast of Spain, a port which the Royal Navy had seized and which the Spanish now held; for while Wellington threatened the French communications from Vitoria through Bayonne, he intended to secure his own. Once across the Esla, the base of operations would be transferred to Santander, not only shortening the land lines of communication from Portugal across this most difficult of terrain, but also reducing the vulnerable sea passage from England by 600 kilometres.

While the allied armies assembled in northern Portugal, the French remained ignorant of allied intentions until a remarkably accurate report from a spy reached Joseph's headquarters on 20 May. Fortunately for the allies, Joseph's principal subordinate, Marshal Jean-Baptiste Jourdan, deceived by the knowledge that Wellington's headquarters had not moved, issued no orders for any changes in dispositions. The armies thus remained dispersed on anti-guerrilla operations and along their lines of communication. This ironically presented a potential difficulty for Wellington: as his army pushed the French back on their own reinforcements, the French would grow stronger – there were 125,000 troops available in north Spain, 175,000 if Suchet could link up – while the allied strength would undoubtedly be reduced by straggling and casualties during the long march. Wellington's need for speed and security was thus absolutely vital: either he would break the French decision-making cycle, or he would be defeated with no prospect of being able to withdraw. Thus the French must be confronted with a dilemma that they could not solve: remain dispersed to fight guerrillas and be destroyed by the allied armies, or concentrate and let loose the guerrillas. This dilemma would effectively ensure that, even with full knowledge of the allied intentions, the French would be quite unable to react in time and thereby would be surprised.

*   *   *

As Napoleon pursued the allies after Lutzen, the armies of the coalition began their march into Spain. Wellington had not expected the march across the Tras-os-Montes to be easy, but it proved even worse than had been feared. Even so, on 22 May the right wing began its advance towards Salamanca. On the 26th contact was made with the French division of General Eugène Villatte on the Tormes and a fight went on all day as Hill's troops drove the French away from Salamanca towards the Douro. To Jourdan, everything seemed to point to an allied advance directly into Spain through Salamanca and he issued orders for a concentration to meet it. This was no easy matter to achieve, given the dispersion of the French armies. Reille's Army of Portugal had one division at Valladolid, another on its way there, its cavalry on the Esla and the rest

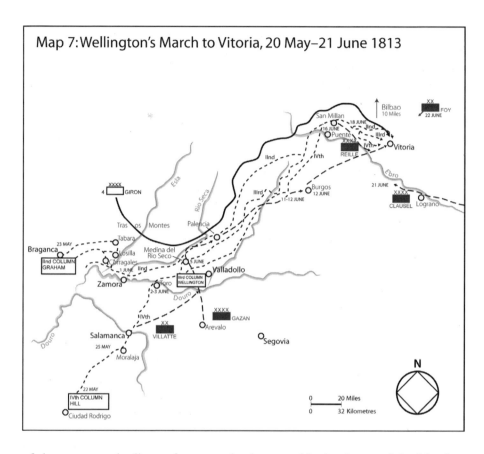

Map 7: Wellington's March to Vitoria, 20 May–21 June 1813

of the army on the lines of communication or with the Army of the North – and that army was closely engaged with the guerrillas. The Army of the South had one division on the Tormes at Salamanca and the rest of the army split between Avila and Madrid. Finally D'Erlon's Army of the Centre was spread between Zamora, Toro and Valladolid.

But on reaching the Tormes, Hill halted, threw out a cavalry screen – and waited. He waited while the left wing completed its 320-kilometre outflanking march to the north. The going was hard indeed, for the roads were few and little better than tracks; guns and wagons had to be hauled by hand over the steep and rugged terrain – at frequent intervals they had to be dismantled and carried while men and horses scrambled for a foothold on the rocky crags. By the 28th Graham's corps, in three columns, had crossed the Spanish frontier and was marching hard for the Esla. The next day they reached the flooding river, which they crossed by pontoon and ford. A day later the advanced guard entered Zamora, where Wellington himself had ridden to meet them. Before

Joseph and Jourdan even knew what was happening, their right flank had been turned, just as Wellington had intended.

It was too late for the French to do anything but pull back. On 2 June, realising that the position on the Douro was untenable, the French evacuated Toro, closely followed by the allies; by 4 June the whole allied army was north of the Douro. Losing no time, the army marched north-east in four columns for fourteen days without a halt across the easy going of the Castilian plain, a light cavalry screen out in front keeping in constant touch with the retreating French. In spite of the depredations of war and of the French occupation, supplies were plentiful and the people greeted the army as liberators. Knowing that the English always paid for their wants in gold, peasant farmers would hurry to greet the commissariat officers with chickens, pigs, hoarded grain and wine. Against such a march, as speedy and audacious as anything the *Grande Armée* had ever carried out, the French were, as Wellington had foreseen, quite unable to react in time: it was retreat or be cut off. Valladolid, headquarters of King Joseph himself, was evacuated on 2 June, Palencia on 7 June. Jourdan, accepting Gazan's advice, urged that all troops in the far north should be recalled and an attack mounted in strength towards the allied communications in Portugal, but Joseph would have none of it. Wellington had by now success-fully linked up with the Spanish Army of Galicia, increasing his strength to almost 100,000 men. This brought its own problems, principally demands from the Spanish for ammunition and supplies. Wellington's answer to these demands was characteristic: 'Either stay and do your best, or go back and I'll do my best without you.' He was even sharper with the Spanish war minister: 'Here is an army which is clothed, armed and disciplined, but which cannot be brought into action with the enemy: I am obliged to keep it in the rear. How can troops march without provisions, or fight without ammunition?'

But the French knew nothing of these difficulties. On 9 June Joseph at last sent word to Clausel to join him with every available man from the Army of the North. Probably he hoped that Wellington would advance from Valladolid towards Burgos by the main road, where he might be blocked; but Wellington was still pressing on with the envelopment. On 12 June the allies halted to allow their supplies to catch up, for the Spanish troops were actually starving and had begun to plunder their own people. Hill's column was, however, pushed forward with most of the allied cavalry towards Burgos, forcing Reille's troops covering the approaches to the city to withdraw. Once again, Joseph found himself confronted with the possibility of a battle before he had con-centrated the army, or else retreat. Again he chose retreat. That night, the army left Burgos, blowing up the castle as they went.

Even as they did so, and as the armistice of Pleiswitz was being concluded far away in Germany, Wellington once more ordered the left wing to push on across the Esla. Leaving only cavalry to screen the main Burgos–Bayonne road, the army again left the plains for rough country. Wellington's intention, still keeping his main effort on the left, was to march north, cross the Ebro river between Rocamunde and Puenta Arenas, then turn east and strike the French communications at Vitoria some 30 kilometres behind their main line of defence, thus completing his grand plan. For the next three days the army pushed on. Considering the broken, dry and hilly country through which they marched, and the scarcity of food and water, the advance was amazingly fast: 44 kilometres (28 miles), for example, on 15 June alone, the day on which the army again turned east to cross the Ebro. By 16 June the army had marched over 400 kilometres into enemy territory, but it was still – at least the British, KGL and Portuguese – according to one witness, '. . . in great fighting order, and every man in better wind than a trained pugilist.'

Throughout these days, Jourdan had waited for news of the allied advance along the main road from Burgos and his apprehension grew as his patrols brought no word. It was not until 17 June that his cavalry made contact with the allies near Puente Arenas, and Joseph gave orders to Reille to assemble the Army of Portugal at Osma, ready to move towards Bilbao. Next day, Reille's men met the allies heading east – not north as they had expected – at the village of San Millan. The French, caught off guard, lost 500 casualties. More importantly, however, Joseph realised that the Ebro was already outflanked; he could not risk the loss of his line of communications, nor the huge supply depots around Vitoria. There was nothing for it but to order a general retreat on Vitoria, where he hoped to find the army of General Clausel, the bulk of the Army of Portugal, and at least 4,000 men from the Army of the North. D'Erlon and Gazan too were ordered to fall back on Vitoria, which both did with considerable skill, since the troops concerned could only get to Vitoria through the narrow pass at Puebla and Wellington was far closer to the pass than they. Reille was ordered to delay the allies in order to gain time for the move of the rest. Whether or not Wellington appreciated the opportunity he had of dividing the French forces and defeating them is uncertain, but by the time his army arrived in the vicinity, the French were well on their way. Clausel too was on the march from Pamplona, with four divisions. On 19 June he was at Logroño, where he had news that led him to believe that Joseph was concentrating the armies on the upper Ebro. On 20 June he therefore marched north-west instead of north-east and thus, vitally, failed to arrive at Vitoria on 21 June. Last of all, General Maximilien Foy was ordered to evacuate Bilbao and he too was to march to Vitoria – but he had no chance of arriving before 22 June.

From the French point of view, therefore, the allies held all the aces. They could lay a siege and mask Bilbao and then march to cut the main road to Bayonne, which would force Joseph to march north and possibly evacuate Spain altogether as it would be impossible to feed and supply the armies. Alternatively they might force a battle on favourable terms which, if they won, would force the French to retreat on Pamplona over roads that were impassable to wheeled vehicles. Joseph, having ordered the concentration on Vitoria, was unable to decide which course the allies were most likely to follow, and therefore what measures he should take to pre-empt it – and so he did nothing.

* * *

In the afternoon of 19 June the French armies of Portugal, of the South and of the Centre, with a combined total of 57,000 men, and with at least 20,000 camp followers in their wake, came pouring into the plain of Vitoria. It was a plain only in comparison with the rough ground all around, since it was an oval of rolling land about 17 kilometres long and 10 kilometres broad, funnelling towards the north-east into a bottleneck at the furthest extremity of the plain near Salinas. Here the little city of Vitoria, named for Our Lady of Victories, stood on an isolated hill, clearly visible from all directions and dominating the plain with its two slim, graceful, church spires. The plain itself was drained by the tributaries of the Zadora river, a twisting, rocky mountain stream with alternating shoals and deep pools, fordable in places but with steep banks making passage difficult for horses, guns and wagons. The river flowed generally north-east to south-west; 11 kilometres downstream from Vitoria it made a conspicuous hairpin bend, and here it was crossed by the bridges of Tres Puentes and Villodas. Running south of the Zadora was the main Burgos–Bayonne road, overlooked by the ridge of La Puebla, which was the main French line of communication, and dominated opposite Villodas by a hill known as the Hill of Arinez, a conical mound covered with shrubs and low bushes. At Vitoria this road was joined by the main routes from Bilbao, Logroño and Pamplona, as well as by a number of small, rutted country tracks which crossed the Zadora and its tributaries by a series of fords and bridges in the plain.

Even though neither Clausel's army nor Foy's division had yet arrived, Joseph and Jourdan decided to occupy a defensive position on the Zadora river. It would have made sense to fall back on their reinforcements, but this was all but impossible owing to the enormous baggage trains that were slowly moving up the Bayonne road towards France, laden both with vital military stores and with the spoils of five years' plundering. Thus Joseph aimed to fight a purely defensive battle on a position from which he could either withdraw, covering his baggage, or advance once reinforced: he hoped for the latter. His army had been continuously in retreat since the middle of May in the face of an enemy whom few of the French troops had even seen. His own prestige was at rock-bottom and worse still, he dreaded the rage which he knew would follow from his brother if he evacuated Spain and left France open to invasion.

Joseph had eight infantry divisions and one infantry brigade available, mostly French but including some Spanish troops; 9,000 cavalry and dragoons; and 151 guns, including those held by his artillery park. Altogether this force mustered around 57,000 men by most estimates, which meant that the allied army outnumbered him. To make up for the lack of numbers, however, Joseph had a reasonable superiority in artillery, with large magazines of ammunition and stores in Vitoria. If Clausel arrived, the French total would climb to 72,000; Foy's division would raise it to 76,000. On 20 June Jourdan was taken ill and the disposition of troops was left to Joseph. Expecting Wellington to attack up the main road from Burgos, he placed his main effort there and the army was drawn up in three echelons behind the Zadora river and astride the road. In the first echelon, across the road and west of the village of Arinez, were three divisions of Gazan's Army of the South, with fifty-four guns, their right on the river and their left on the heights of La Puebla. In the second echelon was the fourth division of Gazan's army and Pierre Soult's cavalry. In the third echelon was D'Erlon's Army of the Centre, consisting of two infantry divisions and a dragoon division. One of D'Erlon's tasks was to guard the bridges over the Zadora on the army's northern flank, at Tres Puentes and Mendoza, for which he detached a single cavalry brigade. In reserve just west of Vitoria were the King's Guard division and a cavalry corps of three dragoon divisions, a chasseur brigade and two regiments of lancers well dispersed across the northern part of the plain. He placed no troops on the far bank of the Zadora and, as command of the stream varied from bank to bank along its length, just as with the Spree at Bautzen, this allowed Wellington a free hand to deploy his troops for the attack.

Some 8 kilometres north-east of the French main army, on the upper Zadora just north of Vitoria, was the Army of Portugal. This 'army' comprised only one infantry division, two cavalry brigades and a Spanish division and was placed to deny the northern approach to Vitoria across the bridges at Gamarra Mayor and Arriaga. The main effort of the army was south of the river, but an advanced guard of one infantry and one cavalry brigade was deployed north of the river, later reinforced by the whole of the French infantry division. Finally the Spanish division, supported by artillery, was sent to guard the bottleneck on the Bayonne road at Salinas. Although this force represented an economy of effort, the danger from the north was obvious: cavalry reconnaissance up the Bilbao road on 20 June had identified some Spanish troops, but these were believed to be a deception. However, on the night of 20 June a Spanish deserter came in to the French lines bringing news of a large body of allied troops marching north – news which should have set alarm bells ringing, but Joseph was preoccupied with getting his treasure and supplies away to France. He remembered to order stands erected in the town for the benefit of the townspeople; however, having placed no troops across the Zadora, he did not remember to order the entrenchment of the position, nor the destruction of the bridges over the river.

On 19 June the allied troops were only 14.5 kilometres from Vitoria, and here they rested throughout the day of 20 June. Wellington's plan for the next day's battle was, like his campaign plan, bold and simple: he intended to crown his spectacular march with an equally spectacular battle, a decisive blow that would both cut the French withdrawal route and smash their armies. He had nearly 80,000 men in the main allied army, 100,000 if Giron's Spanish Army of Galicia was taken into account, but only seventy guns. His plan divided the army into four columns. On the right, Hill would command a column of his own 2nd Division, Francisco Silveira's Portuguese division, Pablo Morillo's Spanish division, and a cavalry division of two brigades – 30,000 men all told. Hill's troops were to ford the Zadora well south of the French position, secure the defile and the heights of La Puebla and then push on up the main road to attack the French main body, fixing it in position. Next to Hill, the main effort of the army would be in two columns totalling 31,500 men. While Hill attacked the French, these columns would envelop the right, or northern, flank of the enemy, fall on them and destroy them. The right centre column was commanded by Wellington himself and consisted of the 4th and Light Divisions and a cavalry division of four brigades. The column was to cross the Zadora by the bridges at Nanclares and Villodas and attack the flank of the Army of the South. On its left, the left centre column, commanded by George Ramsey, Earl of Dalhousie, contained the 3rd and 7th Divisions. This column was to move as quickly as possible through the rough ground of Monte Arato, cross the Zadora near the bridge of Mendoza and assault the flank of the Army of the Centre. Once he was sure that the French intended to stand and fight, Wellington intended that Hill's column should begin the attack at 8.00 a.m. on 21 June and that the other columns should be in position at the same time. This meant that the last column, Graham's, would have to make a night approach to cover the ground in time.

Graham's column was placed on the far left of the army and included the 1st and 5th Divisions, Longa's Spanish division, two Portuguese infantry brigades and a cavalry division of two brigades. It was Graham's troops that the deserter had reported to Reille on the night of 20 June, marching north towards

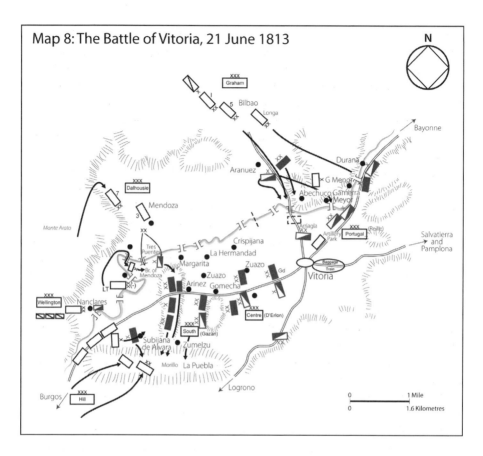

Map 8: The Battle of Vitoria, 21 June 1813

Murgia. Wellington had also sent word to Giron to march on the upper Bayas to support Graham; he did this probably because he had over-estimated the strength of Reille's Army of Portugal and felt the need to add weight to Graham's attack – as things fell out, Giron did not arrive until the battle was over. Wellington's orders to Graham were, however, uncharacteristically vague. He was to maintain contact with the centre columns and be guided by what happened there; he was also told to avoid getting embroiled in a battle in or around Vitoria, but to concentrate on cutting the Bayonne road. This last objective was most likely Wellington's over-riding intention, as the orders to Graham stated that: 'If ... he observes that the troops forming the right of the [enemy] army continue to advance, he will ... turn his whole attention to cutting off the retreat of the enemy by the great road which goes ... to France.' But this primary task was overshadowed by the stipulation to be guided by events in the centre, which must have caused Graham some anxiety. The plan stood a good chance of success but it did contain two flaws: first, the attack was to be mounted over rough ground with considerable distances between the various columns, making communication and coordination extremely difficult. Secondly, like Napoleon at Bautzen, Wellington had not made his intention to sever the enemy line of withdrawal completely clear to his subordinate.

* * *

Early on the morning of 21 June Marshal Jourdan, recovered from his fever, rode out with Joseph to inspect the battle positions. Both were uneasy about the separation of the main army from that of Reille on the upper Zadora and they agreed that this could be overcome if the first echelon troops were moved back, behind the present third echelon position. They had actually sent for Gazan to discuss this move when the first reports began to arrive of Hill's advance. It was clearly far too late to change positions now, so Joseph and his retinue rode forward to the hill of Arinez to observe events.

Hill's attack had gone in as planned but took some time to develop. Morillo's Spanish division was pushed up to secure the right flank of the attack by seizing the high ridge of La Puebla and at first, owing to the difficult going, the Spanish advance was slow; an officer of the 43rd Foot recorded in his diary that: 'the ascent was so steep that while moving up it, they looked as if they were lying on their faces or crawling.' Steep or not, the Spanish troops gained the ridge and, driving the occupying French light troops before them, established them-selves on the crest. Gazan, seeing what had happened, realised that a strong allied presence on La Puebla could envelop the whole of the first echelon of the defence from the south. He at once ordered his advanced guard brigade to counter-attack and sent two other brigades from the first echelon to support the move. This counter-attack almost succeeded, for the fighting was fierce, but Hill had reinforced the Spanish with the Earl of Cadogan's British infantry brigade and this was just enough to hold the position. The severity of the battle on La Puebla can be judged by the fact that Cadogan, the British brigade commander, was killed and General Morillo severely wounded. But Gazan had now seen two things. First, the rest of Hill's column had pushed on through the defile of La Puebla and occupied the village of Subijana without meeting serious resistance. Secondly, the movement of Wellington's own column was clearly visible across the Zadora around the village of Nanclares, threatening the French right. Gazan was sure, therefore, that the attack on La Puebla was not the allied main effort and he said as much to Joseph. Joseph, however, was still sure that the main attack would come up the main road and that Hill's moves proved it; Jourdan declared loudly that the movements on the right were a feint and that the battle would turn around La Puebla. Villatte's division from Gazan's army was therefore ordered to mount a further counter-attack on the heights, supported by two additional divisions, leaving only one infantry division of the first and second echelons actually on the main position. Hill had only so far committed one-third of his corps; his move onto the heights had opened up the French centre and by drawing attention to himself, he was doing exactly what Wellington wanted.

In spite of the slaughter and the undoubted bravery of the Spaniards and British on the heights, the battle of Vitoria was not decided there. It was now 11.30 a.m. and Hill's attack had been under way for well over three hours. Wellington, although satisfied with its progress, had received no reports of progress from either Dalhousie or Graham, both of whom had made slow going over the rough ground. Wellington decided that he could wait no longer and was about to order the Light Division to storm the bridge at Villodas when a Spanish peasant appeared with the astonishing news that the bridge of Tres Puentes, about 3 kilometres away, was unguarded – a scene recorded in the famous painting of Wellington at Vitoria owned by the British Staff College. Wellington at once ordered a British brigade of the Light Division to follow the man and seize the crossing. Concealed from the French by the rocky ground, the brigade set off at a run; at Tres Puentes they found all just as the man had said, but while securing the position they were fired on by some French horse artillery in the vicinity – the second round took off the Spanish peasant's head.

As the riflemen had moved off to Tres Puentes, there were several other hopeful signs for the allies. First, the sound of cannon fire away on the upper Zadora announced the arrival of Graham's corps; secondly and more immediately, Dalhousie's column appeared on the slopes of Monte Arato. Dalhousie, a perhaps surprising choice as corps commander, refused to advance further than the edge of the hills, preferring to wait for formal orders to begin his attack. But Lieutenant-General Thomas Picton, commanding the 3rd Division, would have none of this. He could see the progress of Hill's troops and could also see that the French were utterly unprepared for an attack across the Zadora. Picton was a Carmarthenshire Welshman of unconventional dress, very uncertain temper, colourful language and supreme physical courage. As time went on, his rage and impatience at the delay grew; by noon he could contain himself no longer and, disregarding orders from Dalhousie that the 3rd Division was only to take a supporting role in the eventual attack, sent word back to Wellington that: '... the 3rd Division ... shall in less than ten minutes attack that bridge [i.e. Mendoza] and carry it, and the 4th and Light Divisions may support if they choose.' Turning to his division he cried out 'Come on, you rascals! Come on, you fighting villains!' – and he was away. The advance was furious; roaring across the front of the 7th Division the troops surged across the river by the bridge and a nearby ford and, supported by the fire of the light brigade at

Tres Puentes, blew away the light French covering force of cavalry and horse artillery.

As Picton attacked and Dalhousie dithered, Graham advanced down the Bilbao road. Reaching the village of Aranguiz, his column made contact with the French advanced guard division and halted. Reille himself was with the French troops and was horrified to see the size of the allied column bearing down on him; he quickly decided that here was not the place to fight. At noon Graham had made up his mind to delay no longer and begin the attack, but as his assaulting brigades moved forward, the French withdrew in front of them back to their main position south of the Zadora. The French had fortified the three villages of Gamarra Mayor, Gamarra Menor and Abechuco, which could be supported by the fire of their artillery south of the river. Graham therefore deployed his divisions to clear these villages, which he had to do in order to seize the crossings over the river. On the left Longa's Spanish division successfully cleared Gamarra Menor and pushed on to the Durana bridge, where they came into contact with their compatriots in the Franco-Spanish division of General the Marques of Casa Palacio. As Longa's division had no artillery and the Franco-Spanish troops were well supplied with guns, it was not until after 2.00 p.m. that Longa's men succeeded in storming Durana and cutting the main road. While the two opposing Spanish formations battled it out, the 5th Division deployed in front of Gamarra Mayor and Abechuco, which they stormed. The British troops had to fight hard and suffered heavy losses before they succeeded in clearing the villages, but even when they had done so, it proved impossible to advance across the river in the face of the deadly, accurate fire of the French artillery. Although by the early afternoon, therefore, Longa's men had reached their objective, the rest of Graham's column had been halted.

Even so, at 2.30 p.m. the allies were over the Zadora in strength and Wellington was ready to decide the battle. Joseph had now, at last, realised that the real threat was not on the heights of Puebla: Picton's rapid advance supported by brigades from the 7th and Light Divisions threatened to overwhelm the one remaining infantry division on the first and second echelon positions, since the rest of the infantry from these positions was engaged against La Puebla and the third echelon position was nearly 3 kilometres to the rear. Wellington's own column too could be seen moving towards the northernmost of the two bridges at Nanclares – the whole centre of the French position would be smashed if something was not done quickly. Immediate orders were sent to General Jean-François Leval, who commanded the one remaining division on the main position, to fall back onto a blocking position on the hill of Arinez. The remaining divisions were also ordered to abandon their attacks on

La Puebla and concentrate behind him. Last, the third echelon – the Army of the Centre – was ordered to advance and take up a blocking position between the hill of Arinez and the Zadora, holding if possible the village of Margarita, but if not, then holding the village of La Hermandad. Thus a new line, 3 kilometres long, would be formed, but it would be no easy matter to execute these orders in the face of a determined enemy who could be expected to press home the attack. Moreover the new line was still vulnerable to outflanking movements from either La Puebla or from over the Zadora.

Villatte's division was still heavily engaged against the British and Spanish troops on La Puebla. Some ground had been regained but the British brigade – two Scottish regiments, one English regiment and some Brunswick light troops – had rallied and driven the French back with great slaughter. It was just at this moment that Villatte received the recall order and broke off the attack: this ended serious fighting on La Puebla, much to the relief of the allied troops who had been in action for more than six hours. Even as Villatte began his move, Joseph's hopes of forming a new position between Arinez and the Zadora were frustrated by the speed of the allied advance. Within half an hour Dalhousie's leading brigades had swept the French out of Margarita and the troops were on their way to Zuazo. Picton, still leading the 3rd Division, was urging his men on dressed anyhow in an old blue coat and round felt hat, all the while, according to one witness, swearing 'as loudly as if he had been wearing two cocked ones.' Wellington's column too was moving up the main road from the Nanclares bridge, with infantry leading and cavalry in echelon behind. In the south Hill's men had pushed on past Subijana onto the ground evacuated by the withdrawal of the French first echelon; the troops on La Puebla, in spite of their weariness, were ready to take the new French line in the flank. Wellington was, however, still short of artillery, for very few batteries had crossed the river and this caused some delay as guns were brought up. As they arrived, they were directed into the centre, onto the original ground of the French first echelon, forming a grand battery, and from there they began to pound the new French infantry position.

But Joseph had a still more powerful artillery arm. All his guns had been safely and smoothly moved from the original position and a great battery formed on the slopes of the hill of Arinez. The cannonade from both sides was intense, but in spite of the proficiency of the French gunners it was to be the infantry who would decide the issue for it was clear that the outcome of the battle swung around Arinez. Picton's troops coming in from the north smashed violently into the French line, completely destroying one regiment and driving the rest of the enemy division, which had barely arrived, up the slopes of Arinez hill in disorder. With their new position penetrated before it was properly established, the French had no option but to fall back onto a new line from

La Hermandad through Zuazo to Arinez. Again, their gunners showed great skill in extricating the artillery; they were fortunate too that the allied deployment was as yet incomplete. But this redeployment was also doomed before it was properly completed. The 7th Division assaulted La Hermandad and in ten minutes captured it from the defending German battalions. This new penetration forced Joseph to order yet another withdrawal, this time onto a line from Crispijana through Zuazo and on to Arinez, a line which was now held by all the remaining infantry of the Armies of the Centre and the South in one body. Joseph, however, still had plenty of guns and ammunition, a cavalry corps of 4,500 men and the 2,500 men of the Guards infantry in reserve.

Very soon the allied artillery too was brought fully into action and a new cannonade began to rake the French position. Both sides deployed about seventy-five guns and thus the artillery fire here was the fiercest ever seen in any peninsular battle. The allied fire was quickly followed by a new infantry assault, it being now nearly 4.00 p.m. The allied attack was mounted in three echelons: in the first echelon were Picton's 3rd Division, part of the 7th Division (the rest never arrived until the battle was over) and Hill's 2nd Division. In the second echelon were the 5th and Light Divisions; and in the third echelon Silvera's Portuguese division and the bulk of the allied cavalry. On the right flank Morillo's Spanish division and the British brigade with it advanced along the ridge of La Puebla to get behind the new French line. The attack was by all accounts a truly magnificent sight, recorded with admiration by those who watched from La Puebla or the hill of Arinez. The French artillery fire was heavy and tore many great gaps in the advancing lines, but their infantry defence wavered: for having already been forced out of two positions, the French were as good as beaten. The men had lost faith in their commanders and, worse still, there were rumours that the Bayonne road had been cut by the allies, who would soon attack from the rear as well as the front. As the allied infantry pressed in from the west and the south, the Army of the South began to retire – a retirement which was ordered by Gazan himself on no responsibility but his own, leaving Joseph and Jourdan to their fate. Jourdan later wrote with understandable ire that:

> General Gazan, instead of conducting his divisions to the position indicated, swerved violently to the right, marching in retreat, so as to link up with Villatte; he contrived to draw away, following the foot-hills of the mountain [i.e. La Puebla], leaving the high road to Vitoria far to his left, and a vast gap between himself and Count D'Erlon.

Most narratives agree that from this point on, the French never made anything like a determined stand and this is borne out by the allied casualty lists.

D'Erlon's men put up some resistance around Crispijana and Zuazo, but he knew that he was doomed if he lingered. His troops were quickly forced by the prospect of complete envelopment to withdraw as best they could to a position in front of Vitoria, where every available gun had been mustered. Yet again, a furious exchange of artillery fire broke out, as much to gain time for the French infantry to form as to damage the allied attack, but it could only be for a few minutes: D'Erlon had received the King's orders for a general retreat towards Pamplona.

The orders stated that what remained of the baggage train and the artillery park were to move as soon as possible; the Army of the South would withdraw by the country roads south of Vitoria and the Army of the Centre by the roads north of the city. The Army of Portugal was to hold its position until the main body had passed, when it too was to retire, acting as rearguard. Since all the tracks and country roads specified in the orders converged on the Pamplona road just east of Vitoria, these orders ensured that total chaos would follow. In fact, chaos followed even sooner than that, for the orders to the baggage train and the artillery park had been issued much too late – two hours would have been needed to get them clear – so that all the routes were blocked with a struggling mass of wagons, carriages and civilians. Batteries of artillery released from the battle increased the confusion as they crashed into the traffic jam, trying to force a way through. It was impossible. Around this great blockage, the soldiers of the retreating army pushed their way in complete disorder, struggling over the six marshy-bottomed ravines and scrambling up the intervening wooded crests that lay in their path, hotly pursued by allied light troops. Gazan ordered all his guns to be abandoned to speed things up; the infantry threw off their packs and discarded their weapons; and by a supreme effort the great straggling, struggling mass of the army, in terror of allied pursuit and in no recognisable formation whatsoever, managed to get away down the road, covered by the Army of Portugal which alone maintained some show of order.

It was entirely due to the Army of Portugal that any French troops got away at all. Longa's Spanish division had managed to sever the Bayonne road earlier in the afternoon and it was this significant success which had prevented the French from withdrawing in good order towards Bayonne. The rest of Graham's column had come to a halt soon after 2.00 p.m., with the 1st Division, two Portuguese brigades and the cavalry in front of Arriaga and Abechuco, and the 5th Division at Gamarra Mayor. Graham's failure to press home a serious attack across the Zadora, thus establishing himself in strength in the French rear – probably the result of his uncertainty about the need to conform to movements in the allied centre, mentioned earlier – meant that Longa was on his own. Although the 5th Division made several brave attacks in the face of at least twenty French guns, the allied columns failed to breach the line of the Zadora. Nor did Graham attempt to reinforce the success of the Spanish division by attacking Reille frontally with one division, passing the rest of his infantry and his cavalry through Longa's position and enveloping Reille from the north-east. Thus the real danger to Reille was the advance of the allied columns in the centre, which threatened to take him in the rear, rather than the more passive threat from Graham to his front. Even so, Reille kept his army in good order and, since much of his force was composed of cavalry and dragoons, he was well able to act as rearguard.

There were some striking similarities between the battles of Vitoria and Bautzen. Both envisaged a pinning action, an envelopment and a move on the rear. In both battles, confusion in the orders led to only partial success by the troops moving on the enemy rear, allowing the escape of the enemy army. Here the similarities ended. At Bautzen, the allies made good an orderly withdrawal and lost no trophies. At Vitoria, the French retreat was a shambles: another two hours of daylight would have clinched their destruction. A pursuit of sorts was organised but it had to be called off after only 8 kilometres: growing darkness, broken ground and sudden, torrential rain made a properly organised pursuit impossible. What saved the French as much as the darkness and weather was, ironically, their own baggage train. The pursuing allied cavalry just could not resist the lure of loot and the story of the pillage of Joseph's belongings has been told in detail many times. The exhausted allied infantry, many of whom had marched 32 kilometres since the previous evening, were allowed to rest during the night of 21 June in and around Vitoria. But rest they did not, for their minds were more on loot than on sleep. An orgy of truly bacchanalian proportions developed as the infantry soldiers of four nations joined the cavalry in helping themselves to the accumulated treasures of Joseph's train: clothes, paintings, church plate, jewels, food and wine, and money – the pay of the French armies, 5 million dollars in silver, had arrived at Vitoria shortly before the battle; only 100,000 dollars found its way into Wellington's war chest.

> The consequence was, that they [i.e. the allied troops] were incapable of marching in pursuit of the enemy, and were totally knocked up. The rain came on and increased their fatigue, and I am quite con-vinced that we have now out of the ranks double the number of our loss in the battle ... I am very apprehensive of the consequences of marching our soldiers through the Province of Biscay. It may be depended upon, that the people of this province will shoot them as they would the French, if they should misbehave.

Wellington had aimed not just to defeat the French at Vitoria, but to destroy them. In this he was not completely successful, for the bulk of the army had escaped, but even allowing for this Vitoria was a smashing success for the allied cause not just in the peninsula, but in Central Europe too. Losses were comparatively light on both sides: the French lost 8,000 casualties, the allies 5,000, of whom 3,600 were British and Hanoverian, 900 Portuguese and 500 Spanish. But the French lost 151 guns, the entire artillery of the force save one gun and one howitzer; 415 caissons and 14,000 rounds of ammunition; 2 million musket balls and 40,688 lbs (140 tonnes) of powder – that is, enough ammunition for sixty rounds per man for almost 33,000 infantry soldiers; 100 wagons; and two Colours. Finally Jourdan's own marshal's baton was picked up among the wreckage and sent to the Prince Regent. In return, he sent Wellington the baton of a Field Marshal of England.

* * *

At 10.00 a.m. on 22 June Wellington's cavalry moved out of Vitoria in pursuit of the French. Contact had been lost the previous evening and as the French had continued their flight far into the night, until they were too exhausted to go any further, a gap between pursued and pursuers opened, which was increased by the cavalry's leisurely start. Coming on top of the plundering, this did little to improve Wellington's temper: out of nine brigades of cavalry available, only two had actually been in action on 21 June. The tardy cavalry were followed by the plunder-laden, drink-sodden infantry at such a pace that the French had a breathing space: as early as the morning of 22 June their battalions, regiments and divisions began to reassemble.

Wellington's plan for the pursuit was that Giron's Spanish army, reinforced by Longa's division, would move north into the Basque country, if possible capture the last convoy out of Vitoria, cut the main road to Bayonne and isolate the French troops in the region – these being Foy's division and the garrisons of the Biscayan fortresses. While the Spanish moved north, the rest of the army would follow Joseph towards the great fortress of Pamplona. There was a danger that Clausel's Army of the North, located near Logroño, would continue to march on Vitoria and find the allied hospitals and all the spoils of battle. The 5th Division and a cavalry brigade were therefore left to guard the city, pending the arrival of the 6th Division, which had not taken part in the battle of 21 June. The main allied army marched once more in three columns. The centre column, formed by the divisions under Wellington and Dalhousie, marched on the main road; Hill's column marched on the side roads through El Burgo and Alegria; and Graham marched on Arzubiaga and Audicana. All these routes converged at Salvatierra, where the mountains blocked the exit from the plain of Vitoria, so George Murray suggested that, in view of the likely congestion, one column should march north across country to support Giron and Longa by cutting the Bayonne road behind the system of French fortified posts, thus intercepting either the convoy, or Foy's division, or both. Wellington adopted this idea, sending orders to Graham that he should either destroy the French troops in the Basque region, or force them back across the Bidassoa river into France. However, bad roads and confusion caused a delay in sending the orders, so that Graham's column fell behind its schedule and became badly disorganised too, with its cavalry stuck behind the infantry.

As Graham did his best to sort out his column, the rest of the army pushed on. On 23 June the light cavalry caught the tail of the French retreat, which was moving as fast as only French troops could, and the rearguard division was brought to battle at Araquil near Yrurzun. After a running fight, the French lost 200 casualties, mostly German troops of General Jean Darmagnac's division, and one of the army's two remaining guns. But the rearguard did its work, for the rest of the army was past Pamplona – which was strongly garrisoned – and marching hard for the frontier: Joseph had stopped briefly at Yrurzun and issued orders directing the Army of the Centre to march through the pass of Roncevalles to St Jean Pied-de-Port; the Army of the South was ordered to march through the Col de Velate and the pass of Maya to the Bastan, where it was to establish a blocking position; and the Army of Portugal to march north to Santesteban and the lower Bidassoa river (parallel with Graham's march, as it happened, although neither was aware of the other across the intervening mountains) in order to link up with Foy.

Meanwhile, on the morning of 23 June, while he was still some way short of Pamplona, Wellington had some surprising news: Clausel had not heard of the French defeat at Vitoria and was still marching on the city. The 6th Division had arrived safely at Vitoria, but the 5th had at once marched off to join Graham, so the defending force was likely to face odds of three to one against. The acting commander of the 6th Division, Lieutenant-General Edward Pakenham, called for help from the 5th Division and from Longa, both of whom were still only a few kilometres away, asking them to return as fast as possible. Pakenham, however, need not have feared. Clausel had reached Trevino on the evening of 22 June and there heard news of the battle. He halted and sent out his cavalry, which reported a large body of enemy troops in battle formation. This was more than enough for Clausel, who had no intention of risking a major engage-ment, wanting only to get away and rejoin Joseph as soon as possible. His first idea was to march by the direct route to Pamplona, but as more news came in of the scale of the defeat at Vitoria, guerrilla activity increased. As reports came in of allied troops heading towards him, Clausel retraced his steps to Logroño, picked up the garrison, and headed for Pamplona by a roundabout route. A long, confused and fruitless pursuit followed until on 15 July Clausel, having evaded the chase, rejoined the main French army at St Jean Pied-de-Port with 11,000 infantry, 500 cavalry and six guns. He had lost 1,500 men on his march, mostly from guerrilla activity. The allied main body passed Pamplona on 26 June and on 30 June Wellington gave the army a day's rest, hoping to resume the pursuit on 1 July. However, the army had become so strung out after chasing Clausel around northern Spain that in the event he needed several days to put things right.

In contrast to the pursuit of Joseph and Clausel, the pursuit of Foy had been a brisk affair for Graham and Giron. On the evening of 21 June the last convoy out of Vitoria, escorted by an entire infantry division under General Antoine Maucune, bivouacked at Vergara, where Maucune told Foy that a heavy cannonade had been in progress all day, but he had no other news. Next day, fugitives from the battle began to come in, bringing news of disaster. Longa's division, with only five battalions, was able to catch Foy's division and the garrisons of several forts that he had collected: in all, about 3,000 men. Foy expected to be joined by the garrison of Bilbao and Baron Louis-Paul St-Pol's Italian brigade. Longa too was waiting for reinforcements and so did not attack. In the ensuing pause on 24 June Foy slipped away. Meanwhile, Graham had finally sorted out the confusion in his column and had struck northwards acrossthe Puento de San Adrian; on 24 June his cavalry had made contact with Maucune, although much of his infantry was still strung out on the march. He could see Maucune's covering force division, and also the head of Foy's approaching column; he could also see that Giron was some way behind the French: he decided to attack at once with what forces he had, which consisted of two Portuguese and one KGL infantry brigades. The troops fought well and gained some ground, but Maucune was able to stand for long enough to allow Foy's division to get past. By 3.00 p.m. most of Graham's infantry was up and Giron's troops had also appeared; Graham was beginning to turn Maucune's position around Villafranca, but Maucune, having successfully fulfilled his mission, skilfully broke contact and retired on Tolosa.

There were now 5,000 British, 4,500 Portuguese, and 16,000 Spanish troops available, plus another 6,500 British and Portuguese of the 5th Division on the march, facing around 16,000 French and Italian troops under Foy and Maucune. Graham decided to limit his operations to pushing the French back over the Bidassoa river into France, doing what damage he could to them in the process. On 25 June Graham's men attacked the French, who were in a strong defensive position, with a frontal assault by the British and KGL infantry and a long flank march to the south by the Spanish divisions. A diversionary attack was also made by two battalions, one Spanish and one Portuguese, from the west and north. Graham also sent word to the guerrillas to cut the French escape route along the Bayonne road. It was not until 6.00 p.m. that distant firing announced the arrival of the Spanish outflanking movement and Graham ordered a general attack. Foy was in real danger of being completely surrounded and, probably with only thirty minutes at most to spare, he ordered a retreat. It was just in time, but with darkness coming the French were again able to break clean and slip away up the main road.

When he met Foy, Reille was mightily relieved that the fortress garrisons had been saved, for he now had a reasonable force to defend the Bidassoa. He ordered Foy to retire on Oyarzun in order to cover the frontier and keep open the communications with the fortress of San Sebastian, since this fortress was now isolated. Its defences had been neglected, it was poorly provisioned and armed, but its garrison was a regular brigade of 3,000 men. The new Governor, General Antoine Rey, had only just been appointed and he set about putting the place in order. By 30 June, therefore, San Sebastian, Santona and Pamplona were the only isolated outposts of French power remaining in the whole of northern, southern and western Spain. The French armies, with the exception of Suchet in Aragon and Catalonia, had withdrawn across the frontier, not even attempting to maintain bridgeheads over the Bidassoa. However, Joseph and his lieutenants, for all their many mistakes, had managed to save a considerable army from the wreckage of Vitoria. Although short of cavalry, guns and ammunition, there were at least 70,000 men available to defend the southern frontier of the empire, even without counting a similar number available to Suchet, or the National Guard battalions in France: it was this successful salvage operation that made it necessary for the allies to fight the battles in the Pyrenees.

* * *

Once the French armies had been driven back over the frontier, it became clear to Wellington that an operational pause was both necessary and desirable, for four reasons. First, although the change of base from Lisbon to Santander had taken place as envisaged, the supply situation had not caught up. Wellington's view was that this was due to a lack of escorted convoys and the subsequent predation by American privateers. Lack of supplies meant that the allied armies were having to live off the land, something Wellington did not like. Wellington's view does not, however, stand up to close scrutiny. In spite of difficulties, convoys to and from the peninsula generally made safe passage, especially where military stores and reinforcements were concerned. It is probable that, because of Wellington's complaints, the successes of the Royal Navy have received insufficient credit. Large stocks of supplies had been built up in Lisbon from the summer of 1811 and in answer to Wellington's charges that convoys were not being sent speedily enough, the Admiralty pointed out that a convoy was dispatched whenever eight or ten ships were assembled. To resolve Wellington's complaints, Rear Admiral Byam Martin was sent to Wellington's headquarters, where at a meeting on 13 September 1813 he showed Wellington a list of twenty-two convoy escorts which had arrived in the port of Passages during August alone. Wellington '... admitted a feeling of astonishment at such activity in support of his operations and overall the tone of the meeting was harmonious.'

Secondly, Wellington wanted to clear the French garrisons from the fortresses of San Sebastian and Pamplona since they were strongly held and could interfere with his lines of communication both with the north coast (and so to England) and back towards Portugal. His siege train had arrived at Santander by 29 June and was landed at Passages for San Sebastian from 7 July onwards, again causing doubt about his claims of poor maritime supply. Captain Sir George Collier's squadron of three frigates and fifteen sloops and brigs began the blockade of San Sebastian on 3 July and supported the siege with six heavy guns and sixty sailors to man them, although in the early days the squadron was not strong enough to prevent the French from re-supplying their garrison.

Thirdly, as well as national problems there was a minor but irritating dispute to be resolved among the allies. At the end of June the Spanish Regency removed Generals Castaños and Giron from their commands, a prerogative which was supposed to be in the gift of Wellington alone as Generalissimo. Wellington wrote at once to his brother, the ambassador, in Cadiz to urge him to stop any further moves of this kind. But he evidently decided that, as the armies approached an invasion of France, the preservation of allied unity was all-important. So although distinctly displeased, he confined himself to a series of protests.

Last, and most important of all, there was a great deal of political uncertainty caused by the negotiations in Prague, as the position of Metternich was well understood. If Napoleon could make peace with the allies in Central Europe, who could tell what might happen if he turned all his ire towards Spain? If, on the other hand, war was resumed, then the best service that the allies in Spain could offer to the whole coalition effort would be to continue to tie down as many troops as possible, preventing their redeployment to Napoleon's strategic main effort. Wellington himself put this dilemma, and his solution, very succinctly in his despatches:

> My future operations will depend a good deal on what passes in the
> north of Europe: and if operations should recommence there, on
> the strength and descriptions of the reinforcement which the enemy

may get on our front . . . I think I can hold the Pyrenees as easily as I can Portugal. . . . If the war [in Central Europe] should be renewed, I should do most good by moving forward into France . . . If it is not renewed, I should go into France only to be driven out again.

It was just as well that the victory of Vitoria had given Wellington the stature to deal with interference from London and, to some extent, dictate his own campaign. For the old scheme of diverting resources away from Spain had never entirely died and Wellington again received suggestions that, with the French expelled from most of Spain, their armies could be kept at bay by Spanish and Portuguese formations, stiffened with a few British brigades, allowing 50,000 veteran British and Hanoverian troops to be shipped to Germany. These troops might be enough to induce the allied sovereigns to offer the supreme command of the armies to Wellington: thus England would hold the chief command as well as the purse strings and could dictate allied policy – what chance then for a separate continental peace? If the worst came to the worst and war was not renewed in Central Europe, perhaps Napoleon would settle for a frontier on the Ebro in return for concessions elsewhere? Wellington, however, would have none of this, and such was his position now that the ministry bowed. His wisdom would be proved within a few weeks.

Chapter 6

'*... it was a close run thing*'

The Battles in the Pyrenees, 25 July–2 August 1813

Napoleon received the news of Vitoria at Dresden on 1 July. He had no doubts about the effect of the victory on his enemies' willingness to renew the war in Germany, hence his agreement the following day to the extension of the armistice of Pleiswitz. For this reason, as much as for the loss of his territories and his prestige in Spain, he was furious, forbidding any mention of it in the press: he could scarcely believe that any allied commander – let alone the despised and underrated Wellington – could be capable of a campaign of such audacity and of such devastating consequences. He had firmly believed that all was well in Spain and as late as 24 June he had demanded the withdrawal of another twelve regiments of cavalry from Spain to make good the shortage in his own army, which had been one of the reasons for his agreement to the armistice in the first place. To Napoleon, there could be only one explanation for this disaster, and that was criminal negligence in the high command. That same day he sent orders for the resignation of Joseph and authorised the dispatch of his ablest available lieutenant, Marshal Soult, back to the southern theatre. He arrived a mere eleven days later.

Soult had already spent five years in Spain. He took with him now a commission as 'Lieutenant of the Emperor', letters of credit for a million francs, a warrant for the arrest of Joseph if he saw fit and orders to throw the allies back across the Ebro. He was to 're-establish the Imperial business in Spain ...' He was also secretly authorised, if things went badly, to open negotiations with the Spanish Regency for the return of Ferdinand VII and the removal of all French troops in return for a separate peace and Spain's abandonment of the coalition. Soult was also told to save the isolated fortresses, but it was already too late to save Pancorbo. In the end both Joseph and Jourdan were permitted to leave the theatre of war quickly and in secret, and to retire quietly to the country. For Joseph, who disliked Soult intensely and personally, who considered Soult untrustworthy, perverse and dangerous and who had campaigned long and hard

– without success – to have him removed from Spain, this must have been all but unbearable.

With these issues settled, Soult applied himself to his task. Soult was not much liked by the army, not only because of his well-known taste for loot, but also because although he was a master of organisation and of the operational art, he had been too often beaten on the battlefield. In the present circumstances, though, his good qualities seemed to outweigh the bad and he at once set about re-forming the army. His actions and his energy recalled that of Napoleon after the return from Russia: first, he re-established discipline and morale, placing the blame for past defeats on the shoulders of the discredited high command and issuing a proclamation to the troops urging them to avenge the defeat of 21 June and sweep the allies back behind the Ebro: 'Let the account of [this] success be dated from Vitoria, and the birthday of the Emperor [15 August] celebrated in that city.' This was a clever piece of work, for most of the troops were old soldiers with a good fighting record, although they were now dispirited by long marches, poor rations, and defeat; a British prisoner, Lieutenant Thomas Henry Browne, noted how after Vitoria, the French soldiers cursed their generals and vowed revenge. Soult appealed therefore to their own good opinion of themselves and succeeded in convincing them that they had not been given a fair chance to beat the enemy.

Soult had 72,000 French infantry, twelve foreign battalions (Spanish, Italian and German), but only 7,000 cavalry available to him, not including Suchet's troops and the National Guard. The overall force ratios were therefore roughly even; both sides had the ability to create a local superiority, but the advantage in this respect lay with Soult because of the better communications on the French side of the border and the allied commitment to sieges. Soult immediately set about re-organising the army as Napoleon had ordered, ending the old division into several armies and creating a new, unified, Army of Spain with three corps-sized formations (although in his instructions to Soult, Napoleon had expressly forbidden the formation of numbered *corps d'armée*), a large reserve division containing most of the foreign troops, and two cavalry divisions. Each division was to have two brigades each of 6,000 men and its own artillery. As things turned out, there were considerable differences in the sizes of divisions but Soult was able to make good much of the deficiency in artillery from the large reserves of cannon and ammunition in the arsenal of Bayonne, which was able to supply 140 guns of all calibres to the army. He was less successful with supplies, so that the troops resorted to their usual practice of plundering – this time in their own country. The condition of the men can be judged from the fact that they had to be beaten off the bullocks that Soult had brought up to pull the guns over the mountains, to prevent them killing and eating the animals on the spot.

With his army back in some semblance of order – and this achieved within the astonishingly short period of two weeks – Soult turned to the operational plan. Suchet, who held an independent command, had no enthusiasm for a joint project, so Soult had three courses of action open to him: first, he could attack across the Bidassoa and relieve San Sebastian; secondly, he could attack through the pass of Maya and relieve Pamplona; thirdly, he could attack through Roncevalles, destroy the troops there under Lowry Cole's command and then move on Pamplona. He had news from Rey in San Sebastian that all was well, and so he decided that the relief of Pamplona would be his operational main effort. In the north the reserve division under Villatte would attack the allied formations there, using a series of demonstrations and deceptions that would include bridging operations on the river and the move of his two cavalry divisions to the Nive and Adour rivers. In the centre the corps of D'Erlon would force the pass of Maya and then seize and hold the passes across the Sierra de Aralar, securing the main army against an allied flank attack. The tactical main effort would be on his left, both to maintain communications with Suchet and to use the road network to concentrate rapidly against what Soult saw as Cole's isolated command.

Cole's force was 11,000 strong, although Soult underestimated its strength, and against it he planned to move the two corps of Reille and Clausel. Reille was ordered to force the narrow pass of Roncevalles, while Clausel moved to the east through the even narrower Val Carlos. These two corps would destroy Cole's formation, press on before the allies had time to make a counter-move, and relieve Pamplona. From here Soult would command the main roads, so that he could quickly destroy the allied divisions in the centre and then either move against the allied forces on the Bidassoa in conjunction with his own reserve, or relieve the siege of San Sebastian, or both. Thus the allies would be forced, like the French during Wellington's march to Vitoria, to retreat or be destroyed in detail. Soult began his preliminary moves on 20 July and he hoped to begin the attack on 24 July. It was a daring plan, which fully recognised the weaknesses of the allied position but it demanded surprise, fast marching through difficult country, hard fighting against a determined enemy and a good system of supply. This last requirement was a fatal flaw from the beginning, for the army was still desperately short of wagons and held only four days' supplies: if the troops could not capture the stores of the besiegers at Pamplona within that time, they would begin to starve.

* * *

For the time being, Wellington's policy was one of wait-and-see, based on a strong defensive line. Once he knew that Soult had come back, he had no doubts that there would be a French counter-attack; therefore his army was positioned along the frontier to cover the likely approaches to Pamplona and San Sebastian – Soult's only possible immediate objectives. Wellington's intelligence reports had persuaded him that Soult's immediate objective would be San Sebastian, using the easy approach across the Bidassoa, before pushing on further to Pamplona. As he only had enough heavy guns and engineers for one siege at a time, Wellington concluded that he must, in the light of Soult's probable intentions, first reduce San Sebastian. He therefore placed his main effort here, in the north. Graham's corps and Giron's Spanish army were to cover the Bidassoa river and capture San Sebastian. Next, a corps under Dalhousie held the passes of Echalar and the heights of Santa Barbara above Vera. Hill's corps held the pass of Maya and the minor passes as far east as Les Aldudes. On the right the corps under Lowry Cole held the passes of Roncevalles and Val Carlos. The Spanish reserve corps of Andalusia, under the Irish-Spanish General Count Henry O'Donnell, had arrived, having on its way successfully stormed the French fort at Pancorbo, west of Vitoria. O'Donnell's task was to invest Pamplona, if possible starving it into surrender rather than attacking the formidable defences, releasing the British 3rd and 6th Divisions to be held in army reserve at Olague and Santesteban respectively. Finally, the bulk of the cavalry, which would not be needed in the mountain terrain, was quartered at Vitoria. Wellington still had concerns about his right wing, however unlikely the prospect might be of any moves by the main French army to link up with Suchet in Catalonia, since this would leave him vulnerable to a French move up the Ebro river valley. Two deployments were arranged to deal with this possibility: first, Mina's guerrillas, now embodied as a regular formation, were ordered to screen the Ebro valley; and instructions were sent to Lord William Bentinck in Alicante to launch a demonstration in Valencia province to keep Suchet out of mischief.

The allied force deployed on this defensive line totalled 70,000 British, Hanoverians and Portuguese and at least 25,000 Spaniards, of whom 10,000 were tied up in the sieges. But the line was a long one, vulnerable to a rapid French concentration since the road network was as good on the French side of the mountains as it was poor on the Spanish. This was exacerbated on the Spanish side by the high ridge of the Sierra de Aralar, which tended to isolate Cole's troops. Wellington was not completely happy with the scheme, writing that: 'There is nothing I dislike so much as these extended operations, which I cannot direct myself.' He might not like it, but at the time there was no real alternative. Wellington was, however, reasonably confident that, with these dispositions, the forward divisions would be able to hold on long enough for him to concentrate the rest of the army for a counter-attack if and when Soult came on.

*   *   *

As Soult made his preparatory moves, Wellington still believed that the French main effort would be directed towards relieving San Sebastian. Soult's clever deception measures on the Bidassoa fuelled this belief: 'I have undoubted intelligence that Soult has moved the greatest part of his force towards St Jean de Porte Pied, leaving at Urrugne the boats, which are two complete bridges. It would appear, therefore, that he entertains serious designs to draw our attention from the side of Irun [on the Bidassoa] and then attempt to pass the river.' Thus Wellington felt no compunction in ordering the storming of San Sebastian. Like Soult's attack, this was due to take place on 24 July but was also put off until 25 July.

The fortress of San Sebastian sat on a sandstone plug about 150 metres high, surrounded on two sides by the ocean, on one side by the estuary of the River Urumea, and connected on the fourth side to the mainland by a low sandy spit less than a kilometre long. The plug was crowned by the medieval castle, but the real defences, based on improvements in the seventeenth century for mounting and resisting artillery, were lower down. On the landward side they were supplemented at the end of the spit by outworks based around a fortified monastery. Since the seaward side was unassailable, the weakness of the fortress lay on the eastern side, on the estuary, which was easily fordable at low tide and covered by sand hills opposite, which lay within the range of heavy guns. From this side, James Stuart, Marshal Berwick, had successfully breached the walls and forced the surrender of the fortress in 1719, and although this breach had been repaired, the defences were little different in 1813 from what they had been almost a century before. Wellington had delegated the conduct of the siege to Graham, and the general's plan called for first, the capture of the monastery; secondly the breaching of the walls in the same place as Berwick had done; and lastly the storming of the lower town at low tide across open ground, since no approach trenches could be dug in the tidal flats.

The besieging troops had originally been Gabriel Mendizabel's Basque guerrillas, but these men had been replaced by the 5th Division and an additional Portuguese brigade. The troops had moved into position on 7 July and forty guns had been assembled from the army artillery reserve, supplemented by those dismounted from ships. The battering of the outworks had begun on 14 July and after two days an assault had been tried and repulsed. After another two days of firing a heavier assault by the Portuguese on 17 July successfully captured the monastery. The batteries were now erected for the main attack and the barrage opened at 8.00 a.m. on 20 July. By 23 July 50 metres of wall had been dropped and a second breach made as a distraction; the engineers had also discovered and mined an old aqueduct shaft running under the main defences across the spit, but the delay of two days allowed the defenders to throw up inner defences. The assault was planned for 24 July but the artillery had caused such fierce fires in the streets around the breach that Graham had to put off the attack for twenty-four hours. Rey, inside the fortress, was well able to anticipate the assault.

The attack was planned for 5.00 a.m.: low tide, just before daybreak. The signal for the attack would be the blowing of the mine, which would be followed up by the Portuguese, while the main attack would be mounted across the estuary. The mine was duly fired and did much more damage than had been expected, but the unsupported assault was beaten off. The main attack columns, meanwhile, had moved slowly out of the support trenches and stumbled in the dark across the slippery estuary. The troops reached the breach, but could get

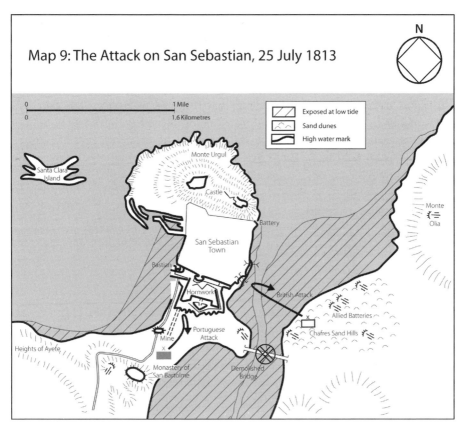

no further as there was a drop of 8 metres from the lip of the breach down into the town and scaling ladders were needed. As soon as the leading assault troops halted, the French opened a devastating fire that killed every man in the breach; with the first impetus lost, any chance of success vanished and after thirty minutes the troops were ordered to pull back. The casualties had been severe: 571 killed in the breach, 330 from the Royal Scots alone.

While the assault was in progress, Wellington had stayed at his headquarters in Lesaca, not wanting to interfere with the battle, but listening to the sound of the guns and trying to judge whether the attack had succeeded. At 11.30 a.m. a message came in, saying that the assault had failed. Wellington ordered his horse and galloped off to San Sebastian to see Graham; the two decided that the siege would be continued using new guns and more ammunition expected from England, which would be used to batter down the main defences for an assault from the landward side. While he was away from the headquarters, the Quarter-Master General George Murray heard firing coming from the east; soon afterwards a despatch arrived from Dalhousie at Echalar to say that the pass of Maya had been heavily attacked but was holding – Murray sent a warning order to the 7th and Light Divisions and some additional artillery to reduce their notice to move, but made no other changes to the dispositions. Wellington was back by 8.00 p.m. and he approved Murray's orders, but without more information he felt unable to issue further orders. At 9.00 p.m. an eight-hours-old report came in from Cole, saying that the pass of Roncevalles had also been attacked, but it too was holding. Wellington still believed that Soult's main effort would come across the Bidassoa and he therefore sent a message to Graham warning him to stand by for attack and to be prepared to mask the fortress while fighting a defensive action. For Wellington could 'hardly believe that, with 30,000 men, he [Soult] proposes to force himself through the Passes of the mountains.' He did, however, send orders to O'Donnell to detach one division from the siege of Pamplona and support Cole; he also sent word back to Vitoria for the cavalry to move up to Pamplona. These orders sent, he went to bed.

* * *

Wellington had slept for only two hours when a despatch from Hill arrived. Hill's troops had been in contact all day and had been driven from the pass of Maya with the loss of four guns and 1,300 casualties. Only the intervention of a brigade of the 7th Division had prevented disaster. Hill had withdrawn but was still in a position to stop further progress by D'Erlon. Soult's real plan was revealed and Wellington issued orders accordingly. The 6th Division was to leave one brigade to secure the town of Santesteban while the main body marched to Elizondo to make contact with Hill; the 7th Division was to march to Sumbilla and make contact with the 6th; the Light Division was to be prepared either to reinforce Graham, or to march east. Wellington rode off with his staff to Irurita where he found Hill, well posted with 9,000 men and no French troops in sight, and there he heard of the events at Maya. Hill's force had consisted of the 2nd Division – one Portuguese and two British brigades under Major-General Sir William Stewart – and Silveira's Portuguese division of two brigades. The corps was dispersed, with the two British brigades in the pass of Maya, the Portuguese brigade of the 2nd Division under Major-General Sir Charles Ashworth in the pass of Ispegui 11 kilometres east of Maya, and Silveira's division further east still, maintaining contact with the troops at Roncevalles.

D'Erlon's three divisions had been ordered to push the allies hard, for Soult believed that success at Roncevalles would force the troops at Maya to retreat or be surrounded; D'Erlon was then to rejoin the main army as soon as possible. But the British and Portuguese troops did not fall back until night had fallen, after one of the bloodiest battles of the Peninsular War. The attack had opened with a demonstration by some National Guard troops towards Silveira's Portuguese, which was thrown back, but it did draw Hill away from Maya to investigate. This was hardly surprising, but Stewart, who was responsible for Maya, left his command and also went to see what was happening. He could not be found when the real action started, so command at Maya devolved onto Major-General Sir William Pringle, a brigade commander who had arrived from England only two days before.

Even if Stewart had been there, things might not have gone any better than they did, for his disposition at Maya was hardly a triumph of tactical planning. The position was a broad, grassy saddle about 1.5 kilometres long and 800 metres high, flanked by peaks reaching another 300 metres higher. The road from Urdax to Elizondo crossed the saddle at the western end, and a track from Maya to Espellette crossed it at the eastern end. Another track running away westwards, still called the *Chemin des Anglais*, allowed communication with the 7th Division. The main road was guarded by a British infantry brigade under Colonel John Cameron, supported by a Portuguese artillery battery, but the eastern track was covered only by a company from Pringle's brigade, while the main body was in Maya village, 4.5 kilometres or one hour's march away. Posted halfway between the brigade and Pringle's company were four light companies, about 300 men. There was a good deal of dead ground on the approaches to the position and the French could easily scout the position.

As a result, D'Erlon decided to force the eastern track with two divisions – those of Generals Jean Darmagnac and Louis Abbé, attacking in echelon, with the third division, under Jean-Pierre Maransin, waiting at Urdax. By 10.00 a.m. on 25 July enough movement had been seen to make Pringle bring up the light companies. They had only just arrived when the first attack of the Maya battle opened at 10.30 a.m. A swarm of *tirailleurs* advanced on Pringle's position, followed by the leading division in column. The speed of the French advance caught the defenders by surprise and forced the small garrison of the Knoll of Aretesque into a tight perimeter, where it held out for an hour, until 260 of the 400 men were casualties, at which point the survivors surrendered. The rest of Darmagnac's division meanwhile marched up to the saddle, at the same time as Pringle's brigade came up from Maya. This signalled the start of the second phase of the action, a series of piecemeal attempts by the three battalions of Pringle's brigade and supporting troops from Cameron's brigade to push the French back. Pringle personally led an attack on the French right flank and an horrific fire fight ensued at less than 100 metres, in which the French suffered more casualties than the defenders; but with odds of twenty to one against, the British were shot to pieces. Within a few minutes, two-thirds of the brigade were casualties and the rest pulled back. The third phase of the action opened with the French pushing along the lateral track from the Aretesque, while Maransin's division moved up the road from Urdax. Cameron had attempted to block the lateral with another half-battalion, leaving only two half-battalions to block the main road. The half-battalion on the lateral succeeded in halting the French, but it was soon turned on both flanks and forced back.

By 2.00 p.m. it was obvious that there was no chance of stopping D'Erlon on the Maya position. Stewart re-appeared, to survey the wreckage of his division. To his credit, he saw that the only hope of avoiding annihilation was to conduct a delaying battle on the main road to allow time for the arrival of the 7th Division, to whom urgent messages for help had been sent. Stewart immediately gave orders for the formation of a new blocking position about a kilometre further south, which was achieved, although with the loss of the four guns of the Portuguese battery – the only guns lost by the Anglo-Portuguese army in the whole Peninsular War. From this new position, the fourth and final phase of the battle was opened. The French did not press home the attack just yet and this allowed Stewart a breathing-space of perhaps thirty minutes. Darmagnac's men had made ground, but the stubborn allied defence had depleted their strength and D'Erlon ordered an echelon change: Maransin's division took up the lead, with Abbé in support, and the new attack was launched at 3.00 p.m.

In its new position, Pringle's brigade had formed two firing lines about 300 yards apart, each of which delivered a volley and then retired behind the other. This effective fire and the irresistible temptation to loot the allied camps delayed the French advance for over an hour; when the attack was resumed,

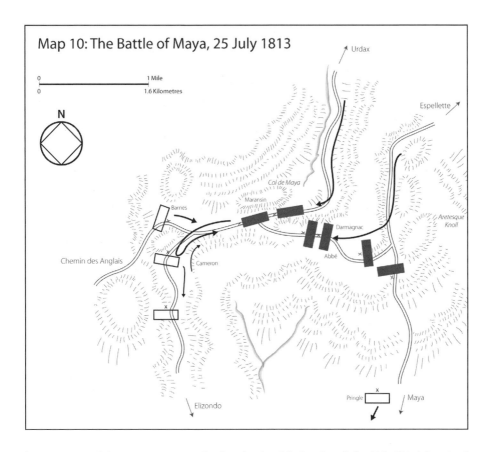

Map 10: The Battle of Maya, 25 July 1813

it was met with a counter-attack, for the lead brigade of the 7th Division had arrived. This attack was temporarily successful, but it was too little to stop the force against it. Slowly the British troops gave way. By 6.00 p.m. it seemed that all was lost, but at that moment the second brigade of the 7th Division under Major-General Edward Barnes marched up. Although the brigade mustered only 1,500 men, Barnes at once led it in a crashing counter-attack onto Maransin's right flank, which, catching the French completely unprepared, flattened the lead battalion. The remaining men of Cameron's command at once gave a loud hurrah and joined the charge. The result was astonishing: Maransin's leading brigade broke and fled, taking the supporting brigade with it, so that the whole division was soon running hard back uphill towards the saddle. D'Erlon assumed that the whole of the 7th Division must have arrived and he committed a brigade of Abbé's division across the saddle. But Stewart did not press the issue; it was enough to have checked the French advance and as dark came at 8.00 p.m. the firing died away.

The day's losses had been horrific, especially on the allied side. Some 1,500 British officers and men were casualties or prisoners out of a force of 6,000 engaged. The French losses had been heavier, 2,100, but this was out of a force of 20,000. D'Erlon reported to Soult that the battle was won but it had been the most desperate he had ever seen. The British troops had fought for ten hours, facing odds approaching twenty to one at times and they were so exhausted that they had scarcely strength to move. When Hill arrived at 9.00 p.m. he brought news that Roncevalles had been attacked and Cole was retiring: the weary soldiers had therefore to summon their strength and march back to Elizondo, 10 kilometres away, or be surrounded. It was there that Wellington met them, and told Hill in no uncertain terms to stand fast and to keep in contact with the 6th and 7th Divisions: for since Hill was now in no imminent danger, Wellington had decided to amend his orders. The 7th Division would support Hill in place of the 6th, and the 6th would march towards Pamplona. Since most of the 7th Division was already close by, this made sense. Wellington himself, shaken by the news of Cole's retreat, which had reached him almost by chance at 8.00 p.m. on the 28th, rode on over the crest of the Col de Velatte to see what had happened. D'Erlon was not following up yet: after the counter-attack late on 25 July he was certain that on the 26th the allies would come at him in strength and that he would have to fight a defensive battle. All day on 26 July he sent scouts towards Elizondo and Vera, and when that evening he had news from Soult that Roncevalles had been evacuated, Hill had been given twenty-four hours start.

*   *   *

Soult had selected two routes for his attack at Roncevalles. Of these, the main road through the pass was quite passable for guns, wagons and horses; this road ran up from Venta d'Orisson on the French side, across the watershed and down into Spain past the Abbey of Roncevalles, where lay the tomb of Roland. This route was given to Clausel. The second route, given to Reille, was a different matter. It was separated from the main route by 5 kilometres across the deep Val Carlos, so there was no chance of mutual support between the two corps. The route itself was no more than a herdsmen's track, impassable for wheeled vehicles as it wound along the steep, narrow Airola ridge until it joined the main watershed at Linduz. From Linduz a lateral track running along the Ibaneta ridge connected the two routes. Also at Linduz, a second lateral track ran off to the west towards the Alduides valley and thus the area was the convergence of a series of ridges commanding sweeping views of the French side of the mountains. Because of this, Soult knew that the allies had already seen Clausel's concentration and that they would expect an attack up the main road; but he hoped that Reille's attack would achieve surprise. This would be vital, for, given the terrain, Reille's three divisions would have to leave their cavalry, artillery and wagons with Clausel's corps on the main road and then advance in a column with a frontage of *two men* for 6 kilometres. The only available artillery support would come from eight mountain guns carried on mules. On the main road Clausel's corps was to be committed in echelon of divisions, followed up by the cavalry, then the guns and transport of both corps. It too was a very long column indeed but the road was good and the slopes each side allowed at least some deployment.

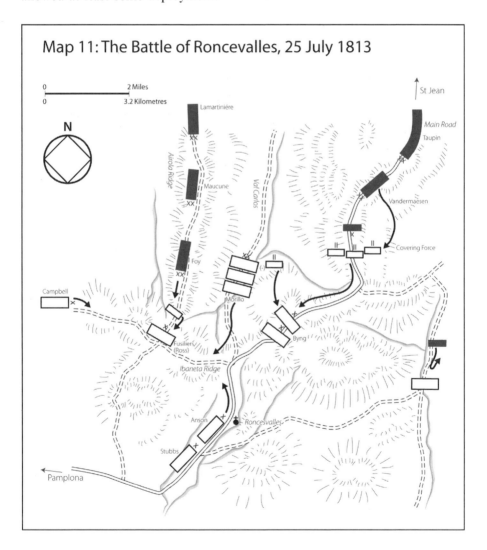

Map 11: The Battle of Roncevalles, 25 July 1813

On the allied side, Cole, in his first command at corps level, had been left in no doubt about Wellington's intention. On 23 July a despatch from Murray had instructed him that:

> ... you should support Major-General Byng in the defence of the Passes as effectively as you can ... you will be good enough to make arrangements further back also, for stopping the enemy's progress towards Pamplona, in the event of your being compelled to give up the Passes ... A sure communication should exist with General Sir Thomas Picton ... in order that he may make such arrangements ... for giving support ...

This had been followed up by a still sterner order on 24 July:

> Lord Wellington has desired that I should express still more strongly how essential he considers it that the passes in front of Roncevalles should be maintained to the utmost, And I am to direct you to be so good as to make necessary arrangement for repelling effectually any direct attack that the enemy may make ...

Responsibility for the pass of Roncevalles had originally been delegated to Morillo's Spanish division and Sir John Byng's brigade of the 4th Division, and the original dispositions had placed the bulk of the troops to defend the main road. Subsequently, Cole himself had assumed personal command. Byng and Morillo between them had a total force of 2,000 British and 3,800 Spanish troops, who were deployed with a covering force of three British light companies and a Spanish light battalion well forward; two British and two Spanish battalions deployed across the main road 3 kilometres behind the covering troops; and a further Spanish battalion detached to guard the flanks on a small path on the right flank. The rest of Morillo's division, with a British battalion, was down in the Val Carlos. On assuming command, Cole had brought up the British Fusilier Brigade to Espinal, about two hours' march away; the rest of the 4th Division – one British and one Portuguese brigade, with an additional Portuguese brigade – were all within six hours' march. On the night of 24 July Wellington's despatch had arrived and the covering troops had been engaged in some skirmishing; then a Spanish informer brought news of a likely French attack up the track to Linduz. Cole therefore ordered the Fusilier Brigade to Linduz, and this was achieved in the dark: by 6.00 a.m. on 25 July the brigade was in position.

The first firing began soon after the Fusiliers had arrived. This was the deception attack by the National Guard. A second deception was mounted on the Spanish battalion holding the allied right, but neither attack achieved any real effect. At 7.00 a.m. Clausel's column appeared in front of the allied covering force and tried to push it aside, but failed. For three hours the allied light troops pinned down the leading French brigade so effectively that the whole of Clausel's column began to pile up. The Spanish and British troops, well concealed in the rough terrain, stood immovable, inspired by the personal presence of General Morillo. One officer, George L'Estrange of the 31st Foot (a veteran of Albuhera, who later commanded the troops at the so-called Peterloo massacre), described the action thus:

> As soon as we could distinguish anything to the front, we saw that the French were coming up ... They continued to bring up their columns for several hours. I conclude that the miserable state of the roads did not admit of any very rapid movements ... General Morillo ... sent out a lot of the Spaniards to skirmish in the front; and we were ordered to defend our position to the last extremity ...

Eventually the whole of the lead French division had to be deployed to the east across the steep hillsides and, seeing this, Byng ordered the covering force to break clean and withdraw. The delay imposed had been remarkable, for it was now approaching 3.00 p.m. and allied reinforcements were well on their way. To the dismay of the French, their enemy's main position was even stronger than that of the light troops and Clausel had decided that the only possible avenue of approach was another long outflanking movement to the east – but at 5.00 p.m. a dense fog came down, obscuring everything and making all movement impossible.

At the western end of the position, at Linduz, fighting had been even heavier. For nearly four hours the Fusiliers had rested after their night march, listening to the sounds of firing on the main road. Cole himself rode past, with the encouraging news that another British brigade and a Portuguese brigade were marching up in support. At midday signs of approach up the track were seen and heard and Robert Ross, the brigade commander, sent forward a company of Brunswick light troops and part of a British battalion to reconnoitre. The Germans got to within 200 yards of the approaching troops and saw that they were French but in no particular formation after the hard climb – just a straggling herd coming up the path at a point where the crest was only 30 yards broad and well covered with trees and shrubs. The leading French battalion, seeing the Brunswickers, deployed and opened fire, forcing the sixty or so Germans to pull back. Needing more time to deploy his brigade, Ross ordered the British troops he had sent forward, a company of the 20th Foot, to charge with the bayonet. The English captain, George Tovey, described the affair:

> ... we came so suddenly on the head of the enemy's infantry column ... that the men of my company absolutely paused in astonishment, for we were face to face with them and the French officer called to us to disarm; I repeated 'Bayonet away! Bayonet away!' and rushing headlong among them, we fairly turned them back into the descent of the hill ...

After only a minute Tovey, seeing the rest of the French battalion coming up, broke off the action and withdrew – but he had gained the time needed: the whole of the 20th Foot had deployed in line and opened a steady fire on the approaching French column, causing heavy losses. But French strength continued to mount and the fire fight increased in intensity, at a range of no more than 100 yards, until the 20th were forced back behind the rest of the brigade, now fully deployed on the Ibaneta ridge. As the French followed up the 20th, devastating volleys from the 7th and 23rd Fusiliers felled first the leading battalion and then the rest of the leading brigade. After that, Foy's division made spasmodic attacks all afternoon, but all failed and no attempt was made to outflank the British position. At 3.30 p.m. Maucune's division appeared, but by 5.00 p.m. when the fog came down it was still not ready for action.

Neither Clausel nor Reille had made any real progress; even if they had succeeded in forcing out the defenders, Cole's reserves had come up soon after noon. The battalions from the Val Carlos had also withdrawn onto the main position so that the allies presented a continuous line of 11,000 troops on a 5 kilometre front: a formidable position, probably unassailable without artillery, and made stronger still when Campbell's Portuguese brigade deployed on the left flank. The morale of the allied troops was high after their successful action – but Cole was uneasy. He estimated the French strength – correctly – at more than 30,000; nor did he expect support from Picton's 3rd Division, marching up from Olague, before early on 26 July at the very best. He was unnerved too by the fog, under cover of which anything might be happening, and took counsel of his fears. In spite of his successful defence and strong position, he decided 'that he could not hope to maintain the Passes against the very great superiority of the forces opposed to him – amounting to between 30,000 and 35,000 men.' He therefore decided to retreat under cover of the darkness and fog. In the early hours of 26 July the whole position was abandoned. The French did not hear the movement and by dawn the whole corps was marching towards Pamplona, aiming for a junction with Picton's 3rd Division at Zubiri. Sir John Byng, the brigade commander, agreed with Cole's decision, but an irate Wellington clearly felt that Cole was wrong and that he had disobeyed explicit instructions:

> Sir Lowry Cole ... retired, not because he could not hold his position, but because his right flank was turned ... all the beatings we have given the French have not given our generals confidence in themselves and in the exertions of their troops. They are really heroes when I am on the spot to direct them, but when I am obliged to quit them they are children.

All in all, the day's fighting had not ended well for either side. The allies had abandoned or lost the vital passes, whose possession would guarantee the time which Wellington needed to concentrate his dispersed army against Soult. But Soult too was in trouble for he had banked on an easy passage of the mountains; instead the French had been forced to fight hard and had taken heavy losses. Surprise had been lost but, worse still, so had valuable time.

* * *

When the fog came down at Roncevalles, Soult must have felt his position to be hopeless, but as day broke on 26 July he realised from reconnaissance reports that, amazingly, his enemies had melted away. His dispatch by semaphore to Napoleon at Mainz was thus one of victory: the passes were forced, D'Erlon had captured four guns and several hundred prisoners and he hoped to be in Pamplona by 27 July. The news reached Napoleon by semaphore on 1 August at the same time as the news of the repulse of the attack on San Sebastian. Napoleon, in optimistic mood, sent to Foreign Minister Maret in Paris, telling him that:

> You had better circulate the news that in consequence of Marshal Soult's victory over the English [*sic*] on July 25th, the siege of San Sebastian has been raised and thirty siege guns and 200 wagons taken. The siege of Pamplona was raised on the 27th: General Hill, who was in command at that siege, could not carry off his wounded, and was obliged to burn part of his baggage. Twelve siege guns (24-pounders) were captured there. Send this to Prague, Leipzig and Frankfurt.

Sending the message to Prague was aimed squarely at the Congress, which was still in session, as much as it was about rallying public opinion in France.

Wellington had sent detailed orders to Picton as soon as he heard of Cole's withdrawal, telling him that the French must at all costs be held in front of Zubiri, where the 3rd and 4th Divisions would be reinforced by the 6th and one of O'Donnell's Spanish divisions from Pamplona. He would come personally to take command. But these orders were soon overtaken by events. Soult's orders to the army for 26 July were an exact replica of those of 25 July, and we can only guess at the carnage that would have ensued if Cole had stood his ground. Reille was ordered to force the pass and then follow the mountain crest to support D'Erlon by taking the allied troops at Maya in the rear – 17,000 men in single file on a steep crest spread over 9 kilometres. Reille tried to follow these orders, but the fog was still thick and the Basque guides did not speak French; in despair, Foy's division, which was in the lead, took the most obvious path. After 3 kilometres this brought the corps down to the main road at Espinal, where the troops tagged on to the rear of Clausel's corps, ignoring the orders to move towards D'Erlon.

In front of Reille's men, the leading battalion of Clausel's corps moved cautiously up to the abbey of Roncevalles but found no sign of the allies; cavalry patrols were sent forward and these soon came up to the allied rearguard, which was bivouacking at Espinal. Clausel ordered his infantry to follow, but the fog was still heavy and it was 3.00 p.m. before General Eloi Taupin's division could get forward. As the division began its move the fog lifted, revealing the whole of Cole's command in a good blocking position on the high ground behind the Erro river around Lizoain. Picton arrived soon afterwards, with the head of his division only 5 kilometres, less than an hour's march, behind him. Picton was looking even more eccentric than at Vitoria, wearing a top hat and blue frock coat and carrying a rolled umbrella. 'Here comes old Tommy' was the word in the ranks of the 4th Division, who knew what Picton was like. 'Now boys, make up your minds for a fight.' But there was no fight on the Erro. Picton, after talking to Cole, agreed that the position was too vulnerable to being outflanked, especially as the enemy was 35,000 strong. Picton decided to hang on until night, as the French were obviously well strung out on the line of march, then slip away again. He sent word to Wellington telling him that in the circumstances, he felt that the only defensible position was on the heights of San Cristobal, just east of Pamplona. By 11.00 p.m. the whole corps was on the march: Wellington's message to hold the ground it had abandoned did not arrive until the column was approaching its destination.

The position chosen by Picton was a good one, but it was within 2 kilometres of the hostile fortress of Pamplona, allowing no depth to the deployment and making the defence vulnerable to a sortie from the fortress in conjunction with a frontal attack. Cole therefore suggested that the position be moved 3 kilometres further north, between Sorauren and the River Arga. This would make use of an excellent position along a steep ridge, 300 metres high and 3 kilometres long, dominated by the heights of Oricain and connected to the outlying ridges of the

Pyrenean *massif* by a prominent col. This ridge offered a strong defensive line on reverse slopes, with secure flanks anchored on two river valleys. The deployment was a defence in two echelons. Forward of the first echelon a covering force of *Caçadores* and British light troops was thrown out; next, the first echelon was placed along the Oricain feature, with two British and two Portuguese brigades in line, supported by KGL artillery and a third British brigade on the highest part of Oricain. The extreme right of the line was fixed on the hill of Zabaldica, which was held by two Spanish battalions sent up by O'Donnell. The second echelon was placed along the original line of the heights of San Cristobal. This was held on the left by a division of O'Donnell's Spanish corps, the rest of which masked the fortress of Pamplona; Morillo's Spanish division in the centre; and on the right the two British and one Portuguese brigades of Picton's 3rd Division. The extreme right of the second echelon was protected by a cavalry division of four brigades which Wellington had earlier ordered up from Vitoria.

The deployment had been completed well before the French appeared, for they had been badly held up by traffic congestion on the one decent road through the rough country. At 9.00 a.m. on 27 July Clausel's leading division came up in front of the Zabaldica, but Reille's corps, having detoured off the main road to try to avoid the congestion, had made even slower going across country than Clausel's men. Clausel at once put his corps into assault formation on a ridge opposite the allied first echelon. He could see troop and vehicle movement in the area of Pamplona and felt sure that the allies were raising the siege: the position opposite him must therefore be only a facade. He asked Soult straightaway for permission to attack, but Soult did not believe that the allies would give up Pamplona so easily and rode forward himself to see how events were unfolding. As it happened, his arrival coincided with that of Wellington.

*　　*　　*

As he rode eastwards, rumours of Picton's and Cole's continued retreat reached Wellington and so alarmed him that he sent a galloper back to Hill to warn him that if things went badly, a retreat to the Yrurzun–Tolosa line might be necessary, but no moves were to take place without his specific orders. In the meanwhile, though, the 6th Division was to march to Olague, Silveira's Portuguese division to Lanz and both divisions and the Light Division were to be ready to move fast if needed. Further down the road at Ostiz, Wellington met Major-General Robert Long with his light dragoons. Long confirmed that Picton had abandoned his position at Linzoain and now intended to fight close to Pamplona. The French were on his heels and a fight might start at any moment. Ostiz is only 6.5 kilometres north of Sorauren: there might just be time to get to Picton before fighting began. Wellington left George Murray to direct troops as they came up and galloped off with his staff, gradually out-pacing them all except Fitzroy Somerset (later Lord Raglan of Crimea fame), his Military Secretary.

As he came towards Sorauren, roughly parallel to the French line of advance, Wellington could see the whole position with the French less than 2 kilometres away. He dashed on to Sorauren bridge where, in the face of the oncoming enemy, he stopped, dismounted and wrote out a despatch for Murray. Fitzroy Somerset rode off with the order: it warned the 6th Division and all available artillery to approach by a safe but roundabout route to the Sorauren position, where it should arrive the next morning; the 2nd and 7th Divisions were to move up to Lanz and Lisazo. Murray had the order thirty minutes later. Wellington, now alone, rode on up the steep track out of Sorauren just as the French cavalry came in to the village at the other end. As he rode into the allied position he was at once recognised by the Portuguese light troops, who set up

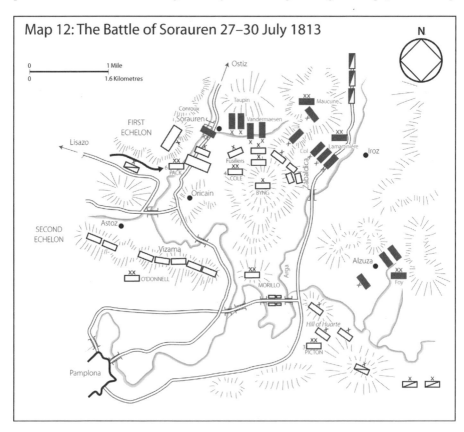

Map 12: The Battle of Sorauren 27–30 July 1813

a cry of 'Douro, Douro!', which was soon joined by cries of 'Nosey!' and 'Our Arthur!' from the British. It was not long before these cries, as much feared by the French as the cries of '*Vive l'Empereur*' were by their enemies, drifted across to the assembling French divisions.

Wellington could see that only about half the French army had arrived. He said afterwards that if only Cole had sent back proper information at regular intervals then much trouble could have been avoided, the army concentrated and the French stopped much sooner. With the French strung out and still deploying, Wellington considered an attack – and an attack might have succeeded, as Soult refused Clausel's appeals for a French assault. Instead, he took his dinner and a siesta while Clausel, leaning against an oak tree, beat his forehead with suppressed rage and muttered 'who could go to sleep at such a moment?' All that Soult did on 27 July was, first, to order a reconnaissance by combat onto the Zabaldica, which was kicked out by the defending Spanish battalions; and then to order Foy's division against the right of the allied second echelon on the hill of Huarte. The two French regiments sent forward suddenly found themselves facing an entire British division – and they fell back in haste. As they went, a violent thunderstorm swept down from the mountains, ending all action that day.

Meanwhile, the two commanders had been refining their plans for the real fight next day. Soult, after a conference with his corps commanders, decided that Foy's division would hold its position to screen the British division (Picton's) on the hill of Huarte, while the remaining five divisions would mount a general attack on the allied first echelon position. The main effort would be on the right, where Clausel's three divisions would attack between Sorauren and the col, while Reille's remaining two divisions would attack the col itself and the Zabaldica position. Most of the army artillery and the cavalry were still jammed on the road and thus very little was available to support the attack, nor did it seem likely that D'Erlon's corps would put in an appearance. Thus success depended on a sudden, all-out blow before allied reinforcements arrived. Wellington meanwhile made very few changes to the initial dispositions, for he was more concerned to get orders away to speed up the arrival of the 6th and 7th Divisions, the whole of Hill's corps and the artillery. These orders were sent off at 4.00 p.m., and with this done, Wellington went to bed and slept well.

* * *

The battle of Sorauren lasted in one way or another for three days and was in the end perhaps more decisive than Vitoria: by the end of the battle and the subsequent pursuit, the French Army of Spain had all but ceased to exist. The first day of the action, 28 July 1813, dawned fine and clear after the storms of the previous night, so that the allied covering troops had an excellent view of the whole French position. Soult spent the morning bringing up and laying out his assault divisions, disentangling his cavalry from the traffic jams on the approach road and bringing up four howitzers and some mountain guns which were the only French artillery available. On the allied side, the 6th Division had marched early and fast and reported its arrival by 10.00 a.m. Wellington ordered the division forward onto the left of the first echelon around Sorauren village, thus securing his left flank against what would obviously be the French main effort. Dalhousie and Hill, however, had been badly slowed by the storms in the mountains and so did not appear at all on 28 July.

The 6th Division came into the line at noon, just before the time fixed by Soult for the main attack. The approach of the division alarmed Clausel, who feared that he was about to be attacked in the flank; thus the first move of the battle was an advance by General Nicolas Conroux's division at 12.30 p.m. against the approaching 6th Division. The attack was engulfed by allied fire on three sides and quickly forced back into Sorauren village, at which point the action paused briefly until Soult's grand attack began at 1.00 p.m. The French came up the steep slope towards the allied position in echelon of brigades, preceded by their usual swarm of skirmishers. The sequence of the attack rippled from west to east and Clausel's initial momentum on the allied left drove in the covering troops and actually reached the summit in front of the Fusilier Brigade, before being thrown back in disorder by allied volley fire and counter-attacks. In only one place did Clausel's corps manage to breach the allied line, between the Fusiliers and Campbell's Portuguese brigade, and although a penetration was made, the attacking troops had lost all cohesion: the severe climb, the devastating effects of volley fire and the high casualties among the officers caused the French formations to disintegrate into groups of individuals. By this time, Reille's attack on the main position was also in progress across the col: it never reached the allied line but was thrown back everywhere with dreadful losses. Seeing this, Wellington decided to put an end to Clausel's foothold in the line and he ordered two British battalions to charge the French left flank, while Byng's brigade was brought up from the support position to block off the penetration. The counter-attack came in at the run and such was the impetus that the French, although in superior numbers, were swept away down the hill.

Subsidiary French attacks on the flanks fared no better. Lamartinière's division had attacked the Spanish troops on the Zabaldica, supported by the available artillery, an attack directed by Reille in person: it was a complete disaster. The Spanish met the oncoming troops with such a blast of fire that three assaults were all ruined. Conroux's division was in contact with the British 6th Division around Sorauren and such was the fierceness of fighting here that even the divisional commander, Major-General Denis Pack, was badly wounded.

But although fighting went on for another hour or more, the crisis of the day had passed. French officers tried to re-form battalions and commit them once more to hopeless assaults but all was in vain. By 4.00 p.m. fighting was over and the French retired to their original positions; there was no allied pursuit, for Wellington was still expecting the arrival of more troops, without which the force ratios were not high enough for him to attack: the French were beaten, to be sure, but not broken and the ground was no more favourable for Wellington's men to attack than it had been for Soult's. The first day of Sorauren had been a classic defeat of column by line and a classic demonstration of Soult's tactical ineptitude. Wellington said of it that it had been 'fair bludgeon work': 2,600 British and Germans had been killed or wounded along with 1,100 Portuguese, 200 Spanish and at least 4,000 French.

* * *

While the battle of the 28th was being fought at Sorauren, D'Erlon, Hill and Dalhousie were all trying to obey their superiors by joining their respective main bodies. Hill had received Wellington's orders in mid-afternoon on 27 July and marched for Lisazo with two British and one Portuguese brigades of his own division; Silveira's division, which mustered only one brigade; and one British brigade of the 7th Division. Dalhousie too had received his orders and marched with his remaining British and Portuguese brigades. But the thunderstorm which had struck the troops at Sorauren hit the marching troops even harder. The columns became so entangled with carts, guns, struggling horses and panicking mules that in the darkness there was no chance of going any further; there was nothing for it but to sit down in the cold and dreary mud and wait for the dawn. When it came, the troops struggled off again. In Lisazo, Hill collected his corps and sent word to Wellington that he had no chance of arriving at Sorauren before early on 30 July. Dalhousie, on the other hand, had fared rather better. Marching all night, he reached Lisazo at noon on 28 July. Here he picked up his detached brigade from Hill and, after six hours' rest, marched his division on to Sorauren, where it arrived that night – complete, after a remarkable feat of marching over two nights on hard roads.

The storm which had stopped Hill also kept D'Erlon from discovering the allied moves. When he did at last push forward early on 29 July, he found Hill gone. He began to move his corps forward, pushing a Portuguese brigade, which had orders to delay the enemy, in front of him and picking up allied wounded and stragglers as he went. His light cavalry soon made contact with Hill's column and also established communications with patrols from Soult's main army. But D'Erlon did not press Hill as he greatly overestimated his enemy's strength – nor did he follow Soult's orders of 23 July which had specifically instructed him to 'seek to reunite as soon as possible with the rest of the army.' Dawn on 29 July therefore found Soult's army at Sorauren in much the same positions as on the previous evening, with D'Erlon's leading division still more than 16 kilometres away. Wellington's situation was much better: the 7th Division was close by and Hill's corps was within one march: by the end of the day, Wellington was sure of superior numbers.

Soult must have realised the logic of the arithmetic and probably planned to withdraw after the battle of 28 July: he sent off his guns and baggage towards Roncevalles that night. But crucially for him, 29 July was the last day for which rations were available. However, his view changed dramatically when he received the news that D'Erlon was only half a day's march away and he hit on a very risky stroke indeed: he would switch the direction of his attack away from Pamplona and towards pushing his army between Wellington and Graham, forcing Graham to lift the siege of San Sebastian. D'Erlon would act as the advanced guard of the army, attack Hill's corps, turn the allied left flank and cut the main Pamplona–Tolosa road. The rest of the army would link up with D'Erlon and here was the risk, for to do this, the army would have to march across the front of their enemies at a distance less than a kilometre. Having offered Wellington another Busaco on 28 July, Soult was about to present the opportunity for a second Salamanca on 30 July.

Soult calculated that in spite of the lack of rations, supplies were on their way – but again this was a high-risk assumption given the state of the roads and the sheer size of the logistical problem. Foy thought that the plan was designed to save Soult's face with Napoleon rather than as an act of war, but the orders stood. D'Erlon was reinforced with a division of dragoons and ordered to attack Hill at Lisazo; Clausel was to leave Conroux's division in Sorauren to cover the move of his other two divisions and Conroux would be relieved by Maucune, who would cover the move of the rest of Reille's corps. The whole move was to be made in the dark during the early hours of 30 July and by dawn the army would, Soult expected, be clear of Sorauren.

Wellington's strength increased that night by two significant additions: the 7th Division arrived and was placed in a concealed position on the left of the 6th Division; and with the 7th much of the British artillery also arrived and was despatched to its parent divisions. Wellington issued new instructions to Hill, accepting the delay in his arrival and telling him to establish a blocking position around Lisazo in case of a French envelopment of the allied left. He also sent orders to the Light Division and an additional cavalry brigade to march to a position close to the Tolosa–Yrurzun road.

The French move began at midnight on 29/30 July when Clausel's rear two divisions moved off, leaving their fires still burning. By dawn they were on the Sorauren–Ostiz road, waiting for Conroux's division to catch up, but Conroux was not relieved until dawn, much later than Soult had ordered, and thus there were two entire divisions in and around the village of Sorauren, in broad daylight and in full view of their enemies. Foy's division was following Maucune, but Lamartinière had not moved and in this vulnerable position the French troops were suddenly bombarded with wholly unexpected salvoes of artillery fire, bringing ruin and confusion everywhere.

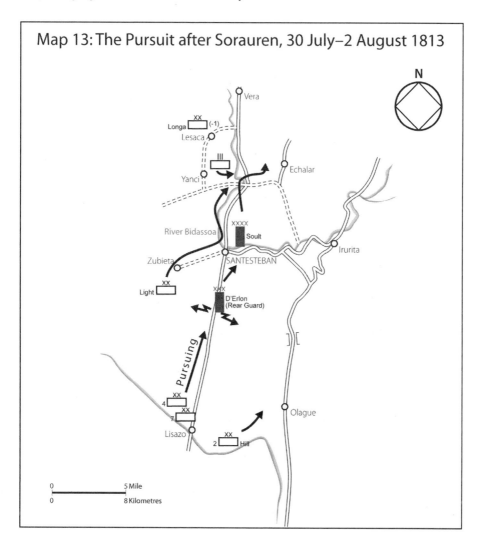

Map 13: The Pursuit after Sorauren, 30 July–2 August 1813

Even in the darkness, the French move, so close as it was to the allied lines, had been overheard and the whole allied army stood-to an hour before dawn. Wellington himself was abroad early and, seeing the French strung out, he issued the order for a general attack. The 6th Division and Byng's brigade attacked Sorauren village, while the rest of the 4th Division and the Spanish troops on Zabaldica went for Foy's column. Picton moved his division towards Lamartinière's division up the main Roncevalles road, intending to cut off the French withdrawal route. Most of the French army was thus caught in column of route by artillery fire and infantry attack, unable to fight back. As Foy later wrote: 'We had not been intending to fight, and suddenly we found ourselves massed under the fire of the enemy's cannon. We were forced to go up the mountain side to get out of range; we should have to retreat, and we already saw that we should be turned on both flanks.'

At least Foy's men could fall back, but the battalions in Sorauren village could not. Surrounded on three sides by British and Portuguese troops, one brigade managed to get clear but the rest of the two divisions were practically exterminated: the total casualties amounted to 3,400 killed and wounded and 1,700 prisoners out of a total of 8,000. The remnants rallied to Foy up on the hillside. Further away, Clausel had halted his two divisions halfway between Sorauren and Ostiz and deployed a two-battalion flank guard above the Ulzama river. At 8.30 a.m. the 7th Division came up from its concealed position, pushed the flank guard aside and closed in on Clausel's column, pouring in a withering fire on the stationary troops. Clausel could not stay still, nor go back to Sorauren: there was only one thing to do. Disengaging as best he could, he marched his column forward up the Olague road away from D'Erlon and towards France.

Wellington issued fuller orders once the initial attack was under way, abandoning the defensive and returning to the offensive, in the belief that Soult could do nothing except retire – and that this retirement would chiefly be through the pass of Maya. Picton was to continue his envelopment towards Roncevalles; Cole was to attack the enemy frontally between the Ulzama and Arga rivers; the 6th Division, O'Donnell's Spanish Division and Byng's brigade were to pursue up the Olague road, co-operating with the 7th Division, which was to remain on the east bank of the Ulzama. The same orders were also sent to Hill, telling him to move towards Olague and Lanz if possible. Hill was also allotted Silveira's Portuguese division, Morillo's Spanish division and the Spanish Regiment of Abispal, detached from O'Donnell, to support him, although 7,000 of these supporting troops were still 16 kilometres to his rear: although they marched hard and as soon as they had their orders, they arrived late in the day.

As Wellington's attack developed, things went no better for Reille than for Clausel. Abandoning Maucune's division to its fate in Sorauren, he tried to form a position with the divisions of Foy and Lamartinière, but Picton's attack threw him into a panic. Terrified at the prospect of being surrounded, Reille gave orders for the immediate escape of the whole corps across country. With these orders, the troops all but ran – with the result that, although in a shambles, by 1.00 p.m. Reille's men had escaped their pursuers and halted near the village of Esain. After restoring some kind of order and gathering up a mass of stragglers, Reille headed off towards Olague, which he reached at dusk with only 6,000 men: Foy's division had disappeared completely, having lost its way and marched through Iragui. From there, Foy continued his retreat the next day to Cambo in France, taking no further part in any fighting. As the French fell back towards Olague, so the allies followed up both on the road and east of the River Ulzama, turning every blocking position which the French tried to occupy. By dusk Clausel was at Olague, where he was joined by Conroux's few survivors – a total force of perhaps 8,000 men out of his original 17,000 – and Reille's 6,000.

What of D'Erlon and Hill, or Soult himself for that matter? Soult was not actually present at Sorauren on 30 July as he had ridden to join D'Erlon very early, before dawn, and so missed the wreck of his army. Reports from deserters and prisoners told him that three allied divisions were reinforcing Hill; Soult therefore meant his advanced guard to crush Hill as soon as possible and he was sure of success. Hill was, however, well aware of D'Erlon advancing towards him and had drawn up the 9,000 British and Portuguese troops available in line on a wooded ridge about a kilometre south of Lisazo, with a covering force of light troops. D'Erlon, with 18,000 men, planned that Darmagnac's division would attack frontally, after which he would envelop the enemy's left flank with two divisions attacking in echelon – Abbé leading, followed up by Maransin.

Darmagnac's attack began as planned, but the attack was repulsed. Abbé's first attack also went awry; advancing through the woods, the division missed its way and it too assaulted the allied position from the front and was also repulsed. Seeing his mistake, Abbé sent another brigade further round the allied flank and this brigade might have succeeded completely but for the committal of Hill's reserve brigade, which threw back the attack and gained enough time for the whole allied division to pull back very steadily across a valley and through a stream, closely followed up by the French, until the allies came to a halt on a new line just in front of the village of Yguras. Here another frontal assault by Darmagnac's division was stopped.

It was now 4.00 p.m. and D'Erlon was forming up his corps for a further assault when, at the critical moment, the Portuguese and Spanish troops from Ollocarizqueta appeared: this was enough to persuade D'Erlon to break off the action. He had forced his enemies back and gained a local tactical success, but he had not beaten them as Soult had intended – however, with a force ratio of only two to one it is unlikely that he could have done more than he did. And what he had done counted for nothing, since Soult's main army was a disorganised wreck camping miserably and without rations around Olagne.

This unpleasant truth dawned on Soult as he rode towards Olagne. In effect, D'Erlon's corps was his only effective combat force; food and ammunition were low and morale was in tatters. There was nothing for it but to abandon the grand plans and retreat as fast as possible back into France, using D'Erlon's corps not as advanced guard but as rearguard. The quickest route for the shattered main body was from Olagne to Elizondo and Maya – the route which Wellington had guessed at – but instead, Soult's orders told D'Erlon to hold his position while the rest of the army marched across country to Lisazo, from there to the pass of Arraiz and so to Santesteban. This was another very risky move and it relied on the steadiness of D'Erlon's men to hold off what would doubtless be a merciless allied pursuit.

* * *

The three-day battle at Sorauren is often compared with Busaco, but in fact it might more usefully be compared with Vitoria. Soult had aimed at inflicting the sort of crushing defeat that Wellington had handed to Joseph in June, but there was no chance that Soult, with his bull-headed forcing of the passes, loss of security and logistic fragility, could hope to emulate the speed, security and brilliance of Wellington's flank march to Vitoria. Nor could Soult match Wellington's mastery of the tactical battle. In both cases the defenders had been drawn up in echelon on ground suitable for the defence, although Joseph had had a secure fortress at his rear while the allies were forced to mask Pamplona and its hostile garrison. But the two attack plans show that the jibes at Soult were well deserved: his clumsy, brutal, frontal attack with insufficient forces does not stand any sort of comparison with Wellington's imaginative enveloping attack. But both battles had one thing in common: at the end of the fighting, the French army was in full retreat towards the mountains. This time, Wellington had no intention of letting them slip away.

* * *

At 1.00 a.m. on 31 July the tired remnants of Clausel's and Reille's two corps marched off as best they could, leaving a trail of stragglers as they went. D'Erlon hung on until daybreak and then sent the divisions of Darmagnac and Maransin away, leaving Abbé's division as rearguard. Wellington was still working on the assumption that the French line of retreat would be through

Elizondo, and as a result the orders for the pursuit meant that well over half the available allied troops were sent down routes on which there were no enemy forces at all. By the end of the day this situation had become clearer. When Hill, whose corps had joined the main army, realised the real situation, and with the news of the smashing victory over the main French army at Sorauren the previous day, he decided to attack the French rearguard under D'Erlon at once. D'Erlon's troops gave ground slowly and repelled two allied attacks with dreadful losses, until a dense fog came down late in the afternoon, which this time allowed the French to slip off. Hill, mistakenly as it turned out, marched his troops towards Maya, leaving only the 7th Division to follow Soult. Wellington, meanwhile, sent further orders to the Light Division to intercept Soult's probable withdrawal route.

Because of the misdirection of the allied pursuit, the opportunity for the French to escape completely came on the night of 31 July/1 August with a march along the gorge of the Bidassoa river. The march began early, at 2.30 a.m., with Reille's infantry leading, then the entire cavalry and baggage with the remains of Clausel's infantry and finally D'Erlon's corps as rearguard once more. On this line of march the only allied troops capable of blocking the route were Longa's Spanish division on the heights of Vera. The allied pursuit too began early on 1 August and by 7.00 a.m. the French infantry, marching on the slopes around the road to avoid the baggage, were flanked by the allied infantry from the ridges above Sumbilla. Soon the whole of Clausel's command was in flight across the hills towards Echalar. Reille's corps at the head of the column was in trouble too: when the French arrived at the bridge of Yanci, they were ambushed by Longa's division troops, causing the whole column to bunch up and stop. Reille's leading troops assaulted the Spanish position, but the firing was misinterpreted further back down the column as an allied attack: dragoons panicked and galloped off down the road, getting hopelessly mixed up with the baggage and infantry. It took Reille himself to sort out the turmoil and get the column moving again but the Spanish, having been forced off the bridge, returned and continued firing on the French, then followed this up with a vigorous attack that caused anarchy down the French column as far back as Sumbilla. At last a whole French brigade was committed, which pushed the Spanish back after a battle in which the Spanish troops acquitted themselves like heroes. It seemed that, although practically a mob, the French would get away across the mountains, for by late afternoon Darmagnac's division, the last of D'Erlon's rearguard, had reached Yanci. But suddenly a furious burst of firing broke out as a swarm of green-jacketed skirmishers rushed towards the French: it was the British Light Division.

After three days of march and counter-march, hearing always the sound of distant firing, the Light Division had received Wellington's order to intercept Soult. The order came in to General Karl Alten at Leyza in the hours before dawn on 1 August: he was 23 kilometres from Yanci along heartbreaking roads, the division was already tired and short of food, and the weather was blazing hot August sunshine. The division marched at dawn; at 4.00 p.m. it reached Sumbilla and saw the enemy rearguard engaged with the 4th Division. Alten decided to push on the remaining 12 kilometres to Yanci, but his men were completely blown. After a short rest, one brigade pressed on and so came to Yanci in time, where till dark the riflemen poured a dreadful fire into the retreating French until the 4th Division arrived. The French rearguard division lost 500 men killed and 1,000 who surrendered; the rest of the division scattered over the mountains in their attempts to escape. But there was no question of further pursuit: the exhausted men of the 4th and Light Divisions slept where they dropped.

That night Soult gathered up the wreckage of his army on the mountain slopes behind the village of Echalar along the frontier. With the allies so close, he could not risk being caught in column and had no option but to turn at bay in a defensive position. The remains of Clausel's divisions formed his centre astride the road from Echalar, with Reille's command extending his line westwards. D'Erlon's three divisions held the eastern part of the line. Altogether, he had only about 25,000 tired, hungry and dispirited men on his position: the remainder were killed, wounded or in allied hands – or else scattered across the countryside. Wellington himself had come across to take command of the operation at Echalar, but he had only 12,000 men in three divisions. Nevertheless, Wellington decided to assault the formidable French position, 500 metres high and against odds of two to one: under normal circumstances, suicidal. However, the allied troops were in tremendous spirits in spite of their tired condition and they were sure that the French were as good as beaten before fighting began: proof perhaps of Napoleon's dictum that 'the moral is to the physical as three is to one'. Wellington ordered the 4th and 7th Divisions to make a frontal attack while the Light Division executed a long flank march through Vera to envelop the right flank.

The 4th Division began its attack early next morning, 2 August, but its move was slowed by massive amounts of discarded French baggage in front of the position; it was the 7th Division marching east which came up to the French first. Dalhousie saw straightaway that the enemy was completely unprepared for an attack – soldiers were sleeping or cleaning weapons, or, in the case of a lucky few, cooking breakfast – and so rather than wait for his whole division, he launched the leading brigade at once. As Dalhousie had expected, Conroux's troops would not stand. As the British came on, the French turned and ran; with allied troops appearing on his flanks, both of which were disintegrating, Soult could only order a retreat: the army broke contact as best it could and fell back on Ainhoue.

* * *

The French army was back once more on French territory, exhausted after hard marching, hungry and sadly depleted, its morale broken by defeat. Soult, seeking shamefully to shift the blame for the defeat from himself to the troops, wrote to Paris that

> I deceived myself ... that the troops had their morale intact and would do their duty. I mistook the sentiment of shame for their recent disaster [i.e. Vitoria] for that of steadfastness. When tested, they started with one furious rush, but showed no power of resistance ... since I first entered the Service I have seen nothing like them ... The spirit of these troops must be terribly broken ...

Soult was saved from complete annihilation only because Wellington had withheld orders for a move across the frontier at the last moment. The reason he did so is clear from his correspondence: the Congress of Prague was still in session and, however tempting, there would be no allied invasion of France until it was certain that war had been resumed in Central Europe. So the allies settled down once more to the sieges after an interval of nine days' fighting which had cost them 7,000 casualties and the French 13,000. It had been, in Wellington's words, '... rather alarming, certainly, and it was a close run thing.'

'*... you may as well win it by yourselves*'

The Battles on the Frontier, August–October 1813

Only ten days after Soult had been chased back over the frontier at Echalar, the armistice of Pleiswitz ended. It was not until 3 September, because of the length of time needed to pass the information back to London and then to Spain, that word came to Wellington that the armies of Austria now marched alongside those of Russia, Prussia, Sweden and England. Until then, as far as Wellington knew, his was the only allied army engaged against the French, and now was not the time to risk it: the situation was no different from that which had made him hold back before Soult's attack. Besides, an invasion of France could only succeed if mounted from several directions simultaneously. For the time being he would repair the damage to his army and prepare for the next round.

The effective strength of the allied armies in the northern Spanish theatre was now 59,500 British, German and Portuguese troops, and 25,000 Spanish. Of these, Graham's corps, consisting of the 1st and 5th British Divisions and Longa's Spanish division were still laying siege to San Sebastian. With Giron's Spanish corps of three divisions, Graham also held the line of the lower Bidassoa river. O'Donnell's reserve corps and Morillo's division were besieging Pamplona, while the rest of the British, Portuguese and German troops held the frontier. The depleted 2nd Division was posted at Roncesvalles, where no enemy activity was expected, supported by Silveira's Portuguese division. The 6th Division held Maya, supported by the 3rd Division at Elizondo. The Light Division occupied the heights of Santa Barbara and the 7th Division was posted between the 6th and the Light. Finally the 4th Division was held in general reserve. The main effort of this defence was on the northern coast, in order to conclude the siege of San Sebastian, and here the bulk of reinforcements were sent as they came in. These included the British Guards Brigade from Oporto; a new infantry brigade from England and Gibraltar; and around 800 individual reinforcements. Longa's Spanish division was also strengthened with the addition of three battalions from O'Donnell's corps. As well as these forces, the Anglo-Sicilian army was still active in Catalonia, for Wellington remained apprehensive that Suchet would march his 30,000 troops across to join Soult. He need not have worried, for Suchet valued his independence too highly; nor would Napoleon consider leaving the approaches to south-eastern France unguarded.

Advice and guidance to Bentinck still took up much of Wellington's time, as well as rebuilding the strength of the army, in which he was remarkably successful: by mid-August the armies were only 1,500 men short of their strength in July. However, Wellington also still had to deal with the difficulties with the Spanish alliance. The June dispute over the diminution of his powers of appointment and dismissal was now resolved: Wellington agreed that Castaños would be replaced and that Giron would be succeeded by General Don Manuel Freire – who was to prove a fortunate choice. Giron was moved to take command of the Andalusian reserve corps in place of O'Donnell; O'Donnell applied for sick leave, but in reality he retired to nurse his wounded pride. He had suggested the formation of a unified army that would include all Spanish troops in the theatre of operations, under his command. In the light of his experiences since 1810, however, Wellington saw no reason to upset the present arrangements, which were working well, and said as much. Concerns remained, however, over the state of the Spanish formations, ill paid and supplied as they were by their government and maintained with rations and ammunition which should have gone to British and Portuguese troops.

Operationally, Wellington was still chiefly concerned with the two sieges. Pamplona was a blockade rather than a siege, conducted by the 10,000 men of Giron's reserve corps, which consisted of two Andalusian infantry divisions, later replaced by a division from Del Parque's 3rd Army and Carlos d'España's Castilian division, and a corps cavalry regiment. These 10,000 men tied up by the blockade were needed to replace Hill's men at Roncesvalles in order to release the British and Portuguese regulars for service on the Bidassoa. But there was little chance of an early end to the blockade, for the Spaniards had no heavy siege artillery and could only hope to starve the garrison out. The fortress had been constructed in the seventeenth century on the *trace italienne* and it was accounted one of the strongest places in Europe, and the French governor, General Louis Cassan, had no intention of giving up so formidable a fortification without a fight; frequent sorties were made by the garrison into the surrounding farm land to forage and thus extend the ability to resist. Seeing the preparations for the Battle of Sorauren on 27 July, Cassan had attempted a serious sortie, which was thwarted by the vigilance of the besiegers. For two days the garrison stood to arms but to no avail and it says much for Cassan's strength of character that he kept his men going for another three months after this disheartening anti-climax. By the end of September the garrison was on half rations, everything edible in the surrounding fields had disappeared, all the horses had been killed and eaten, followed by the dogs, cats and rats. On 24 October, with desertion rife, Cassan asked for terms. On 31 October the ragged skeletons of the garrison marched out into captivity.

The siege of San Sebastian had meanwhile begun again in earnest with the arrival from England of twenty-eight new guns, 62,000 round shot and 17,500 barrels of powder. Although Wellington had intended to mount a new attack from the landward side, the engineers considered that the main attack should again be mounted across the estuary and Wellington agreed. New batteries were built, supplemented with mortars and howitzers; however, Wellington forbade a general bombardment of the town, as it was full of Spanish civilians. The bombardment of the defences began again at 9.00 a.m. on 26 August and the fire was overpowering, not only damaging the walls but also silencing French counter-battery fire. After four days' pounding, a major breach of 300 metres had been made in the south-east wall and a smaller breach further north: an assault was imminent. Lieutenant-General Sir John Oswald, commanding the 5th Division, thought that an assault across the estuary would only repeat the slaughter of 25 July; and Wellington therefore called for volunteers from the 1st, 4th and Light Divisions to storm the place; 750 men came forward, but Oswald was so infuriated by the insult that he swore that they would be nothing but supports to his own division, which would take the town. Unhappily, Oswald was due for relief and his replacement, Sir James Leith, actually arrived only two days before the assault. Oswald, to satisfy the all-important code of honour among gentlemen, stayed on as honorary ADC to Leith to help him complete the assault plan. This called for an assault by Major-General Frederick Robinson's British brigade of the 5th Division, supported by the 750 volunteers, two Portuguese brigades and the 5th *Caçadores* to act as sharp-shooters. The assault would be mounted in two columns on the main breach, with a Portuguese column assaulting the smaller breach; the time was fixed for 11.00 a.m. on 31 August – low tide was at noon. Thus the assault was in broad daylight and was watched as if it was a demonstration by crowds of military and civilian onlookers. Inside the town, the garrison was down to 2,500 effectives, but Rey's men had managed to maintain the sheer drop from the lip of the breach by clearing away all rubble; and they had constructed and strengthened a new inner wall beyond it. Rey had kept several guns masked to cover the breach and had also placed a large mine under it, intending to blow up the assaulting troops. Fortunately for the attackers, this failed to go off.

The morning of the assault was one of heat and haze. The allied batteries kept up their fire until 10.55 a.m., when the assaulting columns emerged from the trenches at a run. The French response was immediate: accurate musketry and artillery fire, so that just as on 25 July, the attackers reached the lip of the breach and stopped, only to be shot down. The casualties were heavy and included Lieutenant-Colonel Sir Richard Fletcher, the chief engineer, who was killed; General Oswald, who was wounded; and General Leith, who was blown from his horse. By 11.35 a.m. the assault had stalled, but the Portuguese pressed on with their attack on the smaller breach. They too were stopped. Graham, the corps commander, realised that the whole assault was about to fail and that only drastic action would save the day. He therefore ordered every battery to fire over the heads of the assaulting troops, which they did for ten minutes with great effect on the defenders, massed as they were around the breaches: the slaughter was terrific. When the fire lifted again, the assault brigade was able to break into the town; by 1.00 p.m. the troops were in San Sebastian town in strength. The defenders resisted fiercely, but were gradually beaten back. By 1.35 p.m. prisoners were being brought out and after another hour the troops had cleared the town, helped by an explosion in the main magazine, which blew up just as the allied reserve brigade was committed, annihilating many of the defenders.

About 1,300 men of the garrison escaped with Rey into the old castle, which formed the citadel, taking with them 450 wounded and 350 allied prisoners; but by this time the general disorganisation of the assault, heavy casualties among the officers and a sudden heavy storm put an end to the fighting – and started the sack of the town. All the plunder, drunkenness, rape and destruction of Badajoz and Ciudad Rodrigo were repeated, although the extent was deliberately overstated by the Spanish authorities; when a raging fire broke out and destroyed most of the town, the English were accused of having started it deliberately. The old castle held out for another nine days. For three days mortars and howitzers pounded the rock, destroying all the buildings and inflicting heavy casualties. On 3 September Rey was offered terms but refused, so to bring him to his senses, Wellington ordered heavy guns to be brought up. On 8 September sixty-one guns, howitzers and mortars opened up; after two hours Rey hoisted a white flag and the garrison marched out into captivity. So ended the siege, which had not been a happy episode for the allies. Some 10,000 of the inhabitants lost their homes and the casualties on both sides were severe, amounting to 3,500 officers and men killed and wounded among the attackers, without counting the defenders and the civilian population.

* * *

Even before the assault on San Sebastian had begun, the sound of gunfire could be heard from the lower Bidassoa, heralding the start of Soult's final attempt to relieve the fortress. It was an attempt that Wellington expected. Soult was in daily touch with the garrison by boat but could not move any earlier because of the state of the army after the battles in the Pyrenees. However, the lack of any allied pursuit into France gave him four weeks. He recovered 8,000 stragglers, brought in drafts of conscripts and filled up his depleted corps from the reserve division. By mid-August he had 53,000 men and ninety-seven guns, organised into nine French infantry divisions, two cavalry divisions and Villatte's reserve division – which now contained the old Royal Guards and the three foreign brigades of Spanish, Italian and German troops. Soult knew that the allied army was well spread out along the frontier, with the bulk of the British divisions in the centre and right of the line, beyond Vera. He was coming under increasing pressure from Paris to relieve Rey, whose defiance of Wellington had captured Napoleon's admiration, and to guarantee the integrity of French territory. This forced Soult's hand: the most direct approach to San Sebastian, across the Bidassoa, meant crossing some very rough country and fighting through three lines of allied defences – but on the other hand, the defenders were mostly despised Spanish troops, the fortress lay only one day's march from the frontier and the river was fordable in several places.

In 1794 a French army had successfully forced the Bidassoa in this area and it was this operation that Soult intended to repeat. His plan was a direct, frontal attack by Reille's corps, with the divisions of Villatte, Maucune and Lamartinière, across the shallows of the Bidassoa to assault the Galician corps on the heights of San Marcial between the river and the town of Irun. Meanwhile, Clausel's corps would form the main effort, with the four divisions of Vandermaesen, Taupin, Maransin and Darmagnac crossing the river below Vera to smash Longa's division and then envelop the Galicians, who would be forced to retreat or be annihilated. To protect the envelopment from inter-ference by the British and Portuguese at Maya, a strong flank guard was formed by D'Erlon's corps, with the divisions of Conroux and Abbé, who were to form up between Sarre, Ainhoue, Urdax and Espellette. Foy's division had been part of this corps, but the day before the attack it was moved into army reserve, with the cavalry. There were serious risks in the plan: a direct attack was to be mounted on a well defended and difficult piece of ground across a river obstacle, by columns that were so well separated that communication between them would be fragile. The force ratios were unfavourable and the need for a flank guard, as well as the positioning of the reserve on the right of the attack, meant that the main effort was not strong enough to be certain of making a break-through.

Unfortunately for Soult, the movements of his army during August had been watched by the allies and Wellington had guessed his enemy's intention. Wellington wrote to his corps and division commanders, telling them that 'The enemy appears to have assembled a very considerable force towards Irun, opposite our left, and also to have added something to their strength near Vera ... All rumours from them agree that they mean to make an attempt for the relief of San Sebastian.' Wellington's orders were that any attack on San Marcial would be held by Freire's and Longa's divisions, supported by the British and KGL troops of the 1st Division and the two brigades of the 4th Division. These were all seasoned troops, completely confident in their ability to beat the French. On Longa's right was a long stretch of unfordable river, then a series of four fords between Enderlaza and Lesaca covered by the Light Division, the Portuguese brigade of the 4th Division and a brigade of the 7th Division. On the extreme right, the 3rd, 6th and 7th Divisions, with a Spanish division from Giron's reserve corps, were to make a feint, as if to attack D'Erlon's corps.

Soult had originally intended to attack on 30 August but his pontoon bridging was a day late. During the delay the allies observed masses of French troops but even so, the heat haze of 31 August enabled Reille's men to move down to the river and cross it unobserved and to place a battery of thirty-six guns south of Hendaye. It was only when the Spanish pickets were driven in, west of the Bidassoa, at 6.00 a.m. that the alarm was raised. However, while the haze concealed the crossing, it also hindered the French from forming up and pressing on over the rough ground of San Marcial and so the allied troops were able to stand-to. By 9.00 a.m. Reille had two divisions across the river and Soult urged him to press on without waiting for Villatte or Foy. Reille therefore ordered Lamartinière to attack the centre of the heights and Maucune to assault the western end. The two divisions climbed the hill in column, just as at Sorauren, but Freire had kept his troops in mixed order, two-thirds of the way up the slope, with a covering force of light troops well forward. When the French, tired by the stiff climb, approached their line, the Spanish troops fired a volley and charged. This sudden attack rolled the French columns downhill so fast that they did not stop until they reached the river; the Spaniards immediately re-formed and reoccupied their position.

Villatte's division had crossed the river at 11.00 a.m. and Reille prepared to attack again, this time with three divisions in line: Villatte on the right, Maucune in the centre, and Lamartinière on the left. As the French came on, the Spaniards repeated their tactic, beating back Maucune and Lamartinière without difficulty; Villatte's men, however, reached the summit opposite the weakest of the three Spanish divisions. Wellington, who was watching, ordered a British brigade from Irun to support the Spaniards but refused to commit a whole division as Freire asked, as he could see that the French penetration was only local. He was quite right. Villatte's men, realising that they were on their own, fled as soon as the Spanish counter-attacked. One watcher wrote that 'This was the only time I ever saw the Spanish Army behave like Soldiers. The 31st August is one of their proudest days ... their conduct in repelling attacks of the enemy had been admirable ... the Spanish were not assisted and repulsed the enemy alone.' This time, the French fled so fast that they did not stop at the river, but broke the pontoon bridges by overcrowding them and could not be rallied for several hours. They left behind 2,500 dead and wounded. It is said that Wellington had replied to Freire's request for a full division in support, that 'If I sent you British troops, it would be said they had won the battle. But as the French are already retiring, you may as well win it by yourselves.'

More French attacks were prevented by the same storm that swept over San Sebastian and by news from further away which required the move of Foy's reserves: Clausel's attack upstream had been less costly, but no more successful than Reille's. Again concealed by the haze, three divisions forded the river, while Maransin's remained on the French side. Having crossed, Vandermaesen's division was dropped off as a flank guard on the left, so the attack was made with only Taupin's and Darmagnac's divisions: the main effort was fatally compromised. As the haze lifted around 8.00 a.m. the French pressed forward and soon pushed back Colonel James Miller's Portuguese brigade towards Major-General William Inglis's British brigade. But as Clausel's divisions followed up, the 4th Division moved forward. Clausel hesitated, and halted. An hour later he received orders from Soult to re-cross the river, as it appeared that D'Erlon's corps was being attacked in the flank. It was now 3.00 p.m. and as the two divisions began to retire, the storm swept down, disorganising the columns and making the leaders lose their way. They eventually blundered down to the river towards dark. The water level was rising rapidly; Clausel himself with the two lead brigades got across but soon a raging stream 6 feet deep prevented any further crossing, so the rear brigades of Taupin and Darmagnac's divisions and the whole of Vandermaesen's division were marooned on the far bank. Vandermaesen realised that if he was still there next morning, he would be destroyed by the allies and so he marched his 10,000 men to Vera, to cross the bridge there.

At 2.00 a.m. the leading troops reached the bridge, which was held by a company of the Light Division. The British troops opened fire from barricaded positions, bringing the French column to a halt and inflicting severe casualties. This firing was heard by Major-General John Skerrett, in command of the nearest brigade of the Light Division, but he refused to send any help. The battle continued for an hour; Vandermaesen himself was wounded but in the end numbers told and the French forced the bridge and the four French brigades escaped certain destruction. Skerrett was never forgiven for this incident by the Light Division.

The cause of Clausel's retreat and Foy's move was the demonstration by the 6th and 7th Divisions against D'Erlon. Dalhousie's 7th Division, after some initial skirmishing, put in a strong attack on the French brigade at Zagaramundi, pushing the French back to Ainhoue. D'Erlon was sure that he was being attacked all along his line and it was only Dalhousie's order to disengage and march to support the counter-penetration by Clausel's corps that broke off any further action. Thus ended Soult's last battle in Spain. With only 45,000 troops in the main attack, it never really stood a chance against a concentrated allied army nearly twice as strong. The attack cost Soult 4,000 casualties, which he could ill afford, including Vandermaesen and Lamartinière dead and three brigade commanders wounded. The allies lost 2,524 men, of whom 1,679 were Spanish: but Wellington was content to have stopped the attack, especially as the brunt of the action had been borne by the 12,000 Spanish troops, who, in spite of several days of short rations, had been as steady in action as the best of the allied or French formations. Next day, Soult learned that San Sebastian had fallen and that his battle had been fought – and lost – for nothing. Soult blamed his generals and the troops for the failure, while the generals blamed Soult's plan, but the troops had now collapsed into the habit of defeat. By contrast, allied morale was high both in Spain and at home, so that when the news of renewed war came from Prague on 3 September, Wellington was ready:

> I shall put myself in a situation to menace a serious attack, and make it immediately I see a fair opportunity, or if I hear that the Allies [in Central Europe] have been really successful ... I see that (as usual) the newspapers on all sides are raising public expectation, and that the Allies are very anxious that we should enter France, and that the government has promised that we shall do so, as soon as the enemy has been finally expelled from Spain. So I think that I ought, and I will, bend a little to the views of Allies, if it can be done with safety to the Army. Notwithstanding, I acknowledge that I should prefer to turn my attention to Catalonia as soon as I have secured this frontier.

Soult was very much surprised that Wellington did not pursue him into France after San Marcial. With a breathing space, and not able to persuade Suchet to come over from Catalonia, Soult opted for an operational and tactical defensive. He was sure that he would be attacked before winter and so set the army to fortifying a line of defences from Maya to the sea. This line of fortifications ran for 36 kilometres through the foothills of the Pyrenees, divided and dominated by the Grande Rhune, a *massif* rising 900 metres above Vera. From the Grande Rhune eastwards stretched a chain of features, of which the largest was the Petite Rhune at 300 metres, as far as the mountain of Monderrain 600 metres above Roncesvalles. Westwards, the hills ran down gradually towards the coast, following the line of the Bidassoa. Soult felt that the most likely allied approach would be east of the Grande Rhune, so he placed the real strength of his defence there with six divisions in the line: D'Erlon, with the divisions of Abbé, Darmagnac and Augustin Daricau between Ainhoue and Monderrain, with five strong redoubts linked by a continuous system of trenches in their first line and a second line of trenches running from Espellette to Amotz. Clausel, with the divisions of Conroux, Maransin and Taupin, held the front from Ainhoue to the Grande Rhune, including the Insola, Commissari and Bayonette ridges. Conroux and Maransin were well entrenched with two large redoubts east of the Grande Rhune, while Taupin, equally well dug in, lay to the west. The Rhune itself was only lightly held.

Supporting the main effort, Villatte's reserve division occupied a fortified camp around Ascain, ready either to move forward or reinforce the defence. To form this main effort, Soult had had to make economies on his flanks: to the east Foy's division was on the flank at St Jean Pied de Port and General Marie-Auguste Paris's division from Saragossa held the pass at Jaca. To the west Reille's corps with the two small divisions of Maucune and Boyer held the tidal estuary of the Bidassoa; Maucune was in the front line, occupying three redoubts at Biriatou, the hill known as Louis XIV and another known as *Café Républicain*; Boyer was in reserve at St Jean de Luz. Thus on what he felt to be the main area of threat, Soult had 29,000 men and a reserve of 8,000, while the flanks were held in the east by 8,000 men and in the west by 10,000. Four-fifths of the army was deployed in a single tactical echelon without either an effective second echelon or a reserve large enough to block large penetrations – a stark contrast to Wellington's arrangements at Sorauren.

This was a plan that could hardly have suited Wellington's intentions better if he had dictated it himself, for he intended only a limited operation designed to create the conditions for a full-scale invasion later on: he therefore aimed at Soult's weakest point. His plan was based on deception, reinforcing Soult's belief that the main attack would come in the left centre and would aim to drive the French towards the coast. Campbell's Portuguese brigade made a demonstration attack on D'Erlon on 1 October, which brought a concerned Soult hurrying over. On 5 October Wellington issued the orders which would ensure this deception worked: Hill's corps, with the 2nd Division at Roncesvalles,

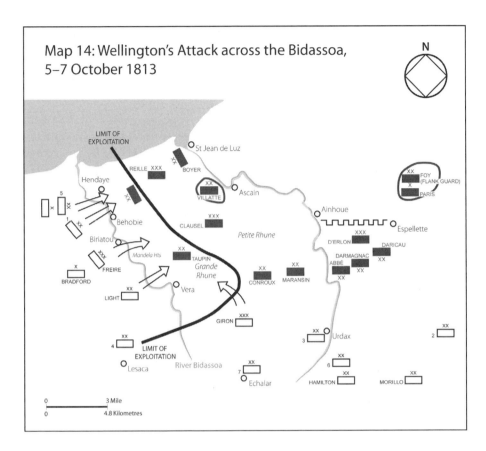

Map 14: Wellington's Attack across the Bidassoa, 5–7 October 1813

the 6th Division at Maya and Morillo's division in support, would hold firm; the Portuguese division commanded by Major-General John Hamilton would hand over in Alduides to Mina's irregulars and move to Maya; Picton's 3rd Division would march to Zagaramundi and Dalhousie's 7th Division to Echalar, both to support Giron, who was to attack the eastern side of the Grande Rhune. Finally Alten, with his own Light Division and Longa's Spanish division, supported by the 4th Division, would attack in columns on the southern and south-western sides of the Grande Rhune. Thus a force of nine British, Portuguese and Spanish divisions would attack on a frontage of 6 kilometres, in a force roughly equal to the defenders, easily enough to make Soult believe that this was the allied main attack. The real main effort would, however, be across the tidal estuary of the Bidassoa, where the French defence was weakest: here a much more favourable ratio of forces was generated. The defenders felt secure in this area behind the kilometre-wide estuary, but Wellington knew that, as well as the three fords near Irun which were passable by infantry at low water, and others upstream around Biriatou, there were three fords near Fuentarabia, known by the local shrimp-fishermen, which were easily negotiable at low tide.

Against Maucune's 4,000 men, Wellington assembled 24,000 British, German, Portuguese and Spanish troops of the 1st and 5th Divisions and Freire's corps. Under cover of night, the 5th Division was to move up to Fuentarabia and at low tide make a dash across the estuary to Hendaye; it was then to move inland and head for the heights of Croix des Bouquets, a known French rallying point 3 kilometres north of the river. Simultaneously, the 1st Division was to make for the fords of Irun, seize Behobie and the redoubt of Louis XIV; while engineers built a pontoon bridge, the division was also to secure the high ground above the river. Freire, with two divisions, was to cross the river around Biriatou in two columns; engineers would build another pontoon here while the Spanish troops seized Green Hill Ridge and the Mandela heights. Major-General Matthew, Lord Aylmer's British and Major-General Sir Thomas Bradford's Portuguese brigades were in reserve.

Throughout the night of 6/7 October the allied troops completed their approach march, covered by another Pyrenean thunderstorm. At 7.25 a.m. on 7 October, covered by the fire of their batteries, the 5th Division crossed the sands of the estuary at the run and entered the river – it was only waist deep. They were across before the French could stand to and the light defending force was soon swept away. Within two hours the 5th Division had reached Croix des Bouquets. On its right, the 1st Division moved equally fast and as the 5th moved up to Croix des Bouquets from the west, the 1st approached from the south. Here a French brigade had formed, joined by fugitives from the front, and Reille himself rode up. Before he could summon Boyer's division, Croix des Bouquets was stormed and captured. The allied success was completed by Freire's corps, which made the same fast progress, linking up with the 1st Division and extending the allied lodgement. By 9.00 a.m. the heights above the Bidassoa were secure and by noon Wellington had halted any further moves except for the Spanish and Portuguese light troops, which continued to harass the retreating French for the rest of the day.

While this quick and easy victory was being won, a heavier but no less successful fight was in progress around Vera and the Grande Rhune. The attack began at 7.00 a.m. with a demonstration against D'Erlon's corps, while Longa and Giron moved up. Giron's leading division advanced on the eastern side of the Rhune, up the ridge of Fagadia, where after several hours' struggle with four French battalions, it gained the summit. Simultaneously, Alten's Light Division advanced from Vera in two columns: Major-General James Kempt's brigade against the pass of Vera and Colonel John Colborne's brigade against the Bayonette ridge. Between them, a detachment of Longa's division occupied a broad wooded ravine, while the main body advanced against the Grande Rhune on Alten's left.

Facing the Light Division's 13,000 men in sixteen battalions, Taupin's whole division of 4,700 men in ten battalions was in the line, occupying two redoubts: the Redoute de St Benôit and the Redoute de la Bayonette, connected by a trench system. Kempt's column reached the summit of Commissari ridge without much loss. Colborne had more difficulty: his whole brigade was needed to force the St Benôit redoubt, then the trenches took time to clear before the troops, led by a swarm of riflemen and *caçadores* moved on to the Redoute de la

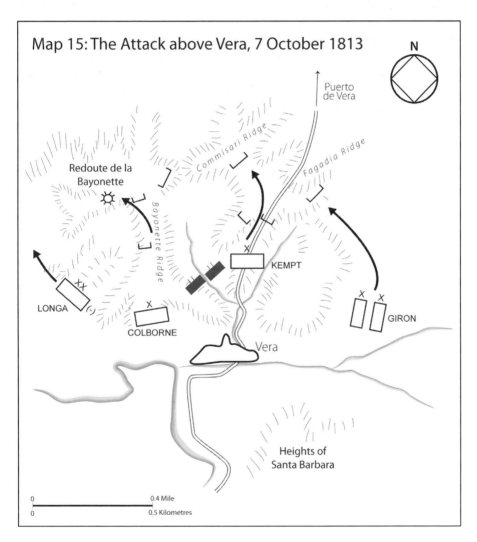

Map 15: The Attack above Vera, 7 October 1813

Bayonette. To Colborne's surprise the defenders of the redoubt ran off; his brigade reached the summit of the ridge just as Kempt's brigade too reached its objective and linked up. A fresh French battalion happened to be moving forward at the same time, but the sudden arrival of both allied brigades forced it to surrender. The rest of the French garrison fled so fast that most did not stop running until they reached Villatte's reserve at Ascain. This penetration by the Light Division allowed Giron's men to establish themselves on the upper slopes of the Grande Rhune, but by this time the summit had been reinforced and all attempts to carry it by storm failed. It was not until the following day that the threat of envelopment from the west by Freire and from the east by the 6th and 7th Divisions forced the French to abandon the whole position. The operation on the Bidassoa cost Wellington over 1,600 casualties, half of them from Giron's division on the Grande Rhune. The French lost about the same number, including almost 600 prisoners, nine field guns and all the mounted pieces in the forts and redoubts. Afterwards Soult, just as at Sorauren, blamed everyone but himself.

'... that equilibrium between insight and promptitude ...'

The Battles of Dresden, Kulm, Dennewitz and the Katzbach, August–October 1813

Napoleon's reaction to the break-up of the Congress of Prague and the accession of Austria to the Sixth Coalition was rapid and thorough, in keeping with the operational defensive he had devised for the southern area of the theatre of war. He ordered the corps of Vandamme and Victor, with the Guard cavalry, to reinforce Prince Josef Poniatowski's VIII Polish Corps around Zittau, to protect his southern flank and threaten Prague. Macdonald was to march to Lowenberg on the Bobr River with V, XI and II Cavalry Corps, while Ney with III and VI Corps moved to Bunzlau. The Guard would march to Lauben. With his forces thus disposed, Napoleon wrote: 'when I am certain that Blücher ... is advancing on Bunzlau and that Wittgenstein and Barclay de Tolly are in Bohemia, en route for Zwickau or Dresden, I shall march in force to carry away Blücher.' This intention was, however, based on the assumption that Blücher had only 50,000 men: his actual strength was nearer 90,000.

Napoleon himself arrived in Görlitz on 18 August, where he learned that the Russians had reached Bohemia and that the Austrians had crossed the Elbe. Uncharacteristically, Napoleon decided on a change of plan: 'It is possible I might enter Bohemia at once and fall upon the Russians and catch them *en flagrante délit*,' he wrote. He himself moved on to Zittau, but after a reconnaissance found that the Austrians, followed by the Russians, were marching west. There would be no allied attack north towards Zittau and even if there were, he was confident that the forces he had placed there, with time to fortify a position, could hold the enemy until he arrived with help. Discounting the possibility of an allied attack towards his centre of operations at Dresden, Napoleon decided to revert to his original scheme of destroying Blücher. By 2.00 p.m. on 20 August he was back at Görlitz issuing orders for an attack next day. This attack, towards Lowenberg, duly took place but Blücher cheated

Napoleon of his intended victory for, in accordance with the allies' agreed plan, he retired in the face of the attack. Napoleon began to follow up what he saw as a retreat.

But on 22 August an urgent despatch reached Napoleon from St Cyr in Dresden. The Marshal stated that the reinforced Army of Bohemia was advancing towards Dresden on the west bank of the Elbe. His position was perilous and he needed help. Napoleon, although not fully accepting St Cyr's fears, realised that the situation was serious and decided to return to Dresden in person with the bulk of the army. The task of dealing with Blücher and securing the army's rear was left to Macdonald with III, V and XI Corps. The situation at Dresden was indeed serious. Schwarzenberg's first objective had been Leipzig, but as he crossed the high ground of the Erzgebirge, he had changed his axis of advance towards Dresden. With only one French formation, XIV Corps, in front of them, the allies made excellent progress and by 25 August the leading Russian divisions had reached the outlying villages immediately south of the city. A strong counter-attack by XIV Corps recovered the high ground around the village of Strehlen but St Cyr was hopelessly outnumbered. The Tsar and Wittgenstein both urged the storming of the city at once, a move which would almost certainly have succeeded, but Schwarzenberg refused. Having no inkling that Napoleon himself was now nearby, Schwarzenberg insisted on delaying the attack until the Austrian army had arrived.

Napoleon was indeed nearby. By the evening of 25 August he was at Stolpen, from where he intended, with a force of 100,000 men, to cross the Elbe at Königstein and fall on the allies' rear while St Cyr continued to hold Dresden. But at Stolpen he received two pieces of news that gave him pause for thought. First, Oudinot's army in the north, marching on Berlin, had been dealt a sharp defeat at the hands of General Bülow, so much so that Oudinot had ordered a withdrawal to Wittenberg-Elbe. With a gap opening up on his northern flank, Napoleon ordered V Cavalry Corps under General Samuel L'héritier from the hard-pressed Dresden garrison to cover the exposed flank. Secondly, General Gaspard Gourgaud had been despatched to Dresden to assess the ability of the garrison to hold off the allies. His report, late at night on 25 August, was so gloomy that Napoleon realised that he must yet again change his plan or risk losing Dresden. He issued orders at once. Macdonald was to continue to hold Blücher; the Zittau position was to be held by Poniatowski's VIII Corps alone. The corps of Marmont, Victor, Latour-Maubourg and the Guard would march at once to Dresden. However, the temptation to hit the allied rear was still strong and so the corps of General Dominique Vandamme was ordered to cross the Elbe at Königstein and attack Pirna. This compromise was to rob Napoleon of what should have been the decisive battle of the war: had Vandamme reinforced Dresden, the rest of the army could have struck a devastating blow on the allied rear, knowing that the garrison was strong enough to hold the allies' frontal attack. While the allies made a tactical error in not storming Dresden at once, Napoleon made a far greater mistake. His decision to switch the bulk of the army to Dresden and confront the allies head-on, although it gained a stunning tactical success, would ultimately cost him the campaign.

* * *

The great city of Dresden, the capital of Napoleon's ally the King of Saxony, had been a fortress until it was dismantled in 1811. In 1813 it was a city of 30,000 people lying on both banks of the River Elbe. The river valley at this point is broad and open and is overlooked by high ground to the north-east and south-west. To the north the Dresden forest came down almost to the Elbe, while south of the river, two streams, the Landgraben and the Weisseritz, flanked the city. Of these, the Landgraben was only a minor obstacle, but the Weisseritz was and is a fair-sized stream with deeply incised clay banks. It was crossed by six bridges and although in dry weather it could be forded in a number of places, in spate, as it was in August 1813, it was an obstacle capable of dividing an advancing army. The city itself has now spread far and wide, completely covering the old battlefield, although some landmarks can be made out. In 1813 the majority of the built-up area of the city lay south of the Elbe in the walled *Altstadt*. Stretching away from this for about 2 kilometres were suburbs or *schlags*, beyond which lay farmland and a network of villages. The last major feature south of the Elbe was the *Grosser Garten*, which is still there, a walled park almost 1.5 kilometres long and ¾ kilometre wide, whose tactical importance lay in the fact that if held by a defender, it enfiladed the approaches to the city from the south-east. North of the Elbe lay the *Neustadt*, surrounded by a ditch and rampart, connected to the *Altstadt* by a stone bridge and two pontoons, which Napoleon had caused to be built either side.

When Napoleon had decided to make the city his centre of operations, he had garrisoned it with St Cyr's XIV Corps. The city had become a storehouse for ammunition, food, forage and supplies of all kinds, as well as home to field bakeries and hospitals. Napoleon had also ordered the repair and improvement of the fortifications, along with those of the outlying fortresses of Königstein and Meissen; although the building programme was not complete, the fortifications were capable of withstanding an assault. The *Altstadt* itself was protected by three lines of defence. Furthest out the French had constructed a ring of five redoubts around the city (marked I–V on the maps), a redoubt in the *Grosser Garten* and two forts north of the river. Of these, redoubts I, II and III were not mutually supporting and redoubt IV was overlooked by buildings, with also a good deal of dead ground around it. Next were the fortifications which St Cyr had erected in the suburbs. Here, houses and garden walls had been loop-holed for musketry, and barricades and palisades erected. With a sufficient force of infantry and light guns, considerable delay could be inflicted on any attacker in this area. Finally, there was the ancient city wall, which St Cyr had strengthened and armed with heavy guns.

St Cyr's garrison consisted of about 20,000 troops. Of these, his own corps of three divisions held the outer defences; a fourth division was detached to hold Königstein. A Württemberg infantry division held the city itself, reinforced by some Dutch, Polish, Saxon and Baden battalions. St Cyr's reserve consisted of two regiments of cavalry, one of which was French and one Italian, supported by two squadrons of Polish lancers, a force probably more multi-national than the attacking allies! St Cyr was certainly under pressure as the allies moved in, but in fact the French position was improving all the time. Between 22 and 26 August the main army marched 195 kilometres – an amazing achievement – so by the evening of 26 August Napoleon believed he would confront the allies with 70,000 men, increasing to 120,000 on 27 August.

Schwarzenberg had at last made up his mind to storm the city on 26 August, and had he done so early in the day he could still have pre-empted Napoleon's arrival. But his plan called for a preparatory reconnaissance in force during the morning, followed by a general attack to begin at 4.00 p.m. The allied assault force was divided into five columns. On the right, Wittgenstein with 10,000 Russians was to attack towards redoubt I in order to draw as much as possible of the defenders' attention. On Wittgenstein's left, Kleist with 35,000 Prussians would attack the *Grosser Garten*. On his left, Count Hieronymous von Colloredo-Mansfeld's Austrian corps, minus one division, would demonstrate towards redoubt III in order to screen the batteries there. Next, General Johann du Chasteler's Austrian corps would occupy Plauen and secure the left flank of the fifth column, 35,000 Austrians under General Count Ignatius Gyulai who would attack the village of Lobtau and then push on north of the Weisseritz, through the suburb of Friederichstadt, to the Elbe. In reserve would be one division of Chasteler's corps at Coschütz, two cavalry divisions and the Prussian Guards. Thus 100,000 allied troops prepared to take on only 20,000 French but, just as at Lutzen, the allies had left significant numbers of troops un-committed: Prince Eugen of Württemberg with his division of 12,500 men secured the right flank of the army near Pirna, but the 50,000 men in the two corps of Barclay de Tolly and Miloradovich remained unallocated. Meanwhile, Napoleon marched at full speed with all his available forces.

Kleist's Prussians on the right were the first allied troops to advance. At 5.00 a.m. in full daylight they attacked the *Grosser Garten* and after three hours'

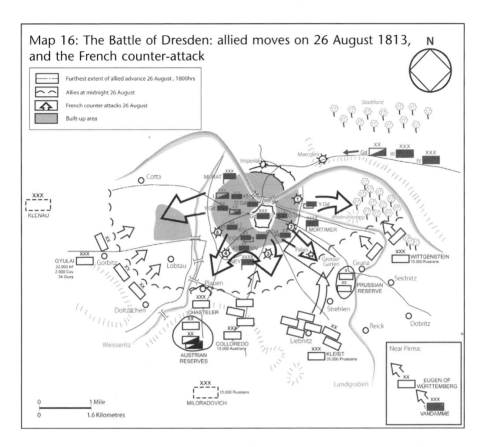

Map 16: The Battle of Dresden: allied moves on 26 August 1813, and the French counter-attack

fighting they had cleared the garden as far as the Palace redoubt. Supported by the Russians on their right, they had taken almost three-quarters of the garden by 9.00 a.m., when they were ordered to pause. The Russians themselves had suffered badly from French artillery fire from the Marcolini redoubt but, keeping in close touch with Kleist's men, they too had made progress. In the allied centre the Austrians made steady progress and by noon they were fighting to take redoubts IV and V, although they had not succeeded in breaking in to either. Out on the left, good progress had also been made and the Austrians had reached the banks of the Elbe.

The allied commanders, however, watching the early moves from the Racknitz heights, were far from encouraged by the apparent progress of the attack. At 9.00 a.m. Napoleon himself entered the city, followed by his Guard, which had marched 140 kilometres in seventy-two hours on rough roads and across country. After this amazing feat of marching, the Guard was immediately committed to reinforce the defenders. Four regiments of the Young Guard and a regiment of the Old Guard under Mortier were sent to the suburb of Dohnesee, while another two Young Guard regiments and an Old Guard regiment under Ney went into Dippoliswalde and Falken, left and right of redoubt IV. The rest of the Old Guard was held in reserve in the *Altstadt*. Napoleon himself at once set out on a tour of the defences and soon the dreaded cries of *'Vive l'Empereur!'* began to reach the ears of the allied soldiers and their leaders. Clearly, if Napoleon himself was here, the *Grande Armée* would not be far behind. Jomini realised that the capture of Dresden was now beyond the ability of the allies and he advised that the attack should be broken off at once. The Tsar agreed but, surprisingly, the King of Prussia thought otherwise. Hours of argument followed, at the end of which it was decided to cancel the planned general attack. But either Schwarzenberg failed to issue the cancellation order, or there was confusion, or it simply did not reach the recipients in time, for the signal guns were fired as planned and the attack went in.

On the allied right the Russians advanced between the Landgraben and redoubt II, supported by the Prussians. Kleist's troops got within 10 yards of the suburb of Dohna but the terrific fire from the defenders, followed by a strong counter-attack, halted the Austrians on Kleist's left and forced a withdrawal. In the centre, between Kleist's men and the Weisseritz, the Austrians had at first made steady progress in spite of the enemy fire. Redoubt III and its supporting artillery halted the attack of the first two Austrian lines until suddenly the guns fell silent – the ammunition was exhausted! Seizing the opportunity, the Austrians charged again, stormed the redoubt and after vicious hand-to-hand fighting threw the defenders out. The attacks on redoubts IV and V were less successful, for steady fire from the defenders and strong counter-attacks blocked all progress. Beyond the Weisseritz too only limited progress was made by the Austrians towards Friederichstadt.

Napoleon, meanwhile, had been active. As well as throwing in the Guard, Marshal Joachim Murat was sent with a reinforcement of eight battalions to take command of the existing French troops in Friederichstadt; more reinforcements were fed in as they became available so that by mid-afternoon Murat had a full infantry division and the whole of Latour-Maubourg's I Cavalry Corps. By the time the allied main attack had been in progress for an hour, therefore, Napoleon's strength was up to 70,000 and he was confident that he had enough forces to keep the allies out. Moreover he now had enough cavalry, with supporting infantry and artillery, for some offensive counter-moves. French morale, too, was high. In spite of the heavy gunfire and the strength of the allied attack, there was only eagerness to confront the enemy. After Lutzen and Bautzen, Napoleon's standing with his army was high and the troops expected nothing short of another crushing success by the commander they believed unbeatable. Between 5.00 and 6.00 p.m., therefore, Napoleon issued orders for a limited counter-stroke, for he was certain that the allied attack would soon run out of steam and the conditions for a successful counter-attack would be there. So it was. At 6.00 p.m. Mortier's Young Guard on the extreme left began their move from the Ziegel suburb. After an hour's desperate struggle, the Russians were driven back to Windmill Hill and by 8.00 p.m. to Blasewitz Wood and Striesen. Wittgenstein was so hard pressed that he personally rode to Barclay de Tolly to ask for reinforcements; a Prussian brigade took post behind Striesen until the village was evacuated at midnight. As the Young Guard moved out of Ziegel, so the rest of Mortier's command attacked from behind redoubt II, driving back the Russians and Kleist's Prussians from their gains in the northern half of the *Grosser Garten*. By 8.00 p.m. the two opposing forces were separated only by the width of the central avenue of the garden, when nightfall brought an end to the struggle.

In the centre the Austrians had only just consolidated their hold on redoubt III when Ney's counter-attack began. The Young Guard's first attempt failed, but a group of fifty men managed to gain a lodgement, from which two regiments stormed the redoubt, taking 400 Austrian prisoners. So fierce had the fighting been that at the end of the day 180 French and 344 Austrian dead were counted in the narrow area around the redoubt. Outside redoubts IV and V the Austrians were also forced back as Ney's infantry drove them across the Weisseritz and as far as Plauen. On the French right, beyond the Weisseritz, the Austrians fought a desperate defence but they too were eventually driven out of the suburbs. Further south Vandamme's corps had crossed the Königstein bridges at about the same time as Napoleon had begun his counter-attack, and had himself attacked the division of Eugen of Württemberg. Although Eugen's men fought well, they were forced out of Pirna by the superior numbers of the enemy and fell back to a blocking position around Zehista. By the end of the day, therefore, the French had regained practically all the ground lost earlier to the allies. The French troops were jubilant at their success, achieved in the face of superior numbers, and were further encouraged by the knowledge that the corps of Marmont and Victor were on their way; they were, too, well supplied with food and ammunition from the stocks in the city. Not so the allies. The troops had fought bravely and well; they still fielded a force of 150,000 men, and they expected reinforcements from the Prussian corps of General Johann Klenau. But indecision, confusion in the orders and the failure to commit enough troops early to the all-out storming of the city had resulted in the loss of all their hard-gained ground. The troops were now short of food, they knew that Vandamme was threatening their rear, they had lost confidence in their commanders – and to cap it all, it began to pour with rain.

As the corps of Victor and Marmont, and the Guard cavalry, arrived at Dresden that evening, the two formations were assigned to the French right and centre respectively. Napoleon thought it most likely that the allies would withdraw under cover of darkness, but if they did not he planned an offensive battle for the next day. His intention was to hold in the centre and attack on both flanks, with his main effort on the right beyond the Weisseritz. He chose this course of action for two reasons. First, he hoped to cut the allies off from the two roads which offered the best withdrawal routes back into Bohemia. Secondly, because of the heavy rain, the Weisseritz was now in spate. If the French could secure the crossings as far south as Plauen, then the allied left could be isolated and destroyed, thus dealing the Austrians in particular a heavy blow. On his right, under Murat, Napoleon therefore massed the corps of Victor, a division of the Young Guard and the whole of I Cavalry Corps reinforced with an additional division – a total of 23,000 infantry, 12,000 cavalry and 106 guns to confront Gyulai's 22,000 infantry, 2,000 cavalry and 34 guns. On the French left Ney, with most of the Guard Corps, mustered 40,000 infantry and 10,000 cavalry against the 24,000 of Wittgenstein and Kleist. In the centre the two holding corps of Marmont and St Cyr mustered 41,000, but with only two brigades of cavalry, against almost 100,000 allies, including the bulk of their cavalry and guns. Thus Napoleon deliberately avoided the allies' invitation to an attritional slogging match by massing his strength on the flanks for an enveloping manoeuvre on terms of local, if not overall, superiority.

At 6.00 a.m. on 27 August Napoleon rode to a position just behind redoubt IV where a tent had been pitched and a great fire lit. Here he stayed until 10.00 a.m., when reports came in saying that the attack beyond the Weisseritz was going well; he then moved on to watch the attack on his left and centre. On the left, Mortier had also moved at 6.00 a.m. and an hour later his men had taken the village of Blasewitz. Moving north of the *Grosser Garten*, from which the Prussians had withdrawn at daybreak, his troops pushed on to Siednitz, where they began to meet serious opposition from Wittgenstein's Russians. After another hour's fighting and several repulses, the French managed to take the village. Mortier then ordered his cavalry to by-pass Leubnitz and, wheeling northwards, to threaten the Russian withdrawal down the Pirna road. In the driving rain this manoeuvre failed to achieve its objectives and the Russians were able to pull back steadily. Napoleon himself arrived in front of Reick at 11.00 a.m.

The Russians in this village were well protected by the Landgraben and were supported by cavalry. Even so, Napoleon ordered the village to be taken. Two French assaults ended in bloody failure until the buildings were set on fire by artillery, even though the rain continued to pour. In the smoke, the Russians did not see that they were being surrounded and they missed the chance to withdraw. None escaped. By noon the French held the village. Napoleon next turned his attention to the centre, where St Cyr's corps was attacking Leubnitz from Strehlen. Here, all French attacks were driven off by the Prussians with heavy losses.

Tsar Alexander, meanwhile, seeing that the action between Leubnitz and the Elbe was going badly, and on the advice of his two counsellors Jomini and Moreau, ordered Barclay and Wittgenstein to counter-attack Mortier, while Miloradovich and Kleist counter-attacked towards Strehlen and Gruna. The order was queried by Barclay but before a decision could be reached, fate intervened. Disgusted by his failure at Leubnitz, Napoleon was on his way towards the right centre and while en route ordered a battery of guns to engage a group of horsemen on the Racknitz heights. The first round passed close to the Tsar, for the group was the allied commanders, and it hit Moreau. The ball tore through his right leg, passed through his horse, and shattered his left leg as

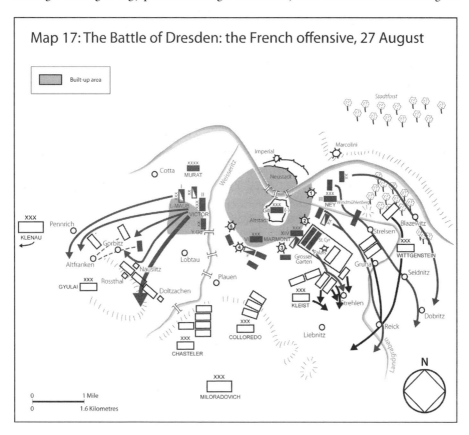

Map 17: The Battle of Dresden: the French offensive, 27 August

well. In agony, he was attended by the Tsar's surgeon, who amputated both his legs – but to no avail. A week later, still in great pain, Moreau died. This incident so upset the Tsar that the counter-attack on the allied right never took place and the French remained in possession of the field.

Away on the French centre right, meanwhile, Marmont's corps had pushed the Austrians back to Plauen, but otherwise had maintained only a holding action. The heaviest fighting of the whole day was further right still, beyond the Weisseritz. Murat began his attack between 6.00 and 7.00 a.m.: Victor's corps, supported by the artillery, crossed the Weisseritz by the Freiburg bridge and divided into four columns. The first column moved south-west towards Dölzschen; by 2.00 p.m. the village was on fire and the Austrian troops were penned hard against the Weisseritz, which in this area flowed through a deep cutting. Here they had no choice but destruction or surrender, while across the river the Austrian reserves could do nothing but look on helplessly. Victor's second and third columns, supported by his corps cavalry, headed towards Rossthal and Wolfnitz respectively. By noon the Austrians had been forced out of Wolfnitz and Ober Gorbitz in disorder. Victor's cavalry could be seen preparing to charge and the Austrians formed square, but the torrential rain had made the Austrians' flints and powder useless. Unable to fire their pieces, they were ridden down or compelled to surrender. Victor's fourth column and, on its right, the bulk of Murat's cavalry, advanced along the Freiburg road, pushing the Austrian troops back towards Pennrich, while the Young Guard infantry, moving south of the road, cut their withdrawal route. Threatened by infantry and cavalry, and unable to use their weapons, a large body of Austrian troops surrendered. Of Klenau's reinforcements there was no sign, for he had marched by a roundabout route and never reached the battlefield in time. Thus by 2.00 p.m. the entire Austrian left beyond the Weisseritz had been smashed. Some 15,000 of the original 24,000 were prisoners, many others were dead or wounded and only a battered remnant of the corps managed to escape towards Freiburg.

By 3.00 p.m. the Battle of Dresden was over. Napoleon, soaked to the skin, his famous cocked hat plastered round his ears, rode into the city followed by 1,000 prisoners. Another 12,000 followed, along with three generals, sixty-four officers of field rank, fifteen captured standards, twenty-six guns and thirty ammunition wagons. Napoleon had gained a remarkable, if almost his last, victory. True, the allies had made many mistakes but Napoleon had again shown his old genius. He had at once realised the advantages which the terrain and his interior lines offered, and he had boldly denuded his centre in order to create local superiority on the flanks, on what was the first occasion in his career when he had not managed to assemble an equivalent or numerically superior force to his opponents. Von Caemmerer said of this that:

> When an army of 120,000 men, in the presence of 180,000 enemies, deploys from a bridgehead, then surrounds the enemy on both wings, and seriously damages both; when it compels a whole division to lay down its arms in the open field, when it brings in immediately from the battlefield 1,300 prisoners, fifteen standards and twenty-six guns, that is a quite undeniable victory.

* * *

At the end of the day's fighting on 27 August Napoleon was sure that another day of combat would follow. He therefore gave orders for the action to be renewed. It was not until daybreak on 28 August that Marmont and St Cyr found the allies gone, their retreat covered by the darkness, rain and mist. An uncharacteristic delay of several hours followed – probably caused by illness – until Napoleon issued new orders for the pursuit. St Cyr was to march on Drohna, keeping in touch with Mortier, who was ordered to Pirna. Vandamme was at the same time to move north of Hellendorf, cutting the road there. Marmont's corps was ordered towards Dippoldiswalde and Murat's two corps towards Freiburg. If Vandamme, Mortier or St Cyr could close up to the allies and stop them crossing into Bohemia, it was in Napoleon's mind that Murat and Marmont could wheel south-east, thus enveloping the enemy. Napoleon himself set off for Pirna and on the way he received despatches from Vandamme, saying that he had no great force in front of him. Napoleon therefore decided to halt the Young Guard at Pirna, return the Old Guard to Dresden, and order Vandamme to push on to Peterswalde. For the time being, the pursuit could, it seemed, be left to his lieutenants, especially as Napoleon was clearly in great pain and far from well, probably suffering the onset of the cancer that eventually killed him.

After the fatal wounding of Moreau, the allied commanders had held a council of war. Frederick William was for continuing the fight; Jomini advised withdrawing south-west towards Dippoldiswalde; the Tsar, the Emperor of Austria and Schwarzenberg were all for withdrawing into Bohemia, and it was their view that prevailed. The orders called for three withdrawal routes to be used: the Russians and Prussians would march via Dohna and Peterswalde; Klenau via Freiburg; and the remaining Austrians through Dippoldiswalde. With some modifications to their routes, Klenau reached Marienberg on 30 August and the Austrians got to Dux in Bohemia on the same date. The Russians and

Prussians too had to modify their route. Covered by their rearguard, they marched south on two routes through Dippoldiswalde and Maxen, the main body having reached Fürstenwalde on 29 August.

Meanwhile, the division of Eugen of Württemberg, now subordinated to General Count Alexander Ostermann, was also ordered to march via Maxen. Eugen himself urged that to do so would leave the Peterswalde road open to Vandamme and allow him to block the allies' route across the Erzgebirge into Bohemia. Fortunately for the allies, he managed to persuade Ostermann to this view. The division had to fight its way to Hellendorf, so that when Eugen assembled the command there late on 28 August, it was strung out, depleted and hotly pursued by Vandamme. Throughout the day of 29 August the withdrawal continued, with Eugen's Prussians turning to fight Vandamme three times. By 10.00 a.m. the division, 14,700 strong, had reached Kulm. Ostermann fortunately had the foresight to send a messenger to the allied sovereigns warning them of the situation; the result was a message from the Tsar ordering Eugen and Ostermann to hold their position between Kulm and Priesten in order to cover the move of the rest of the army – for Eugen's analysis had been quite correct. But the Tsar, the King of Prussia and the Emperor also sent orders to all available troops to march to support Ostermann. By the end of the day about 6,000 of these had reached the village of Priesten. Throughout the day of 29 August the Prussians and French battled around Priesten. The fight swung first one way and then the other as reinforcements arrived to bolster both sides. At 5.00 p.m. Vandamme made what he felt must be a decisive attack, but it was checked by the Prussian infantry and a charge by three regiments of cavalry. Vandamme broke off the action, meaning to wait until the rest of his corps, which was straggling badly, arrived during the night.

The remainder of the allied army continued to withdraw in good order and the French, hampered as ever by a lack of cavalry, did not press the pursuit. The allied commanders themselves converged on Priesten during the evening of 29 August, and by dawn on 30 August their strength had risen to 44,000, while Vandamme had about 32,000. With their superiority in numbers, the allies planned to force Vandamme onto the defensive and destroy him. By 11.00 a.m. this plan had been pressed home so effectively that Vandamme's position was extremely worrying, more so as cannon fire could be heard in his rear. At first, he believed it to be St Cyr or Mortier coming to his aid – but his hopes were soon dashed: it was the corps of Kleist.

Kleist had originally been ordered to support Ostermann, but the routes were hopelessly blocked – all save one: the Peterswalde road. Kleist decided that boldness was his only possible course. He would force his way down the route and fall on Vandamme's rear. After a forced march of eight hours, this is exactly what his bold move achieved. Vandamme's corps was destroyed: 10,000 prisoners, including Vandamme himself, were taken; another 5,000 men were killed or wounded. The allies also took eighty-two guns, 200 wagons, two Eagles and five Colours. Eugen's foresight in blocking Vandamme, the exertions of the allied sovereigns in reinforcing him, and Kleist's boldness had produced the victory which had eluded the allies for so long. As Clausewitz wrote, 'The defeat of a corps may be made up for by the victory of an army, and even the defeat of one army may be balanced or even turned into a victory by the successes of a larger army, as happened . . . at Kulm.'

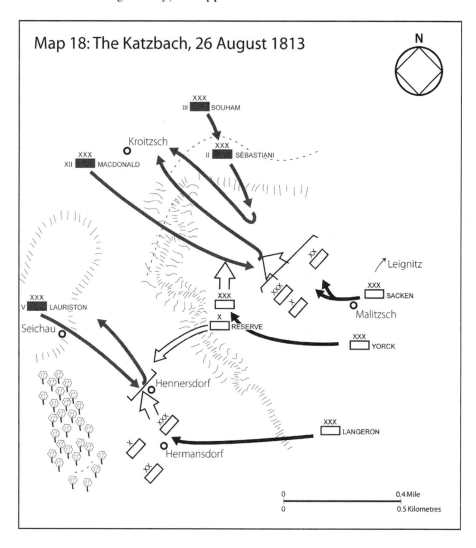

Map 18: The Katzbach, 26 August 1813

There was more to come. The news of Oudinot's defeat by Bülow at Grossbeeren was followed by the news of another allied success in the east. On 26 August Macdonald, who had been left to prevent Blücher's army from advancing westwards, decided to cross the Katzbach and take the offensive. Unknown to him, Blücher had decided on a similar course. Macdonald crossed the Katzbach on the following day and thus, while the main armies were engaged at Dresden, he and Blücher had fought a wholly unexpected meeting engagement in pouring rain. Macdonald had advanced in three well separated columns and the result was that Blücher, with the corps of Sacken and Yorck, was able to generate sufficient local superiority to smash Macdonald. The French had lost 14,000 prisoners, thirty-six guns and 110 wagons. It seemed that the allied plan of defeating Napoleon's lieutenants was vindicated. St Cyr's gloomy prophecy too seemed fulfilled and it was hardly surprising that Napoleon took the news badly – for the situation at the operational level had been transformed. Mortier and St Cyr were censured for not supporting Vandamme, but Mortier certainly had only received his orders on 30 August, too late to affect the action. So now, far from having lost the initiative at Dresden, the allied Army of Bohemia was intact and its morale revitalised; the Army of Silesia and the Army of the North were threatening from the north and east; and the Reserve Army of Poland would soon be hastening westward. For all its success at the tactical level, Dresden had already become, in the context of Napoleon's campaign, a wasted victory.

In the aftermath of the reverses at Grossbeeren, Kulm and the Katzbach, Napoleon conducted a thorough-going review of his operational plan and the courses open to him. These courses he reduced to two. First, he could block the allies in the north and east and concentrate the bulk of his army for a march south in order to destroy the Army of Bohemia and seize Prague. Secondly, he could block to the east and south while directing most of his forces against the Army of the North and Berlin. His review seems to show that he was in favour of attacking northwards, for this course offered the chance of returning to the original campaign plan, with the bonus of dealing a hard blow against Bernadotte. It also offered new sources of forage, which was becoming scarce in the south. Last, but perhaps most important, it offered the advantages of a central position. Operating on interior lines, Napoleon felt he could take Berlin in three or four days and then be able to move against any developing allied threat, defeating the allied armies piecemeal before they could unite. The remarkable thing about both possible courses is that Napoleon, uncharacteristically, still continued to fix his eyes on territory as much as on his enemies: his belief in Berlin as a decisive point in the shattering of allied unity was clearly still very strong.

This northward option could not, however, be implemented, for Vandamme's defeat had deprived Napoleon of many of the forces he had planned to use to hold the southern flank. Then came the realisation that Macdonald had been comprehensively beaten on the Katzbach, so that Blücher could not be ignored. The drive on Berlin would go ahead, but in much reduced strength and without the Emperor himself. Furious at Oudinot's incompetence, Napoleon placed Ney in command, a move which provoked deep resentment from Oudinot. However, Ney, without the influence of Jomini, was by no means a trustworthy lieutenant. Ney received his orders on 2 September. These orders directed him to march first on Baruth and then on to Berlin, which he was to reach by 10 September. Ney found his new command north of Wittenberg-Elbe, with Bertrand's IV Corps on the right, Oudinot's XII Corps in the centre and Reynier's VII Franco-Saxon Corps on the left. Originally Napoleon had planned to support these troops with an additional corps positioned at Luckau, but events elsewhere, especially the need to reconstitute I Corps, prevented this. Ney's orders for 5 September directed XII Corps, followed by IV, to march towards the small town of Juterbog. VII Corps was to march north and then east towards Baruth, forming a strong flank guard.

Opposing Ney, the Army of the North was well dispersed with a Prussian forward detachment under General Boleslas Tauenzien, a veteran of Jena, on its southern flank; Bülow's Prussians in the centre; and to the north the Swedish corps of Field-Marshal Kurt Stedingk, with General Ferdinand Winzingerode's Russians. Fully expecting a French attack, Bernadotte's intention was that Tauenzien would occupy a blocking position around Dennewitz, with part of his force deployed forward at Zahna in order to delay a French advance. Once the French had closed up to Dennewitz, the rest of the army would close in from the north on the enemy's flanks and rear.

During 5 September both armies moved as they had been ordered. Tauenzien's advanced guard met the French at Zahna and was driven out. Ney at once ordered the advance to continue on the 6th, except that while IV and VII Corps continued to march on Oehna, Oudinot was to wait for IV Corps to get clear of the town before himself marching on its left flank. It was about 2.00 p.m., therefore, before XII Corps began to move, so that the three French corps became well separated during the course of the day. IV Corps had marched at 8.00 a.m. and at 11.00 a.m. the leading regiment reached Dennewitz, to find Tauenzien's Prussians on rising ground north of the village, well supported by cavalry and artillery – although much of the Prussian infantry was *Landwehr*. Bertrand decided to attack at once, which he did with some success, driving in both Prussian flanks. But Tauenzien's men, with great courage and deter- mination, held their ground long enough for Bülow's corps to come up and put in a vigorous counter-attack. Although this attack was beaten off by the French, Bertrand was forced back 3 kilometres south-east towards the village of Rohrbeck.

A lull in the fighting followed until 2.30 p.m., when the leading division of Reynier's corps arrived. Ney, who had also arrived, ordered a further attack, which retook some of the lost ground and at one point threatened to pierce the Prussian position. Moreover Oudinot's corps was by now at Oehna, while Bernadotte's Swedes and Russians were still several kilometres away – Ney had a perfect opportunity to reinforce his success in the centre and smash the Prussians. He threw it away. Oudinot, instead of being ordered to the village of Görsdorf, was ordered to march up on Bertrand's right flank. Still piqued at having Ney placed over him, Oudinot obeyed this order to the letter. By the time he had closed up to the battlefield by a roundabout route, Bernadotte himself appeared at the head of his main body, seventy battalions of Russians, Swedes and Mecklenburgers, and a fierce allied counter-attack smashed into the depleted corps of Reynier and Bertrand. The whole French force, Oudinot's unmarked corps included, broke and fled in wild confusion – nor did the French stop running until they were on the Elbe. Although the allied losses were considerable, around 10,500 killed and wounded, Ney had lost 22,000 killed, wounded and prisoners along with fifty-three guns, 412 wagons and three Colours. The remnant of his force was so disorganised that it could scarcely any longer be called an army.

*   *   *

If Napoleon had been angry with Oudinot, his rage against Macdonald after the Katzbach knew no bounds. While Ney's army had moved north, the Emperor had set off for Bautzen with his Guard, Marmont's VI Corps and Latour-Maubourg's I Cavalry Corps. By 4 September he was at Hochkirch, meeting the stragglers and fugitives from Macdonald's demolished army. These were being pursued closely by the 10,000 men of Blücher's advanced guard so, true to form, the Emperor at once went over to the attack. Murat with III Corps and Latour-Maubourg's cavalry was ordered to move on Wurschen; Macdonald with V and XI Corps and General Horace Sébastiani's II Cavalry Corps was to move on Murat's right; while the Franco-Polish VIII Corps under Prince Poniatowski acted as flank guard to the south at Lobau. The Emperor himself moved with Macdonald while the Guard and VI Corps were held in reserve.

The wily Blücher soon realised who was opposing him. Who else could have turned Macdonald's defeated rabble around in such a near-miraculous way? In accordance with the agreed allied plan, Blücher at once ordered a retirement. The French followed as far as Görlitz, by which time Napoleon had guessed the Prussian's intention. Declining to accept the bait and be drawn into Silesia, Napoleon left Macdonald to shadow Blücher once more while he returned to Bautzen with the Guard and VI Corps. When he reached Bautzen, Napoleon's initial intention was derailed by news from St Cyr that the Army of Bohemia was advancing once again against Dresden. This was partly true, for a body of 60,000 Austrian troops was moving on the east bank of the Elbe against Macdonald's southern flank – Schwarzenberg hoped that, in combination with Blücher, he could force a battle on terms favourable to the allies which would complete the destruction of Macdonald's army. At the same time Barclay de Tolly was moving with the combined Russian and Prussian contingents of the Army of Bohemia on the west bank of the Elbe. Barclay's move was essentially a deception designed to tie up French forces that might otherwise be sent to tip the balance against Schwarzenberg and Blücher, and to reinforce this, Barclay was ordered to retire if Napoleon himself appeared. It was this deception that had attracted St Cyr's attention.

Napoleon reacted speedily, meaning to force a battle if he could. He set out at once with his Guard to join St Cyr, who on 7 September had placed his own corps in a blocking position around Pirna. Here Napoleon joined him on the following day and at supper that evening he received news of Ney's defeat. In contrast with his anger at Oudinot and Macdonald, he took the news well enough, ordering Berthier to tell Ney to take up a blocking position on the east bank of the Elbe at Torgau. He then talked at length to St Cyr and, accepting his point of view, decided to march towards Teplitz and so cut the allied communications back into Bohemia. This movement began early the next day but, like Blücher, Schwarzenberg soon guessed who was behind this aggressive move and ordered a hasty counter-march. By 10 September his Russian and Prussian corps were assembling near the scene of Vandamme's destruction, although the Austrians were still far off. At 11.00 a.m. that day Napoleon himself arrived. St Cyr was for an attack at once in order to destroy this portion of the allied army but, surprisingly, Napoleon, the man who had taken such risks at Jena and the crossing of the Alps, hesitated. Perhaps he felt that moving into Bohemia while Bernadotte followed up the defeated Ney towards Dresden risked having his forces destroyed piecemeal, or perhaps he thought the force ratios unfavourable, for the French had had difficulty with their artillery on the rough roads. Whatever the reason, he seemed to lose interest and left St Cyr to press the allies while he himself returned north. On the 17th he was back again, for although he was pushed northwards initially, St Cyr had launched a counter-attack which took the French once more to Kulm. By now, however, the Austrians had been able to bring together a formidable force. Napoleon's troops were growing desperately weary, and he had still not resolved the problems with the artillery. Napoleon hesitated again: the opportunity for battle slipped away.

If Napoleon appeared *distrait*, it was because there were worrying trends further afield. Throughout the autumn campaign, French communications had been harried mercilessly by German partisans and flying columns of Cossacks and Bashkirs, whose activities were almost out of control. At Weissenfels on 12 September, for example, a column under General Johann Thielmann had taken 1,000 prisoners and twenty-six guns. Six days later the same column took 200 prisoners in Mersebeck. At Altenburg on 28 September Thielmann again, with seven Cossack regiments and some *Freikorps*, drove out the French garrison and took another 1,000 prisoners. This pattern was being repeated throughout Germany and the result, combined with battle losses, sickness and straggling, was alarming. Since the end of the armistice of Pleiswitz, the French had lost 150,000 men killed, wounded and taken prisoner and another 50,000 sick and straggling. The supply situation was also bad and raiding was being exacerbated by deteriorating roads and bad weather, so that French troops were reduced to only one-quarter of the daily bread or biscuit ration and had almost no meat. Then there was bad news from Napoleon's allies. After the battle of Kulm the Italian Tyrol had broken out in revolt and declared for Austria. After Dennewitz the Danes had abandoned Davout in Hamburg and retired to Lübeck on the Baltic coast. In Westphalia Ataman Alexander Chernikov's Cossacks had driven King Jerome Bonaparte from his capital and declared the end of the puppet kingdom. Even worse, although he did not know it, the Bavarians had concluded an armistice with the allies on 17 September. On 8 October, having received promises of territory from the allies, Napoleon's oldest ally in Germany formally changed sides. Thus only Saxony, with its army forming the bulk of VII Corps, remained with Napoleon; but the troops were disgruntled that their country was bearing the brunt of the war and were only kept in the ranks by the personal presence of their king, Frederick Augustus.

Napoleon was forced to turn his attention to this drastic situation. First, he ordered the move of large quantities of flour and other stores to Dresden by barges on the waterways, the transfer of which was to be protected by Marmont and Murat with their entire corps. Next, he set about securing the rear areas. General Charles Lefebvre-Desnoettes' division was reinforced to 4,000 cavalry at Freiburg and 2,000 at Lorge – a diversion of resources that Napoleon, with his chronic lack of cavalry, could ill afford. This force was ordered to clear the Cossacks from the west side of the Elbe; a division of Victor's corps was moved to Freiburg; and the newly formed IX Corps of Marshal Jean-Pierre Augereau was ordered to march to Jena from Würzburg to keep the crossings over the Saale open. Next, a partial reorganisation of the army took place. Oudinot

te 1. 'The French Conscripts', engraved by Matthew Dubourg (fl.1813–20) and John Heaviside
rk (c.1771–1863), from *Historic, Military and Naval Anecdotes,* published by Edward Orme
74–c.1820), 1817 (aquatint), Atkinson, John Augustus (1775–1831) (after).
vate Collection/The Stapleton Collection/The Bridgeman Art Library STC 88707)

te 2. A contemporary picture of English military and civilian dress in 1813 and the process of
ruiting the raw material of the army in a country where conscription did not exist as a formalised
cess for the regular forces. Reproduced from R. & D. Havell, *The Costume of Yorkshire* (1814).
permission of Science, Industry and Business Library, New York Public Library, Astor, Lennox and Tilden Foundations)

Plate 3 (*left*). A contemporary illustration of British soldiers of the 6th (Warwickshire) and the 23rd (Royal Welch Fusiliers) in the uniform of 1813, by Charles Hamilton Smith. (*Author's collection*)

Plate 4 (*right*). A contemporary illustration of the British Royal Artillery in the uniform of 1813, by Charles Hamilton Smith. (*Author's collection*)

Plate 5. A contemporary illustration of the British Royal Wagon Train in the uniform of 1813, by Charles Hamilton Smith. (*Author's collection*)

Plate 6. A contemporary illustration of line and light infantry soldiers and a light dragoon of the King's German Legion in the uniform of 1813, by Charles Hamilton Smith. (*Author's collection*)

Plate 7. A contemporary illustration of infantry soldiers and a hussar of the Duke of Brunswick-Oels's Corps in the uniform of 1813, by Charles Hamilton Smith. (*Author's collection*)

Plate 8. A contemporary woodcut of the Battle of Lutzen in May 1813, printed and published by Pellerin of Épinal. (*Author's collection*)

Plate 9. Tsar Alexander I, the Emperor Francis I of Austria and King Frederick William III of Pruss meet at the opening of the Congress of Prague. In the background are the allied generals.
(© *Bildarchiv Preußischer Kulturbesitz/Kunstbibliothek, SMB/Knud Petersen*)

Plate 10. Wellington at the Battle of Vitoria, 21 June 1813, by Thomas Jones Baker; the original is in the British Joint Services Staff College. (*Author's collection*)

Boney receiving an account of the Battle of *Vittoria* — or the Little Emperor in a Great Passion

te 12. Austrian troops storming a redoubt during the Battle of Dresden in the War of the Sixth
alition, 26 August 1813, c.1820 (colour litho), German School (nineteenth century).
vate Collection/Sammlung Hecht/The Bridgeman Art Library DHC 379977)

te 13. Close-quarter fighting on 18 October as the allies close in on Leipzig.
Bildarchiv Preußischer Kulturbesitz/Kunstbibliothek, SMB/Knud Petersen)

Plate 14. The Battle of Leipzig, detail of Napoleon in the foreground, 18 October 1813 (gouache on paper), French School (nineteenth century). (*Bibliotheque*

was called away from the north to command a small corps of two divisions of the Young Guard, while I Corps, destroyed at Kulm, was partly re-formed by drafting divisions from other corps, especially from XII Corps, which Napoleon disbanded and redistributed to make good losses elsewhere. With these precautions in hand, Napoleon hoped to be able to join Ney at Torgau but again the allies forestalled him: for the first time he may well have had the distinct impression that he had lost the initiative.

In the midst of all the French reorganisations, Blücher had begun to move again and quickly drove in Macdonald's outposts. Two divisions of the Young Guard were ordered forward at once and Napoleon wrote that as soon as the weather improved, he would come himself. On 22 September he wrote to Macdonald, ordering him to carry out a reconnaissance in force. On 23 September he himself joined Macdonald as promised and, advancing towards Bischofswerda, met and drove back Blücher's force. But yet again,

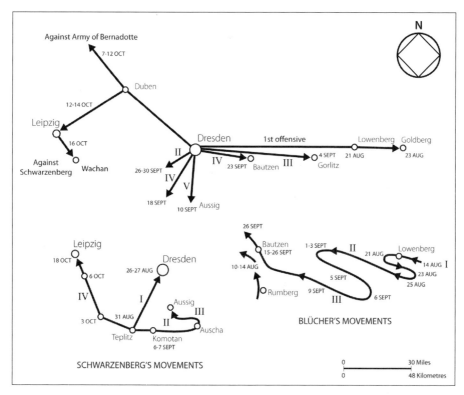

Figure 4: Diagram showing a summary of Napoleon's moves between August and October 1813.

Napoleon hesitated to deliver a decisive blow: to be sure, Bernadotte was again threatening Ney around Wartenburg, but Napoleon seemed to have lost his old drive. As Yorck put it:

> The fact is, that that equilibrium between insight and promptitude, which he himself pointed out as most desirable in a general, was no longer present, and we thus understand why irresolution, with wavering, inconsequent, illogical action, and therefore failure, were the result.

Clausewitz put it another way:

> ... did not Bonaparte, who used to rush at his enemies like a wild boar, twist and turn like a caged animal when the ratio of forces was no longer in his favour in August and September 1813, without attempting a reckless attack on any one of his enemies?

Reviewing the state of his army and the events of the past three weeks, the unpalatable facts must have become clear to Napoleon: he was exhausting his own dwindling troops and achieving nothing. The allies' refusal to offer battle to the Emperor himself, while wearing down his subordinates, was succeeding remarkably well – so much so that Napoleon was being kept off-balance and was compelled to dash hither and thither to assist one or other of his marshals to react to an allied move, but then usually arriving too late and with too little force to achieve any decisive result. Faced with this situation, the Emperor came to a decision – not, as Yorck suggested, at his own initiative, but in response to the allied moves. His decision was to abandon all territory in the east, including the distant garrisons on the Oder and Vistula, and to pull his army back behind the Elbe, maintaining strong bridgeheads at Königstein, Pilnitz, Dresden, Meissen, Wittenberg-Elbe, Torgau and Magdeburg. Husbanding his remaining 260,000 men and 784 guns, he would watch the allies, and, if they took the offensive, he would concentrate and compel them to fight. Napoleon began his moves on 24 September and by the end of the month his army was deployed in accordance with the plan.

The allies too had recast their plans and were about to begin the series of moves that would bring victory at last. The Army of Poland was on the move; Bennigsen was ordered to join the Army of Bohemia and this combined force was then to advance through the Erzgebirge towards Leipzig, cutting the French lines of communication both westwards towards the Rhine and northwards up the Saale and the Elbe. Blücher was ordered to cover the flank of Bennigsen's march as far as the Erzgebirge and then march north to join Bernadotte. This second army would then force the line of the Elbe and drive the French back towards Bennigsen. Coincidentally, Blücher began his move on 25 September, at the same time as Napoleon's redeployment. Moving rapidly, his army crossed the Elbe on 3 October and drove Bertrand's corps from its positions at Wartenberg, while Bernadotte's army crossed the river between Wittenberg and Dessau. To Napoleon, it seemed that the allies had divided their forces and delivered him the opportunity for a series of blows successively against each main army. After some careful deliberation, Napoleon decided to leave Murat with II, V and VIII Corps and some cavalry to block the Army of Bohemia south of Chemnitz; St Cyr was given the task of defending Dresden against the *Freikorps* and the threat of Bennigsen, with his own XIV Corps and the new I Corps. Napoleon was clearly in two minds about committing a large force in Dresden but in the end he believed the future potential of a base of operations against Schwarzenberg was worth tying up two corps. This was a decision that arguably cost Napoleon the battle of Leipzig, by not obeying his own instincts and oft-repeated principle of concentrating every available man and gun for his main effort against the enemy army and ignoring considerations of ground or internal politics. Thus on 6 October, when he moved north against Bernadotte and Blücher, he went with 150,000 men: not a superior force, but one almost exactly matched.

Napoleon's cavalry reports had led him to believe that Blücher was positioned around Duben, with Bernadotte further north, which was substantially correct. His intention was force his army between the two allied bodies, create a local

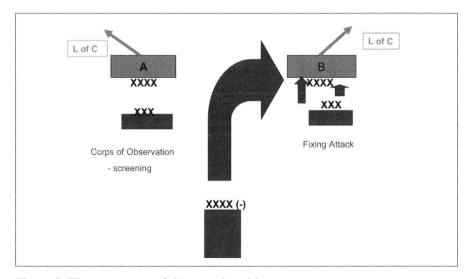

Figure 5: The manoeuvre of the central position.

superiority against each one and defeat them sequentially before they could unite – the well-worn manoeuvre of the central position.

Blücher, with his superior cavalry, quickly identified Napoleon's intention so that, although the French soldiers accomplished the colossal feat of marching nearly 140 kilometres in two days, they found only Blücher's rearguard division at Duben. Disgusted, Napoleon considered pressing on towards Berlin, but news from the south, where Murat had met Schwarzenberg, caused him to hold back. Blücher, meanwhile, slipped away: not east towards Berlin, but rather west, so that he reached Halle on the Saale river on 12 October. Bernadotte had initially fallen back towards the Elbe and would have gone further still had not Blücher, who disliked, despised and mistrusted Bernadotte nearly as much as he hated Napoleon, insisted that both their armies continue to march towards Leipzig so as to join Schwarzenberg – but Bernadotte wavered. In the end Blücher marched alone, followed after a pause of several days by a doubtful and disgruntled Bernadotte. South of Dresden, meanwhile, Schwarzenberg had begun to march on 7 October, leaving Chasteler's 10,000 Austrians to guard Bohemia. The supreme commander was finding the Erzgebirge heavy going: even against 240,000 men, the rough terrain allowed Murat to conduct a skilful delaying operation with his three corps. On 10 October Schwarzenburg had the chance to attack and destroy Murat's force at Borna, but missed it. And so, slowly, the army moved north-west, while Murat retired in front of it, maintaining contact with his cavalry. It seemed as if Nemesis was imperceptibly but irresistibly drawing all the armies towards one place: Leipzig.

Chapter 9

'*... the vital moment of our sacred war*'

The Battle of the Nations: Leipzig, 13–19 October 1813

In Napoleon's army at Leipzig there were Frenchmen, Italians, Neapolitans, Spaniards, Portuguese, Dutch, Belgians, Swiss, Poles, Croats, Illyrians, Saxons, Württembergers, Westphalians, Bavarians and host of contingents from smaller German states. Against him fought Prussians, Russians, Hungarians, Austrians, Czechs, Slovaks, Slovenes, Mecklenburgers, Swedes, English, Cossacks, Bashkirs and Kalmachs. In all, well over half a million men battled for six days. It was the largest engagement of the Revolutionary and Napoleonic wars and the greatest – and bloodiest – battle in Europe before the First World War. History knows it as the Battle of the Nations: surely, it could have no other name.

Like Dresden, the city of Leipzig has spread out so far in modern times that the site of the battle is completely obscured; even fewer features remain at Leipzig than at Dresden, other than the road pattern and some traces of the old city. In 1813 Leipzig had a population of about 30,000. Like Dresden, Leipzig too had been a fortress in former times and the old wall still stood around the *Altstadt*, which was about a kilometre square. Five gates opened into the wall and beyond them, the suburbs had begun to spread. Some of these suburbs were of substantial stone houses and garden walls, although those to the north and west were poorer quarters with narrow, winding streets and squalid, crowded dwellings. The most notable feature of the city's location was the water obstacles: the Elster, Pleisse and Parthe rivers, which conveniently divided the ground around the city. To the east and south, between the Parthe and Pleisse, lay a series of low ridges that were eminently suitable for the defence. Here the country was generally open, so that cavalry and guns could move freely, although some ponds and marshes made low-lying areas difficult to pass. The highest feature in this area was the Galgenberg, although the Kolmberg was conspicuously crowned by an old Swedish redoubt, a relic of the Thirty Years' War. Most of the villages outside the suburbs lay in this area. These were solidly built farming communities, of which the most important were Markkleeberg, Sommerfeld, Liebertwolkwitz and Stötteritz. The Parthe river flowed past this area in a generally north-westerly direction and it was a sluggish, tortuous stream with steep and in places marshy banks, making it an obstacle to troops.

South and south-east of the city, between the Pleisse and Elster, lay an area of marshy ground protecting the defences of the city. The two streams flowed generally south to north and were inter-connected by a mass of boggy channels, with some woods and gardens in between, making this a very difficult area indeed for troops in rigid formations and virtually impassable for the movement of wheeled vehicles and guns. As the Elster flowed north-west of the city, it made a right-angled turn towards the west and was joined by the Luppe, a small stream also flowing from the south, and the combined stream then meandered through an area very similar to that between the Elster and the Pleisse. Further west, towards Lindenau, the country became almost a level plain, while to the north, between the Elster and Parthe rivers, the land was also relatively flat and well drained except along the banks of the Elster, which were marshy.

As well as the water obstacles, another significant feature of Leipzig was the convergence of routes from all directions. Of most significance was the road west through Lindenau, since this afforded the only real withdrawal route for the French army. Over the marshy ground this route was carried on a causeway that had five stone and several wooden bridges in a space of only 2 kilometres. The largest bridge, over the Pleisse, lay just outside the Rannstadt gate of the city. There were other bridges too, further south, but in order to make the ground between the Elster and the Pleisse even more of an obstacle, these had been demolished and this had the additional effect of cutting the only alternative withdrawal route, which was the road towards Lutzen. Napoleon had ordered the existing defences of the city and those in the suburbs to be improved by loop-holing and the building of palisades, and some earthworks and small redoubts had been constructed around Lindenau. Altogether, the position provided the opportunity for the French to fight on interior lines in a strong defensive position and a line of retreat at their backs, while the allies would have to approach over some very difficult ground.

On 13 October Schwarzenberg had reached Markkleeburg close to Leipzig and there, for a whole day, the cavalry of both sides fought the largest cavalry engagement of the year. Murat's cavalry was so closely massed and the allies' so dispersed that neither side was able to achieve a decision and the fight, which was in essence the opening action of the battle of Leipzig, was inconclusive. But by this time the possibility that the allies might unite at Leipzig was very real, if not imminent, and Murat's despatches had woken Napoleon to the fact that he had to act very quickly indeed. Napoleon also realised that the strength of the allies was so great that he had no choice but to adopt an operational – and possibly a tactical – defensive: something he almost never did. On 12 October he had sent Marmont with his VI Corps and the Guard to Taucha near Leipzig with orders to support Murat. At 3.00 a.m. on 14 October Napoleon followed this with orders to all corps for a general concentration of the army at Leipzig, as well as specific orders to Macdonald to march with all speed: 'I hope you will arrive here in good time today. It is necessary to cross the river at once. There can be no doubt that during tomorrow – the 15th – we shall be attacked by the Army of Bohemia and the Army of Silesia. March with all haste . . .' Napoleon also believed that Bernadotte was some distance away and therefore that he might be able to destroy the Army of Bohemia before the arrival of the Army of the North.

Napoleon entered Leipzig at noon on 14 October and immediately rode to join Murat, whose clever delay battle had succeeded in retaining control of much of the ground of tactical importance close to the city. Napoleon's reconnaissance soon convinced him that an allied assault was imminent: his concentration was not a moment too soon. By nightfall on 14 October 157,000 French and client troops were already available, while a further 18,000 under Reynier were expected within forty-eight hours. But Davout was still in Hamburg with 25,000 men, and St Cyr was in Dresden. Along with the other Elbe garrisons, this meant that 30,000 French troops were being effectively masked by 20,000 men under Ostermann, whom Bennigsen had detached, and were not available to Napoleon in anything like a meaningful time frame.

The allied Army of Bohemia, immediately south of Leipzig, numbered 203,000 Austrians, Russians and Prussians. Blücher was approaching from Halle with 54,000 Russians and Prussians, while Bernadotte's 85,000 Russians, Swedes and Mecklenburgers moved in from the north-east; Bennigsen too was within striking distance. Schwarzenberg, King Frederick William and Bernadotte remained uneasy about fighting Napoleon in person, but the fiery spirit of Blücher and the determination of the Tsar were equal to the challenge. It was clear that a major and probably decisive engagement would be fought on terms highly advantageous to the allies.

Even with his back to the wall, Napoleon had no intention of fighting a purely defensive action. On 16 October he counted on having close to 160,000 men, including 27,000 cavalry and the huge total of 690 guns. His plan was to hold off the expected advance of Blücher, and possibly Bernadotte, in the north with III, IV, VI and VII Corps, all under Ney's command, while the garrison of Leipzig, about 7,000 Germans and Italians under General Jean-Toussaint Arrighi de Casanove, would hold open the line of communication – which might possibly become the line of withdrawal – through Lindenau. His main effort, however, would be placed between the Pleisse and Parthe, where almost 120,000 men would be assembled for an attack on Schwarzenberg's main army. Here II, V and VIII Corps, supported by III Cavalry Corps, would pin the allied army frontally with a strong attack, while XI Corps and the II Cavalry Corps under Macdonald would turn the allied right and draw off the reserves. The *coup de grâce*, a smashing blow in the centre, would be delivered by the Guard Corps, IX Corps and either IV or VI Corps drawn from Ney's command at the appropriate moment, followed up by I and V Cavalry Corps and supported by as many guns as could be assembled. In short, this would be a classic example of the decisive Napoleonic battle.

The allies, too, planned to go on the offensive. Schwarzenberg's initial proposal placed the allied main effort in the constricted and marshy ground between the Elster and the Pleisse. This plan met with violent opposition and eventually the Tsar told Schwarzenberg that he could do as he pleased with the Austrians, but that the Russians must come east of the Pleisse. The modified plan called for the reinforced corps of Gyulai to assault to the west of the Elster and seize the Lindenau position, thus cutting the French communications. The corps of General Maximilian von Merveldt would attack towards Leipzig between the Elster and the Pleisse. At the same time Blücher's army was to attack from the direction of Halle. The main effort was placed against the line of villages Markkleeberg–Wachau–Liebertwolkwitz, which would be the objective of a column under Barclay de Tolly. The Russian and Prussian Guards were held in reserve at Rotha, but the Austrian reserves under General Vincenzo Bianchi were placed west of the Pleisse. This plan, however, contained several flaws. First, as the armies of Bernadotte and Bennigsen, and indeed a number of Austrian formations as well, had not yet come up, the total allied strength was only just over 200,000, including 40,000 cavalry, a force ratio of only 1.25:1 over the French – even though the allies deployed nearly twice as many guns. For a successful attack at least 3:1 was generally considered necessary and, if possible, 5:1. Secondly, a considerable number of these allied troops were held in reserve, in positions from which they would be unable to influence the main effort and the real ratio was therefore closer to evens. Thirdly, while two-thirds of Napoleon's forces would be massed for his main effort, the allies committed only one-third, about 77,000. Finally, the bitter lesson of the Weisseritz at Dresden had not been learned, for the Elster cut off Merveldt's corps from the rest of the army.

If anyone doubted that the decisive moment of the War of Liberation had arrived, their doubts must have been set aside by Schwarzenberg's general order to the army – an unmistakable cry for allied unity:

Brave Soldiers!

We come to the vital moment of our sacred war; the hour of decision beckons, prepare for combat. The bond that unites our warlike nations in a single cause will bring us success on the field of battle. Russians! Prussians! Austrians! You all fight in a righteous cause, for the freedom of your country, for the immortality of your name!

All for one, one for all! It is with this great and potent cry that we must open the sacred struggle; keep faith with this and victory will be yours.

Karl, Field Marshal
Prince of Schwarzenberg

Redeployments occupied both sides for the whole of 15 October, but that night the French troops watched as the sky was illuminated by a blaze of rockets fired by the allies – a signal announcing the imminent union of all the armies and the beginning of battle. The next day dawned cold and wet with a thick mist, so the allied attack was put off until 8.00 a.m. At 9.00 a.m. Napoleon arrived at the Galgenberg and saw that the allies had pre-empted his attack. He therefore reinforced the threatened areas of his line at Wackau, Markkleeberg and Liebertwolkwitz with additional artillery and most of the infantry of the Guard – and waited for the allied attack to spend itself.

For the conduct of the main allied attack, Barclay de Tolly had delegated responsibility to Wittgenstein. Hoping to turn the left flank of the French position, Wittgenstein had spread the five formations available for his attack over a frontage of 9 kilometres: this dispersion, combined with the weather, meant that visual contact – and therefore the cohesion of the attack – was immediately lost. The Tsar, arriving on the high ground south of Guldengossa at 9.00 a.m. at once saw the weakness of the attack and ordered up the Russian and Prussian reserves to the area of Gräbern and Guldengossa. He also sent word to Schwarzenberg, who was west of the Pleisse and therefore not present at the main effort, to send the Austrian reserves to support the attack.

Eugen of Württemberg's division was the first allied formation to advance. By 9.30 a.m. Eugen was in Wachau, but was stopped from getting beyond the village by heavy French artillery fire. The French II Corps also immediately counter-attacked Wachau and for the next one-and-a-half hours a furious hand-to-hand struggle raged in the village. Wachau changed hands several times, for Eugen was determined to hold his position, but by 11.00 a.m. he was forced to withdraw just to the south of the village. On Eugen's left Kleist's

Prussian corps stormed and took Markkleeberg but again French artillery fire stopped him from exploiting northwards. His attempts to support Eugen by attacking on the west side of Wachau were also repulsed with heavy loss. At 11.00 a.m. Kleist still held Markkleeberg, but his corps was badly mauled. Over on Eugen's right Gortschakov's Russians had advanced on the south side of Liebertwolkwitz without waiting for General Johann von Klenau's Austrians to support them from the east. Neither the Russian infantry nor General Carl von der Pahlen's cavalry division could make any progress in the face of the French artillery and both fell back. Eugen therefore, under pressure as he was, extended one of his brigades to try to maintain contact with the Russians. Klenau, meanwhile, had not begun his attack on the east of Liebertwolkwitz until 10.00 a.m. By 11.00 a.m. his left was in the village and his main body had succeeded in occupying the high feature of the Kolmberg. From there he could see the ominous signs of a French advance developing around Holzhausen; he therefore asked for help from Pahlen and received fourteen cavalry squadrons in support.

Napoleon had every reason to feel satisfied with the course of events so far. The main allied attack had been held, while west of the Pleisse, Merveldt's men had been thrown out of the Dölitz–Lösnig area by vigorous counter-attacks. Macdonald and II Cavalry Corps were moving into position for the planned attack on the allied right and it was these troops that Klenau had seen from the Kolmberg. Napoleon also expected the arrival of the corps of Souham and Marmont from the north to reinforce his main effort, so he now prepared to pass from the defensive to the offensive. He sent orders to Macdonald to storm the Kolmberg and then turn the allied right. Once this movement was complete, Napoleon intended to let loose a general attack: Oudinot with the Young Guard was to advance on Auenhain; Lauriston on Guldengossa; Mortier and the Old Guard towards the Nieder Holz. This attack would be supported by the fire of a huge battery of guns, positioned between Wachau and Liebertwolkwitz, which would mangle the allied centre. Having thus penetrated his enemies' position, Napoleon planned to commit the corps of Souham and Marmont, when they arrived, to drive the allied left into the Pleisse and their right off their communications with Dresden, thus winning the battle.

Shortly before noon Macdonald began his attack on the Kolmberg. In spite of a gallant charge by some Austrian cavalry, this attack was completely successful and Klenau himself narrowly escaped capture when his horse was shot from under him. The repulse of Klenau's corps forced the withdrawal of Gortschakov and Pahlen, and consequently Lauriston's troops were able to clear Liebertwolkwitz. Kleist too was forced out of Markkleeberg by the Young Guard. He was reinforced from the allied reserves and counter-attacked, but was forced back again. By 2.00 p.m. he had just a toehold in the southern edge of the village. Only Eugen of Württemberg, with two-thirds of his division dead or wounded around him, still held his ground. Thus by 2.00 p.m. the allies had been to all intents and purposes driven back to their start line – it was Dresden all over again and it seemed that all that was needed now was for Napoleon to complete another stunning victory. His I Cavalry Corps and the Guard cavalry were massed around Meusdorf; Oudinot and Lauriston were forming attack columns between Wachau and Markkleeberg; and south of Liebertwolkwitz, Victor was ready with Mortier's Old Guard behind him. Although there was still no sign of Bertrand, Marmont or Souham, Napoleon was so confident of success that he sent word for the bells of Leipzig to ring for a victory.

At 4.00 p.m. Macdonald's troops resumed their advance towards Siefertshain, Klein Posna and University Wood in order to complete the turning movement on the allied right. Some progress was made and by dark the French held the Nieder Holz. But an unexpectedly stiff fight had been put up by Klenau's Austrians in Siefertshain – and in Gross Posna too – so that by dark the French advance had been stopped. On the allied left, too, the fortunes of battle began to change. Poniatowski's VIII Corps and Augereau's IX Corps advanced against Kleist, who, in desperate straits, retired on Gräbern. As he did so, the Austrian cavalry reserve arrived from over the Pleisse and at the same time the French Guard cavalry and part of III Cavalry Corps appeared on the plain just north of the village. The Austrians at once charged, driving the French back, but themselves suffered heavy losses and were in turn driven back on Gräbern. The French infantry pressed forward again but, fortunately for Kleist, the Austrian reserve infantry under Bianchi, following up the cavalry from over the Pleisse, debouched from Gräbern just at the right moment to check the French advance. This move had the additional effect of relieving pressure on Merveldt, so that he at last managed to cross the Pleisse; and it had the further effect of checking the advance of Oudinot and Victor towards Auenhain. By 5.30 p.m. the French right was in dire straits – so much so that Napoleon committed a division of the Old Guard and one division of Souham's corps, which had at last come up, to stabilise the situation. By dark Bianchi's advance with Kleist advancing on his right had almost reached Dölitz, but here it was halted. Merveldt, too, whose troops had actually entered Dölitz, was halted and then thrown back. Merveldt himself, being rather short-sighted, rode into the midst of some Poles of VIII Corps, whom he mistook for Hungarians, and was captured.

While the French left had made limited progress and the right was being repulsed, Drouot's great battery continued to fire on the allied centre. Behind the battery I Cavalry Corps was massed, waiting its moment. At 2.30 p.m., while the cavalry action on the French right was in full swing, the corps commander, General Jean-Pierre Doumerc, who was standing in for the wounded Latour-Maubourg, ordered a division of French and Saxon cuirassiers to charge from the western end of the great battery. This charge carried away one of Eugen of Württemberg's weak battalions and captured twenty-six guns – but it did not stop there. Cutting through Eugen's men, the cavalry arrived in front of the high feature of the Wachtberg, where Tsar Alexander and the King of Prussia were watching the progress of the battle. For a moment it seemed that the allied monarchs might be captured – but the impetus of the French charge was spent. As the cuirassiers struggled through the ponds at the foot of the Wachtberg, they were themselves charged by the Cossacks of the Tsar's bodyguard, followed by thirteen squadrons of cuirassiers from the Russian reserve. Those French and Saxons who managed to escape fled back behind the battery, pursued by the Russians, who were beaten off only by the fire of Drouot's guns.

In spite of the counter-charge, Eugen's division was in tatters and it had now been forced right back to a line between Auenhain and Guldengossa. At Guldengossa the Tsar ordered the assembly of a battery of ninety-four Russian guns, bigger even than Drouot's battery, and there too the Russian and Prussian Guards from Prince Constantin's Reserve Corps were marching in support. This was more than enough to stabilise the allies' situation so that, although Macdonald had gained ground, the majority of the allied position had been salvaged. The result of the day's fighting on the southern front was, therefore, a bloody draw – thanks to the determination of the allies. Had Napoleon been reinforced as he had expected, it would have been a different story and so it is now necessary to look further afield in order to understand why the additional French forces had not appeared.

*   *   *

West of the Pleisse, Gyulai's task was to attack Lindenau, linking the corps of Merveldt with Blücher's attack from the north-west and if possible drawing French troops away from the allied main effort. Gyulai did not expect to be able to take the fortified position of Lindenau and so decided to mount a demonstration only. At about 8.00 a.m. his scouts reported fighting south of Leipzig and so the Austrians began to advance. By 10.30 a.m. they had closed up to Klein Zschocher, which was taken after a fierce struggle with a French forward detachment. The Austrians pressed on again to where the French garrison troops under Arrighi were drawn up across the Lutzen road between Lindenau and Plagwitz, with their artillery in redoubts and a small body of cavalry holding their left. Gyulai's artillery at once began to bombard the French infantry, while his superior cavalry drove the French horsemen, who attempted to attack, back behind their guns. The main body of the Austrian infantry advanced on Plagwitz, but repeated attacks on the place failed in the face of well-placed French artillery. On Gyulai's left, however, the Hessen-Homberg division was able to capture the village of Leutsch. Beyond lay a mass of ditches and streams covered by the fire of French batteries in Lindenau. Slowly, patiently, the Hessians worked their way through this morass and succeeded in storming the defences of the causeway, only to be thrown out by a counter-attack. A second attack was mounted; it too succeeded briefly but was then evicted again by Arrighi's troops.

At 10.00 a.m. Ney had despatched Bertrand's corps south to support Napoleon as he had been ordered. The corps was on its way when Bertrand received an urgent message from Arrighi, asking for assistance at Lindenau. Since Arrighi was clearly extremely worried about the possibility of losing the only line of communication, Bertrand turned from his route and moved with his whole corps to Lindenau – a position which was so strong that an additional brigade would probably have sufficed. It was Bertrand's arrival that ensured the repulse of the Hessen-Homberg division, which retired on Leutsch. Bertrand, hearing the bells of Leipzig ringing to announce an apparent victory south of the city, then attempted to advance towards Klein Zschocher, only to be twice beaten back by Austrian fire. After this, the action around Lindenau was confined to artillery fire until nightfall, when Gyulai, maintaining small forward detachments in Klein Zschocher, Schönau and Leutsch, withdrew his corps to Markranstadt. He had not captured Lindenau, but he had drawn Bertrand away from Wachau, so his attack had been more successful than he could have hoped.

*   *   *

While Lindenau was being successfully defended, the bloodiest of the three engagements of the day was being fought out north of Leipzig, between the forces of Marmont and Blücher. Ney had ordered Marmont to find a position which would block the northern approaches to Leipzig city and he had selected a defensive line between Lindenthal and Breitenbach, on the very ground where in 1631 Gustavus Adolphus had defeated Tilly. Marmont insisted, however, that this position required 30,000 troops to hold it, as against the 14,000 that he actually had. His corps, VI, was, next to the Guard, probably the best in the *Grande Armée*, composed for the most part of experienced soldiers; it also, like VII Corps, contained several regiments of Saxon and other German infantry, as well as General Jan Henrik Dombrowski's Polish division; Saxon cavalry regiments made up the entire corps cavalry. Napoleon promised Marmont that, if he was attacked, Bertrand's and Souham's corps would rally to help him

– although he had no intention of keeping this promise. But as most of these formations were placed around Euritzsch, Marmont believed him, so he set about fortifying his main position and despatched an advanced guard to occupy the village of Radefeld.

On the evening of 15 October Marmont received a report that Blücher was about to march from Halle. At 10.00 p.m. that night, from the church tower in Lindenthal, he watched the sky lit up by the glow from the camp fires of the Army of Silesia: he at once sent word to Napoleon, and again received assurances of support: all, therefore, seemed well. But early next morning, 16 October, a thunderbolt struck. Napoleon's orders arrived, insisting that, as no significant enemy force opposed him, Marmont was to march south to join the main army and his place was to be taken by Bertrand. Although he knew that his master was wrong, Marmont had no choice but to obey. No sooner had he begun to move than Blücher's advanced guard occupied Radefeld.

Blücher's main body had spent the night of 15/16 October at Skeuditz. Blücher knew very well that he could expect no help from Bernadotte for at least another full day, for the British liaison officer, Major-General Charles Stewart, had arrived in his camp to warn him. Nevertheless, old General *Vorwärts* decided to press on. His intention was to seize the high ground around Radefeld and then decide on the next move once he had identified the French position. He was particularly concerned about the possibility of a French defence on the Döben road and he therefore placed the main effort of his army on the left. His orders called for the Russian corps of General Count Louis Langeron to advance on Radefeld. General Fabien Sacken's Russian corps would follow, with St Priest's Russians following up. Yorck's Prussian corps was to advance down the main road from Halle as far as Lötzschena and then swing north to Lindenthal.

Blücher's main body did not begin to move until 10.00 a.m., but Langeron had no difficulty in occupying Radefeld since Marmont had withdrawn. Still worried about the Döben road, Blücher ordered Langeron to press on so as to dominate the approach from Breitenfeld. Yorck, meanwhile, advanced as he had been ordered. His main body forced the Saxon cavalry to evacuate Lindenthal, while his advanced guard pressed on down the main road, pushing the French out of Stahmeln and Wahren. These moves soon made Marmont aware that continued withdrawal by his corps would be disastrous and he therefore took up a new blocking position between the village of Möckern and the Rietzsche stream, with Dombrowski's Poles and the Saxon cavalry occupying Gross and Klein Wiederitzsch. He still hoped for support from Souham's III Corps, although he knew that Bertrand had been sent south.

It was 2.00 p.m. before Blücher realised the true extent of the French position. He ordered Langeron to clear Wiederitzsch at once but, still preoccupied with the Döben road, he moved Sacken's corps forward to screen the approach. Langeron sent his advanced guard regiment against Wiederitzsch, where a desperate fight soon raged between the Russians and their hereditary enemies, the Poles. By 3.00 p.m. the Poles had been driven from the village in disorder and had fallen back on Euritzsch, when Marmont's Saxon cavalry charged the Russians. Seeing this, the Poles rallied, turned back and with an unstoppable counter-attack threw the Russians out of the village. Once again the Russians attacked and once again the Poles were driven back on Euritzsch, when General Antoine Delmas's division of III Corps appeared, escorting a baggage train. Although the division was less than 5,000 strong, the size of the baggage train gave it the appearance of a corps. The Russians, badly shaken, withdrew north-east of Wiederitzsch until Langeron realised the true size of the new force and resumed the attack, supported now by the leading division of St Priest's corps, which Blücher had ordered forward. This time, there was no counter-attack. Delmas's division and the Poles were thrown back over the Parthe with heavy losses.

Yorck, too, had realised the true extent of the French position and had wheeled his main body south-east from Lindenthal. Once Langeron had moved on Wiederitzsch, Yorck moved on Möckern. His first two assaults on the village failed and there ensued one of the bloodiest struggles of the entire war for the possession of Möckern, surpassing even that of Lutzen. The village changed hands over and over again as both sides sent in reinforcements. At the same time Yorck determined to attack the centre of the French line as well as the village. Here, too, the initial Prussian attacks were repulsed with great slaughter, but as the French prepared to follow up the repulse with a counter-attack, the Prussian artillery set fire to several ammunition wagons, which blew up with tremendous force, spreading death, injury, panic and confusion. Seeing this and gaining heart, the Prussians returned to the attack – but again the French rallied and drove their enemies back. An attempt by one brigade to assist the fight in Möckern met with repulse and near-disaster, but it could have been worse still: Marmont ordered the Saxon cavalry to charge but its commander refused, perhaps treacherously in the light of subsequent actions by the Saxons.

Back in Möckern, Yorck's men had at last succeeded in gaining control of the village and now the climax of the battle had arrived. Marmont personally led his infantry forward to destroy the remnants of the Prussian attack on his centre, but Yorck, realising his peril just in time, brought up his corps cavalry. Charging furiously forwards, the Prussian horsemen swept away Marmont's leading battalions and their supporting Saxon cavalry and crashed into the midst of Marmont's guns. The *mêlée* that followed was merciless: cavalry, infantry and gunners fought hand-to-hand with any and every weapon within reach until at last the French broke and fell back. With Möckern lost, Marmont could do nothing but fall back as best he could as the whole of Yorck's corps pressed forward. As the fall of night brought an end to the fighting, and Marmont's shattered men bivouacked where they stood between Gohlis and Euritzsch, the victorious Prussians broke into a vast, solemn chorus of the great Lutheran hymn *Nun danket alle Gott*. Well they might: Yorck's corps had lost nearly 8,000 men, or one-third of its strength, and Langeron had lost 1,500, but they had inflicted at least 7,000 casualties on their enemies and had taken 2,500 prisoners, fifty-three guns, an Eagle and two Colours. Marmont's corps had lost well over half its strength and could barely think of fighting for another day.

*   *   *

What then was the result of the fighting on 16 October? South of Leipzig it was, on the face of things, a drawn battle. The allied attack early on had achieved some tactical surprise and the Tsar's intervention had ensured that Napoleon's main attack had been held. At Lindenau the French had held open their communications, but Gyulai had successfully prevented Bertrand from decisively reinforcing Napoleon's main effort, while at Möckern Blücher had shut Napoleon in from the north. Nothing less than complete victory would have served Napoleon in his situation but, as it was, he had scarcely held his own. He could expect little further help – only Reynier's 18,000 men – and these, taking into account his losses, would only raise his strength to around 170,000. The allies, on the other hand, could expect the arrival of Colloredo, Bernadotte and Bennigsen, bringing their strength to over 320,000 men.

*   *   *

The night of 16/17 October should have found Napoleon hard at work planning a withdrawal. The route through Markranstadt could easily have been forced, given the relative strengths of Napoleon's main army and Gyulai's corps; an escape to the Rhine would have left Napoleon with an army more than 50,000 stronger for the campaign of 1814 than was to be the case. Instead, the night found the *Grande Armée* in a wet, miserable and hungry bivouac on the battlefield. Napoleon's tent was pitched in the bed of a dried-up pond, where the captured Merveldt was brought before him. Napoleon, who knew Merveldt, spoke to him briefly and then recalled him later that evening. Napoleon asked how strong the allied army was. Merveldt replied that it was more than 350,000 men. Napoleon then asked whether the allies realised that he was there and, if so, whether they would attack again.

Map 19: The Battle of Leipzig: the situation at dusk on 16 October 1813

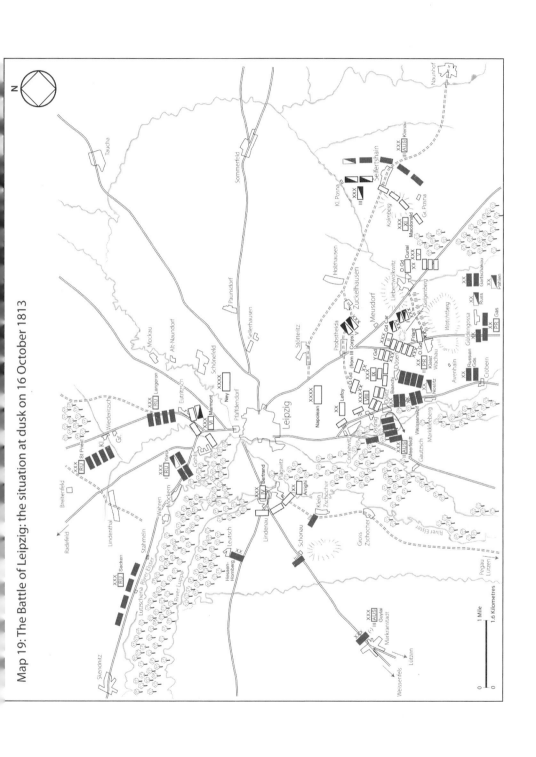

Merveldt replied that they did, and they would. Napoleon then asked 'Shall this war last forever? It is surely time to put an end to it. Austria should speak the word of peace, and not listen to Russia, because Russia is under the influence of England, and England wishes for war. I am ready to make great sacrifices.' Merveldt replied that the Emperor of Austria would not separate himself from his allies and that England wished only for a Europe free from the domination of one power. Napoleon said, 'Let England give me back my islands [i.e. in the West Indies] and I will restore Hanover, Holland and the Hanseatic cities.' But he would not agree to the disbandment of the Confederation of the Rhine nor the loss of his territories in Italy and the Adriatic. Merveldt then told him that Bavaria had gone over to the allies; Napoleon replied that she would repent it. He then proposed another armistice and negotiations for peace, during which he would retire behind the Saale while the Russians moved back behind the Elbe and the Austrians into Bohemia. Saxony would stay neutral. Merveldt told him flatly that the allies would never agree to such terms now and would not leave Germany, even if they could not drive the French over the Rhine. Napoleon replied that to be driven back thus, he would have to lose another battle and that this one was not yet lost. He ended the interview by sending Merveldt back to the Emperor Francis with a letter. Francis was delighted to see Merveldt again, as he had feared him dead, but said that he could speak to him only in the presence of his allies; not surprisingly the Tsar and Frederick William, having come this far, would have none of Napoleon's proposals.

During the night the bad news from Möckern came in. With his losses and his low ammunition stocks, Napoleon now knew that he could not last another day of battle like 16 October and, torn as he was between military necessity on one hand and holding on to his empire in Germany on the other, he made up his mind to withdraw. Even so, probably for domestic political reasons, he decided to keep the field for one more day. For the same reason there was no large-scale bridge-building to supplement the single withdrawal route over the Lindenau causeway. As it was, 17 October was quiet, with only minor skirmishing, for the allies had decided to husband their strength until the entire force had arrived on 18 October, before making their final attack. Napoleon's orders were therefore not issued until 7.00 p.m. that evening. In these orders he told Bertrand to leave Lindenau late that evening and secure the passages over the Saale and the Unstrut rivers at Freiberg, Weissenfels, Merseberg and Bad Kösen. The rest of the army left its bivouacs at 2.00 a.m. on 18 October in pouring rain for new defensive positions, for Napoleon planned to hold a line much closer in towards Leipzig; he had no thoughts of further offensive action. The right wing of the army was placed under Murat's command and consisted of II, VIII and IX Corps; the Old Guard; and I, IV and V Cavalry Corps. This force was to defend the line between Connewitz and Probstheida. The centre was placed under Macdonald's command. With his own XI Corps, V Corps and the Guard cavalry, he was to hold the line between Zuckelshausen and Holzhausen. Ney continued to command the left wing with Reynier's newly arrived VII Corps, III and IV Corps and two cavalry divisions. His task was to repulse the allied attack between Paunsdorf and Schönefeld. Dombrowski's Polish division with two cavalry divisions was ordered to block the approach from Gohlis into the north of Leipzig, while Mortier with the Young Guard and Arrighi's division held open the causeway at Lindenau.

The allied plan for 18 October called for an attack in six great columns. The main effort would be with the assault from the south, on Markkleeberg, Lösnig, Wachau and Liebertwolkwitz. Bennigsen would turn the French left by attacking towards Probstheida and Holzhausen. Blücher would continue to advance on the north-east side of the city, with Bernadotte between Blücher and Bennigsen. Gyulai would once again attack Lindenau from the south. The allied attack began at 7.00 a.m. when, after a night of rain, the day had broken dull and cheerless, but by 8.00 a.m., with the attack well under way, the sun broke through. The allied Column I had to fight hard to push the French forward detachments out of Dölitz, Dösen and Lösnig but by 2.00 p.m. the column, commanded by General Colloredo in the absence of the wounded Prince of Hessen-Homberg, had closed up to the main French position in front of Connewitz. On the right of Column I Barclay de Tolly had closed up to Probstheida, where he paused to allow Bennigsen to complete his turning movement. Bennigsen's column advanced on four axes: Klein Posna, Siefertshain, the Kolmberg and the Nieder Holz. By 2.00 p.m., after some stiff fighting, which included two cavalry actions, he too had driven the French back onto their main position between Zuckelshausen and Paunsdorf. Bennigsen's right around Paunsdorf engaged VII Franco-Saxon Corps and it was here that the celebrated desertion of the Saxon cavalry and two divisions of Saxon and Westphalian infantry took place. In the long run this action did no good to its commanders: General Karl-Friedrich Normann and several other senior officers were subsequently cashiered and banished, while the regiments concerned were disbanded.

Away to the east of Leipzig Bertrand's corps had burst out of Lindenau, throwing Gyulai's attack back over the Elster and the Luppe. By 2.00 p.m. Bertrand had opened up the route towards Weissenfels and was marching hard for the Saale. At the same time north of the city Blücher's men were heavily engaged against Ney at Gohlis, while the corps of Langeron and St Priest, having pushed Marmont's corps back on Schönefeld, awaited the arrival of

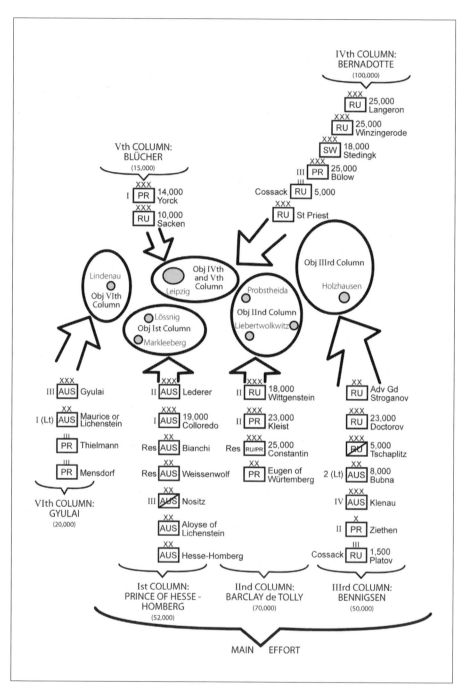

Figure 6: The Battle of Leipzig: the allied attack plan, 18 October 1813.

Bernadotte around Möckern and Breitenfeld respectively, where they had been ordered to support the Swedish advance. All around Leipzig, therefore, the engagement was general, except that there was still no sign of Bernadotte. In fact, by 2.00 p.m. the leading corps of the Army of the North, the Prussian corps of Bülow, had almost closed up to the battlefield, although the rest of the army was still two hours' march behind and did not cross the Parthe until 4.00 p.m.

It was therefore between 2.00 p.m. and 5.00 p.m. that, having closed up to the main French line, the allied attack reached its heaviest. Column I was counter-attacked by Augereau's corps and by Poniatowski. Lösnig changed hands several times and the allies held on with great difficulty. Resuming the attack, Colloredo could not take Connewitz, although by nightfall Poniatowski's corps had been reduced to only 2,500 effective fighting men. Barclay's column attacked Probstheida, which was the vital ground in the French defensive position. Barclay himself wanted to wait for support on his flanks, but the Tsar insisted on an immediate attack. Three attempts were made and all were repulsed with dreadful losses on both sides. The struggle was truly heroic and at 5.00 p.m. the allied monarchs, who were receiving better news from their right, forbade any further attack here. The news was that Bennigsen's troops, supported by the famous British rocket troop of the Royal Horse Artillery, had closed up and captured the villages of Zweiaundorf and Molkau. Here, two other Saxon infantry brigades and a battery of twenty-two guns deserted to the allies. Napoleon afterwards attributed his defeat to this desertion, but as the total strength of the Saxons was only 4,000 men, this was hardly a loss that could have influenced so widespread a battle as Leipzig. A strong French counter-attack was mounted on Bennigsen's troops, which they beat back, but Bennigsen could make no further progress before nightfall.

It was the arrival of Bernadotte which had allowed Bennigsen to go as far as he did. Bernadotte committed only his artillery, saying 'Provided the French are beaten, it is indifferent to me whether I or my army take a part, and of the two, I had much rather we did not.' Even so, Bernadotte's arrival had important consequences in the north. Langeron's attack on Schönefeld from the north was supported by St Priest on his right and by the assaults of Bernadotte's Russians and Prussians from the north-east, towards Sellershausen. Sellershausen was taken, but the numerous and determined garrison of Schönefeld was in a strongly fortified position protected by marshes. When Langeron's men eventually took the place, the artillery ammunition of his corps was exhausted and the troops were almost immediately forced out by a counter-attack. The arrival of Russian and Swedish guns sent by Bernadotte saved the day: Ney, his last reserves spent, was forced back on Leipzig itself with the disorganised remnants of his command.

By dusk the French, although still holding their positions in many areas, had been given a very severe mauling indeed. Their ammunition was almost completely spent, food and water were scarce and casualties had been heavy; all in all, they were in no sort of condition to continue the fight and it was fortunate for them that there was no allied commander capable of exploiting the situation to full advantage. The allied attack, as on the 16th, had been general, with the main effort directed towards the strongest, rather than the weakest, French positions. The army of Bernadotte, strong enough to have achieved decisive action, had arrived too late and when it did, it acted only in a supporting role. As General Alexander Danilevski later wrote:

> Night fell; the sky glowed red, Stötteritz, Schönefeld, Dölitz, and one of the suburbs of Leipzig were in flames. Whilst with us [i.e. the allies] all were intoxicated with joy ... indescribable confusion reigned in the enemy's army. Their baggage, their artillery, their broken regiments, the soldiers who had been for days without food, were stopped for want of bridges over the streams around Leipzig. In the narrow streets resounded the cries of woe of innumerable wounded, as our shot and shell fell upon them. Over the battle field, so recently filled with the thunder of two thousand guns, there reigned the silence of the grave.

*   *   *

The French retreat had begun even while the battle of 18 October had been in full swing. Gyulai had reported Bertrand's break-out during the afternoon and the small Austrian detachment at Weissenfels had been warned to drop the bridge. Napoleon had ordered the retreat to begin at 11.00 a.m. and from that time a stream of traffic began to move down the Lindenau causeway. Everything not immediately needed for the fight was sent off: baggage, artillery parks, camp stores, wagons. At 4.00 p.m. I, III and V Cavalry Corps were ordered west of Lindenau. By evening, news of the retreat reached Blücher and while the rest of the army bivouacked, Yorck's weary corps was sent to occupy the crossings over the Saale river at Halle and Merseberg. Marching all night, the Prussians reached their objectives early on 19 October – but elsewhere there was no coordinated plan led by Schwarzenberg to stop the French and then destroy them by occupying Freiburg, Kösen or Naumberg, or by destroying bridges using the allies' considerable advantage in cavalry and Cossacks. The only formation sent in pursuit, apart from Yorck's corps, was Bubna's Austrian light division. Possibly the allies were only too glad to offer Napoleon the chance to disappear, so as not to have to face him in person when the attack on Leipzig was resumed – for the attack was to be resumed. Schwarzenberg's orders for 19 October were simple: 'All parts of the Army must be ready in battle order at daybreak to renew the battle. In case of the enemy's retreat, the army will advance, as on the 18th, in five columns concentrically on Leipzig …'

Napoleon, meanwhile, had issued orders for the retreat of the rest of his army. The city of Leipzig would continue to be defended by two Baden battalions, one Italian battalion and about 1,200 Saxon troops – the only remnant of the Saxon army left that was still loyal to their King. Macdonald, with what remained of VII and VIII Corps – which contained large numbers of Poles and Germans – and his own XI Corps, was ordered to act as rearguard and if possible hold off the allied attack for another day. The causeway at Lindenau was to be mined and blown up once the rearguard had broken contact and withdrawn. The rest of the army began thinning out from its forward positions at 2.00 a.m. on 19 October; by 5.00 a.m. allied patrols began to bring news of their departure. By a stroke of irony, it was a year to the day since Napoleon had marched out of Moscow.

At 7.00 a.m. the allies began to advance on the city once more and by 10.00 a.m. they had penetrated the suburbs. By 11.30 a.m. the remaining French and client troops had been driven in to the *Altstadt* and although they had stood their ground valiantly until now, with Napoleon himself gone the troops' thoughts turned towards safety. As the allies advanced from the north and south, the one escape route looked in danger. Fighting was desperate at the northern and eastern gates of the city and around the Parthe bridge, with fearful losses on both sides, but by 12.30 p.m. the allies were in the city: all hope for the French rearguard had gone.

Shortly before 1.00 p.m. Napoleon, who was sleeping at Lindenau, was awakened by the roar of a huge explosion: the causeway had been blown. The demolition had been in the charge of the veteran Colonel Montfort of the engineers, who, going to Lindenau to try to discover which corps was to be the last to retire, had delegated control of the demolition to a corporal, along with strict orders not to blow the charge unless the allies were about to capture the causeway intact. But with the roads crammed with troops, Montfort had been unable to get back to the site and the wretched corporal, seeing Russian skirmishers approaching, panicked and lit the mine. It blew up with appalling effect and, as the smoke cleared, the troops left on the far side realised that they must either fight to the death, swim for the far side or surrender. Thousands surrendered, others tried to swim, of whom many drowned. Macdonald managed to swim the Elster on his horse, but Poniatowski, who had only received his

Marshal's baton from the Emperor's hands on 15 October, was weakened by wounds and was drowned.

Just after 1.00 pm the Tsar and the King of Prussia, with Schwarzenberg and their staffs, rode into Leipzig market place. Cheering troops lined the streets, bands played, swarms of ecstatic civilians came out from their shelters in cellars to crowd windows and roofs. In the market square the sovereigns met Bernadotte and Bennigsen; Blücher and Gneisenau arrived a little later, followed by the Emperor Francis of Austria. The only other monarch present was the hapless King of Saxony – who was also titular Grand Duke of Warsaw -- Frederick Augustus. The unfortunate king had refused to accompany Napoleon and had remained in the city to meet his fate. He was arrested in the Tsar's name and later sent to Berlin as a prisoner of war.

The Battle of the Nations was over. The allies had lost by most estimates something like 50,000 killed and wounded. Napoleon's losses were far worse: the allies had taken 15,000 prisoners and 5,000 deserters, many of whom were Poles and Germans. Another 15,000 were sick in the hospitals, but 75,000 more had been killed and wounded. These included six general officers killed, including Prince Poniatowski; eleven generals and marshals wounded, including Ney, Macdonald, Marmont, Souham, Latour-Maubourg and Sébastiani; and thirty-six generals and marshals captured, including Lauriston, Reynier and Prince Emilien of Hesse. French materiel losses included twenty-eight Colours and Eagles; 325 guns – half the French artillery; 900 ammunition wagons; 720 tons of powder; and 40,000 muskets and rifles.

Napoleon crossed the Rhine with an army of 80,000 men, of whom perhaps 60,000 were fit to fight. There can be no doubt, regardless of Napoleon's attempts to disguise the fact, that the French army was comprehensively beaten at Leipzig: only the inadequacies of the allied pursuit allowed the campaign, and the war, to go on into 1814. There were complex political as well as military reasons for this, which will be discussed in a later chapter. But even in defeat, Napoleon was already looking further afield. There was a sense of defeat permeating the *Grande Armée*, especially among the Poles and other allies, which had to be over-come. In the wake of the death of Poniatowski, many Poles especially wished to return home. However, as General Henryk Dembinski later recounted,

> We resolved to accompany the French Army to the Rhine, and share its dangers until the last moment, and then return home. The Emperor welcomed our deputation favourably. He appreciated our chivalrous devotion ... He told the deputation 'Assure your compatriots that when they arrive at the Rhine they will be absolutely free to do as they wish.' Several days later, when we reached the Fulda, our corps

approached the main route at the same time as the Emperor was passing ... He addressed us for a long time, urging us not to abandon him. 'Read the *Moniteur* ... you will see that Poland existed in my thoughts ...' The conversation continued for over three-quarters of an hour, always in a tone of confidence and reproach.

Meanwhile, Bertrand had reached Weissenfels late on 18 October, where orders reached him to occupy all the country between Kösen and Merseberg, as well as Freiburg, and watch the passages over the Saale. He was also to collect all available stores and position these in depots along the army's withdrawal route. At the same time Kellermann, in Mainz, was ordered to collect all available troops, including recruits, at Erfurt and Würzburg, and to provision the latter city. Kellermann was also ordered to call out the National Guard for the defence of France itself, for Napoleon was sure that an invasion was imminent. Last, orders were sent to St Cyr at Dresden to escape as best he could. Torgau and Wittenberg could also be given up, provided that the garrison troops could escape and not be made prisoners.

The French main army retreated slowly on Weissenfels. Napoleon, unsurprisingly, was apprehensive about being pursued and caught, but he need not have been. At Erfurt he rested for two days before once more marching westwards. At Hanau on 28 October he was intercepted by a force of 27,000 Bavarians and 25,000 Austrians, who until recently had faced each other as enemies. The Bavarian commander, Count Karl Wrede, posted his men on open ground on the east bank of the River Kinzig, prompting Napoleon to remark that he had made Wrede a Count, but he could not make him a General! In a remarkable feat of arms, getting a beaten army to win a battle only eleven days after a colossal defeat, Napoleon pushed the Bavarians and Austrians aside. The army then marched on, reaching Frankfurt am Main late on 31 October and Mainz on 2 November, where he pushed out a light screen of cavalry and supporting troops to deceive the advancing allies. Schwarzenberg's armies reached Frankfurt am Main two weeks later and there they halted – of which Clausewitz said that:

> [Napoleon's] feigned defence of the Rhine, then, sufficed to bring the Allies to a halt and make them decide to postpone the crossing until the arrival of reinforcements – a period of six weeks. These six weeks must have been of incalculable benefit to Bonaparte. Without the show of resistance on the Rhine, the battle of Leipzig would have led the Allies straight to Paris.

Chapter 10

'*... to marry ourselves to the interests of Great Britain*'

The Strategic Flanks:
North America and the Mediterranean,
1813

In the week of 18 June 1812 Napoleon's *Grande Armée* had crossed the River Nieman into Russia, heading for Borodino; and Wellington had crossed the Agueda river from Portugal into Spain, heading for Salamanca. Both crossings were to prove fateful, if not decisive. Almost to the day, James Madison, President of the United States of America, crossed a Rubicon of his own by declaring war on Great Britain and beginning the attempt to bring all of British North America under the flag of the United States. Of course, this coincidence of events could not be known at the time and with the benefits of hindsight it is useless to criticise Madison's timing. In the early nineteenth century several weeks were required for news of such events to be passed from eastern Europe to Spain, London and on to Quebec or Washington: it is as far from Halifax, Nova Scotia, to Amherstburg on the western frontier of British North America as it is from Moscow to Paris – even without taking into account the additional factors of weather and season, roads and rivers, wind or horse power that governed the speed of communications. Six months later, in December 1812, with the defeats of Detroit and Queenston on which to reflect, the wisdom of declaring war must have seemed doubtful to many Americans, even more so when the scale of Napoleon's defeat in Russia became clear.

While these enormous events had been unfolding in 1812, and as the campaign in Central Europe developed during 1813, England's main contribution against Napoleon continued to be at sea: a constant blockade of all French and client ports, the maintenance of English trade and the interdiction of enemy commerce, and the seizure of colonies were all principally naval business, and after Trafalgar the French were never again able directly to challenge the Royal Navy's supremacy – in spite of building and manning large numbers of superb ships, resourced as they were with the finest timber, sailcloth, cordage and ironwork that the whole of their continental possessions could supply. Because of this essentially maritime strategy, in which the oceans – seen by many nations as a barrier – were to the English a thoroughfare, the war was taken to the French wherever an opportunity could be found. This inevitably opened up the need to protect the strategic flanks. For Wellington in Spain, the first and most immediate of these flanks was the Mediterranean.

* * *

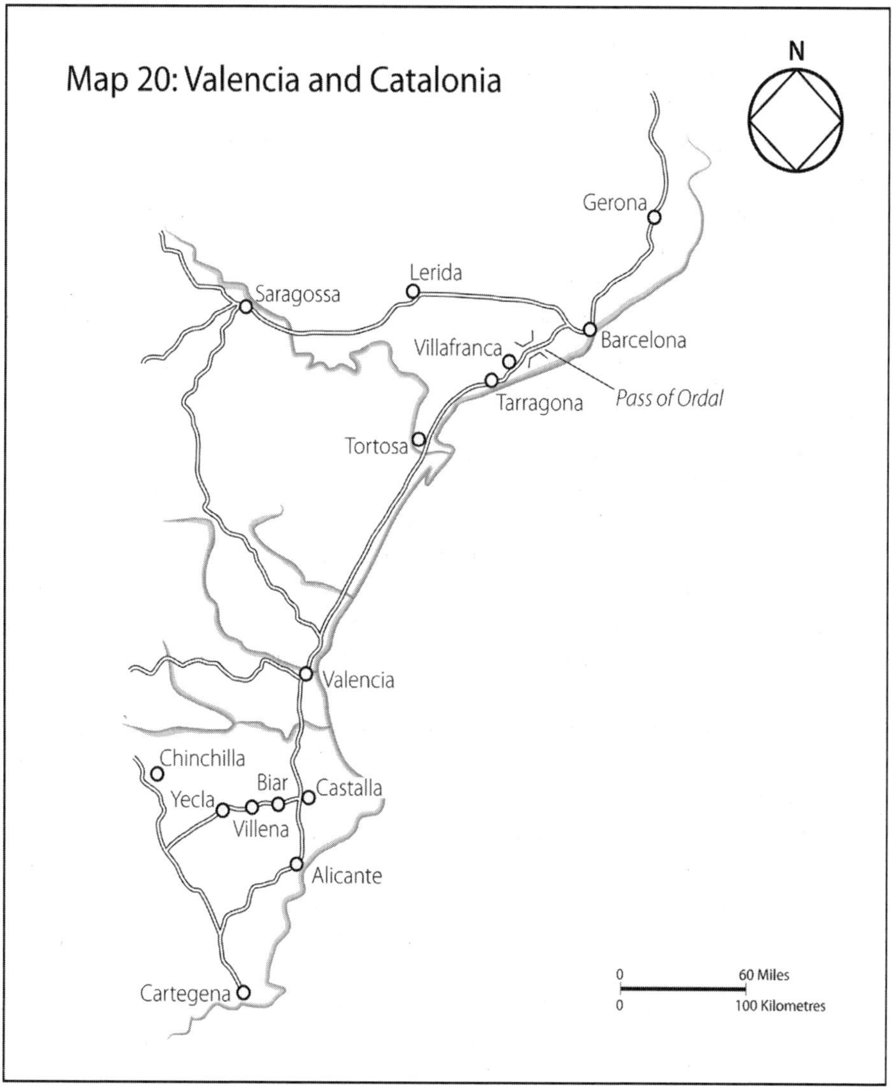

Map 20: Valencia and Catalonia

To keep the force ratios as favourable to Wellington as possible during the campaign of Vitoria, it had been necessary to stop the French army in Catalonia under Suchet from marching to join Joseph. Suchet had 75,000 men altogether, a formidable force, but the majority were tied down in guards and garrisons, leaving a field force of only about 15,000 men for active operations, without exposing the line of communication back into France to guerrilla attack. To keep them thus pinned down, therefore, Wellington had received authority in August 1812 to take the Anglo-Sicilian army at Alicante under his own command. This force of 18,000 men consisted of 7,000 British, 2,000 KGL, 8,000 Spanish and 1,000 Sicilian troops under the immediate command of Lieutenant-General Sir John Murray. All except the Spanish were troops sent by Lord William Bentinck from the British garrisons in Sicily, and it can be seen that it was a highly heterogeneous body. Even below the headline nationality figures there was complexity: the infantry consisted of six British, three KGL, four Italian and two foreign battalions in British service; two cavalry regiments – one British and one Sicilian; and some Portuguese and British artillery. One of the Spanish divisions was Castilian, under the Irish émigré Major-General Philip Roche, and the other Mallorcan (Majorcan), or Catalan, which was in British pay and commanded by Major-General Samuel Whittington, who, to make things even more complicated, was a British officer in the Spanish service.

More serious for Suchet was the added presence of the Spanish Army of Murcia under General Francisco Elio, more than 32,000 strong. Thus, although the entire allied force was numerically superior to Suchet's field army, it was weak in cavalry and artillery and contained some units of doubtful loyalty. Suchet had a high degree of autonomy since Catalonia had actually been annexed to France in February 1812: a Napoleonic ploy aimed at the Catalan independence movement. On the other hand, he was isolated from the rest of the French armies in Iberia and the only enemy he really feared was the Anglo-Sicilian force.

In late February Murray had wanted to go on the offensive and seize Valencia, but his plan had been thwarted by the removal of some of his best troops and by despatches from Wellington that told him to wait for detailed orders. On 11 April, however, Suchet forestalled him and himself went on the offensive. The initial French attack was delayed by a brigade-sized force under Colonel Frederick Adam in the pass of Biar, while Murray concentrated his troops at Castalla, about 35 kilometres north-west of Alicante, in a strong defensive position. The French attacked the next day but were badly mauled, escaping only through the courage of their rearguard. Suchet's main loss, as well as in men, was in reputation, for the battle further emboldened the Spanish regular troops and guerrillas, as well as putting heart into the Anglo-Sicilians. Murray, however, did not follow up his success, preferring to wait for Wellington's instructions.

These instructions soon arrived. Murray was to capture the province of Valencia; establish a secure base on the east coast in order to co-operate with the Royal Navy; and then force the French back from the lower Ebro. Murray's first move was an expedition to capture Tarragona, in the hope of distracting Suchet. This operation was launched in mid-May but French counter-moves to strengthen Barcelona panicked Murray, who re-embarked his troops and abandoned eighteen valuable siege guns, leaving the Spanish forces under General Francisco Copons, who had been co-operating with him, to face the French alone. The only good thing that came out of the adventure was that it did prevent Suchet from joining Joseph's main army at Vitoria.

On 18 June Lord William Bentinck arrived from Sicily to take over command of the army from Murray. He was too late to forestall the abandonment of the expedition to Tarragona and the army re-grouped at Alicante. Suchet, in parallel, was concentrating such forces as he could muster for a counter-move but the news of Vitoria saved Bentinck from a devastating French attack. Suchet retired first on Valencia, then to the Ebro river and eventually back into Catalonia, where his 18,000 men joined the 8,000 under General Charles Decaen. Bentinck followed up as soon as he had recovered the Anglo-Sicilian army, in cooperation with the Spanish forces of Generals Francisco Elio and Diego Del Parque, who would clear out the French garrisons in the fortresses of Valencia while Bentinck captured Tarragona. Initially things went well, but a counter-move by Suchet relieved Tarragona and only the presence of the Royal Navy offshore, supporting Bentinck's strong defensive position on the coast, checked him. Suchet retired once more into Catalonia, dismantling the fortifications of Tarragona as he went.

During August and September Soult wrote several times to Suchet urging him to join forces but Suchet refused. However, rumours reached Bentinck that Suchet had sent troops back into France and he decided to risk another move towards Catalonia. On 28 August the Anglo-Sicilian army began its third advance towards Tarragona, which this time it occupied unopposed. On 1 September Copons arrived with news of a French move northwards, which prompted Bentinck to march with all the forces he could muster: 22,000 of his own men and the division of General Patrick Sarsfield, another Irish émigré in the Spanish service and scion of a famous family who had also served in the Irish Brigade in France until 1789. On 5 September the troops began to move on Barcelona. A week later, on 12 September, the advanced guard under Adam had reached the pass of Ordal, where they were joined by Sarsfield's men – all in all, about 4,000 infantry, a few guns and some light cavalry. Suchet, meanwhile, had been assembling his army into two columns: the first of 10,000 infantry in three divisions, with 1,500 cavalry, under his own command, and the second of 7,000 French and Italian infantry in three divisions under Decaen. His intention was to attack through the pass of Ordal with his own column, while Decaen moved inland to turn the allied flank. Given the strength of the position, Adam and Sarsfield should have been able to hand Suchet the sort of treatment that Soult's men had received in the Pyrenees; however, Adam had not put out a covering force and the French, making a night march, surprised the allies and drove them from the pass. Suchet followed up, expecting to envelop his enemies; however, Bentinck conducted a skilful fighting withdrawal over the next days until Suchet's force ran out of momentum and supplies. The position stabilised around Arbos, about 20 kilometres west of Villafranca, and there the fighting stopped. Suchet dispersed his army, Bentinck returned to Sicily and before any further campaign could develop, Wellington was over the Bidassoa and into France.

*   *   *

Against the English and their maritime strategy, Napoleon's chief weapon was his Continental System. It had been this system, and its effects on the trading relations of the world and on England's ability, through trading revenue, to bankroll the coalitions against Napoleon, which opened the second strategic flank and turned the European war into a world war that also encompassed America, but this war was some time in the making. After a period of friction and confrontation that almost brought war between the USA and France, the Convention of Paris in September 1800 declared friendship and peace between the two countries. But its real significance lay in its provision for free trade and a lowering of tariff barriers, since even in 1800 Britain was piling up a large war debt that could only be serviced by exports of manufactured goods. Since nearly one-third of this export trade was to the USA, any reduction of it must help France. At the same time Bonaparte was engaged in the negotiations with London which led to the Peace of Amiens, and in concluding the second, secret, Treaty of San Ildefonso with Spain (the then owners of the Louisiana Territory), as part of which he took ownership of this vast area.

However, France could hardly take possession of the territory while still at war with England, for to do so would only invite the English first to blockade it and then to seize it; thus the Peace of Amiens provided the opportunity for Napoleon to secure the territory. Napoleon had promised never to cede the territory to a third power, but the news of the transfer seemed to President Thomas Jefferson to renew the prospect of conflict with France. This pushed Jefferson towards the purchase of the territory. He was in no doubt about what would follow the arrival of French ships and troops in New Orleans – 'in that case', he wrote, 'we would have no choice but to marry ourselves to the interests of Great Britain.' The matter was soon arranged and the treaty of cession was signed on 30 April 1803, binding the USA to pay 60 million francs ($15 million), with interest. This came at a time when federal revenue was at most $20 million a year, Gross Domestic Product about $500 million, and represents about $8.4 billion at today's rates: no mean sum, therefore. Spain had at this point no choice but to agree, but the deal was certainly one of the many causes of bitterness between France and Spain which later erupted into

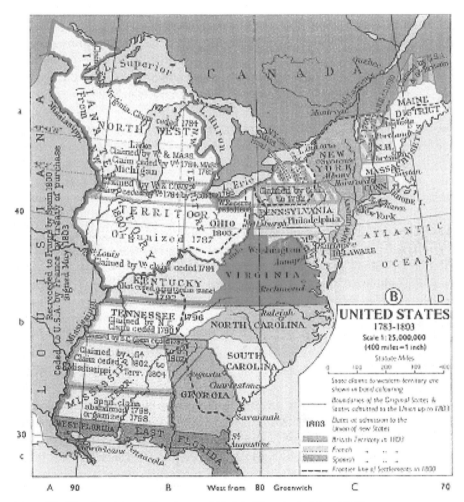

Map 21: The Louisiana Purchase. (*Muir's Historical Atlas*, 1974)

war and drove the Spanish into the arms of their ancient enemy, England. As it was, on 20 December 1803 New Orleans became an American city and the size of USA territory almost doubled.

The collapse of the Peace of Amiens in May 1803, shortly after the Louisiana Purchase had been settled, was also the trigger for Napoleon to push ahead with his Continental System. That it developed as it did, however, was the result of Napoleon's inability to carry through the invasion and conquest of the British Isles. After this, the system was really the only method for him to attack the English directly. In the aftermath of the collapse of the Peace of Amiens, French client states and allies, like Spain and Naples, were obliged to adopt the embryo system; so too was Prussia after the formation of the Franco–Prussian alliance of February 1806. The articles which established the Confederation of the Rhine in July 1806 forbade all those states too from trading with England.

It was not until Napoleon's first alliance with Prussia had overturned into war during 1806, and then war into conquest, that the Continental System was codified in the Berlin Decrees. In these decrees, which had monumental consequences for the Napoleonic state and its clients, Napoleon laid down the doctrine that it was the failure completely to exclude English influence which had led to the continuation of war. To bring the English to their knees, therefore, Napoleon proposed to put the British Isles in a state of exclusion. He was quite clear that in doing so, he was accepting war to the end: either England would be brought down, or his empire would be destroyed – there was no possibility of compromise. Napoleon knew well that the British national debt was enormous: in 1812 it had reached £609 million and by 1814, £725 million – multiply by about 1,000 for today's rates – at a time when Gross Domestic Product was about £330 million per year. It did not approach the same level again until the First World War. Only the export trade could service this kind of debt and thus maintain Britain's ability to sustain war.

The important articles of the Berlin Decrees were first, that the British Isles were placed in a state of blockade; second, that all commerce and all correspondence were interdicted; and third, that all merchandise belonging to England, or coming from its factories and from its colonies, was forbidden. The Milan Decrees in 1807 extended the system by putting pressure on neutral nations – but doing little harm to England. Any ship of any nation that submitted to search by the Royal Navy, or that paid any English dues, would be seized on entering a French port. The decrees, followed by those of St Cloud and Trianon in 1810, created the commercial borders of the French Empire, keeping English goods out but with the intention of letting French industry and commerce fill the gap. This completely Franco-centric system even went so far as to exclude manufactured goods from industrial areas within the Empire when they competed with France. In the industrialised areas of Germany like the Grand Duchy of Berg, for example, the resulting job losses were dramatic: 10,000 by 1810, a contributing factor to the revolts which broke out in the Confederation of the Rhine in January 1813.

The years 1806 to 1812 saw a period of enormous economic strain for the belligerent powers, and all Napoleon's diplomatic and military efforts were directed towards perfecting his system. The client states and allies had no choice but to accept the system, while other states were coerced into it by military defeat; by the time of the invasion of Russia, only Turkey, Sicily and Portugal were *officially* outside it. Not that the client states or reluctant allies were at all in favour of the system – quite the reverse. Louis Bonaparte, King of Holland, tried to gain exemption from it, but received the reply that 'it is the only way to strike at England and to force her to make peace.' But only two months later Napoleon was again writing to Louis that 'I am informed that commerce between Holland and England has never been more active.'

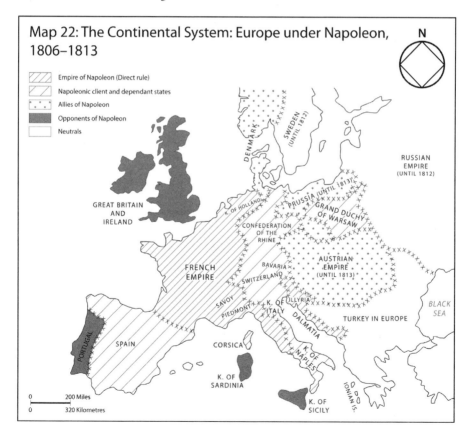

Map 22: The Continental System: Europe under Napoleon, 1806–1813

Where the system worked, and Napoleon kept out British trade, Britain suffered but so too did the rest of Europe, because the Continental System was not a blockade of Great Britain by France: the French navy was incapable of attempting this. Nor was it a blockade of the French Empire by the English: the English government freely issued licences for trading with Europe. The Continental System was a blockade of the French Empire *by itself*. But the Continental System really only worked where the French dominated all the coasts. France and Italy were relatively secure, but Spain, Holland, Belgium and the Baltic were never properly committed. Even so it almost worked, albeit indirectly, as America became more closely embroiled in the affairs of Europe. But the extension of the system by Napoleon's annexation of the north German coast was bound to offend the Tsar because it included the possessions of his cousin, the Duke of Oldenburg, which had been guaranteed by the Treaty of Tilsit. Napoleon therefore directly threatened Russian interests *and* violated the treaty.

Tsar Alexander had, as a result of the Treaty of Tilsit, joined the Continental System but he had never excluded neutral shipping, which of course carried English trade. Tilsit had also bound the Tsar to force Sweden to join the system and the Tsar had done so, by war, in 1809. But after this war the Swedes had continued to trade freely with England and indeed, the more closely Napoleon controlled the north German coast and Denmark, the more the Swedes benefited from English trade both in Sweden proper and in Pomerania. So the Continental System succeeded only in setting most of Europe against Napoleon, but given that only one-third of England's trade was with Europe, while two-thirds was with the rest of the world, it was the indirect effect of the system which most nearly brought disaster to England and which was to bring her into conflict with America.

In response to the Continental System, the English tried to do two things: first, to keep open the seas so that any neutral nation, especially America, could trade with them. The Royal Navy in general did a good job but of course French privateers did their best to counter this: they took 500 British ships per year on average between 1793 and 1815. On the other hand, by 1811 some 4,000 former French ships flew the British flag. Secondly, they aimed to penalise any neutral state which obeyed Napoleon. The mechanism for achieving that was the Orders-in-Council, issued in response to the Berlin Decrees from January 1807. The first order stated that 'No vessel shall be permitted to trade from one port to another, both of which ports shall belong to or be in the possession of France or her allies, or shall be so far under their control, as that British vessels may not freely trade thereat.' Subsequent orders and the system of licences – effectively exemptions – increased the pressure on both neutrals and states within the Continental System to defy Napoleon, and thus English goods continued to reach Europe in neutral ships. As time went on, the licence system and the relaxation of the Navigation Acts became vital measures for keeping Wellington's Peninsular Army fed, chiefly on American grain, even though they became one of the prime causes of war with the USA in 1812.

In America controls imposed by both France and Britain were bitterly resented, although it is doubtful if either Thomas Jefferson, or his successor James Madison, realised that the Berlin Decrees had brought in a total war. In 1807 Jefferson introduced an embargo act that prohibited US trade with all foreign nations. This act did far more harm than good, was widely ignored, and was replaced by the Non-Intercourse Act (1809), which prohibited trade with either France or Britain until each dropped their blockade decrees. This act again did more harm to the US than to France or Britain. Napoleon's response was the Decree of Rambouillet, by which all US shipping entering French ports or found on the high seas was subject to seizure. In 1810 Congress repealed the act, but offered to either power which respected neutral rights the reward of refusing trade with the other. Napoleon's response was that the Milan Decrees would be revoked on the understanding that so would the Orders-in-Council, and in November 1810 Madison gave London three months to repeal the orders and, receiving no response, re-imposed the embargo act. Thus Napoleon, who had no intention whatsoever of weakening his system, hoodwinked the US and pushed her further towards war with Britain. Certainly, given the trade figures outlined earlier, the most dangerous situation for Britain was a successful Continental System and a disruption to US trade: this is exactly what occurred in 1811.

The results for the British economy were dramatic. Lancashire was deprived of raw cotton and export goods began to pile up at ports. British exports to the USA fell from £11 million per year to £2 million and the government found itself forced to pay for vital American grain in gold rather than in goods. Weekly wages for workers fell by two-thirds, and in industrial Lancashire a fifth of the population was thrown onto the rates by unemployment as the mills were forced to close. Credit and gold became unobtainable and there was a run on the pound. Worse still, food prices almost doubled from their pre-war levels because of a bad harvest and the need to import grain from Italy, Poland and even France – which Napoleon permitted in order to accelerate the drain on his rival's exchequer. There were riots in Nottinghamshire, Staffordshire, Lancashire and Yorkshire, which required the diversion of troops from the Peninsula: the situation was critical, for a rebellion in England now would certainly have handed victory to Napoleon. But in fact, relief was already in sight. The embargo and non-intercourse acts had been hugely unpopular in

America, especially in New England, and were widely ignored by merchants, who were happy to continue to use British licences. In this they were encouraged by the English, who after 1812 continued to trade with New England while blockading southern ports from the Gulf coast to Long Island, thus increasing national divisions and anti-war sentiment in New England.

England's real saviour was the Tsar. His famous *Ukase* of December 1810 gave preferential treatment to neutral US shipping and thereby indirectly re-opened the door to English trade. In doing so, he spelled the death of the Continental System. Napoleon's invasion of Russia in 1812 accelerated the process by opening the ports of Russia and Sweden to British ships as well as neutrals: by the spring of 1813 British exports were at their highest level for years – total exports were valued at £118 million for the year 1812–13, while taxation yielded £68 million, or five times the pre-war figure. It was this that allowed England, with a population of only 18 million, to subsidise the armies of the Sixth Coalition that brought Napoleon down.

After the declaration of war in 1812 the only methods by which the Americans could directly attack Britain were the invasion of British North America and privateering. A series of single-ship actions early in the war had been largely favourable to the bigger American frigates but by 1813 British naval superiority had largely confined the small American navy to its bases. On land, after two dramatic failures at Detroit in August 1812 and Queenston in October, the American army had undergone a rapid transformation. The US Army's establishment was increased by Congress to 36,000, or thirty-one regiments, plus 50,000 volunteers – an enormous force far exceeding the small British garrison, but almost totally lacking in competent officers and NCOs. Most of the former were either raw young men or elderly veterans of the Revolutionary War. In the spring of 1812 the government appointed about a dozen other general officers, mostly aged veterans or part-timers from the state militias, none of whom was capable of exercising operational command. Most of these elderly generals had to be replaced within a year: the average age of an American general officer in 1812 was 55; two years later it had fallen to 33. The army was equally deficient in training and in practical experience; equipment too was in short supply, for a good deal of the army's clothing and equipment usually came from Britain.

Part of the problem was that the powers of the federal government were much weaker in 1812 than now – people spoke of *these* United States, not *the* United States – and the federal government had limited means of raising money, customs and excise duties being its major sources of income; these had been much diminished by the embargo acts. There was, therefore, a greater reliance on the military forces provided by each of the states: the militia, which

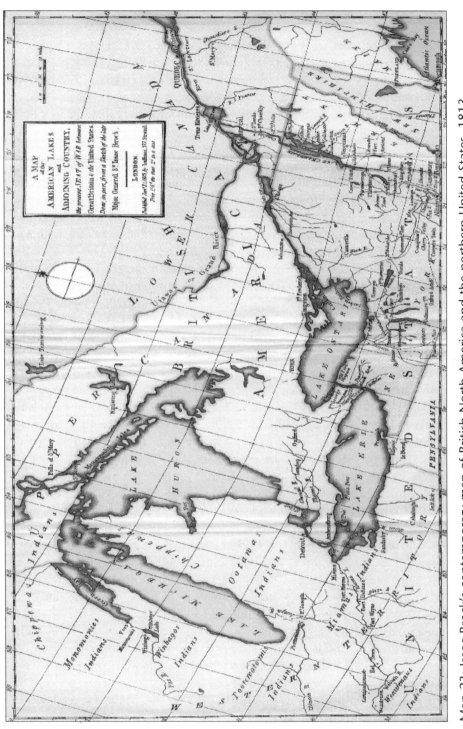

Map 23: Isaac Brock's contemporary map of British North America and the northern United States, 1813.

at a theoretical strength of 100,000, was the traditional bulwark of the American people against oppression. It was this citizen army which, according to popular mythology, had wrested victory from the redcoats and Hessians (the massive French and Spanish military assistance of the later years of the Revolutionary War was conveniently forgotten). Post-revolutionary America had no love for a regular army, but every man between the ages of 18 and 50 was theoretically liable for service in the militia. Almost twenty years of peace, a generation in effect, had eroded the capability of the militia: its discipline and training were lamentable, leading to much friction with regular units; its officers were elected; and men with farms to run were unwilling to tramp off to the Canadas. But not all was gloomy: there remained a strong core of hardy men well skilled in shooting and field-craft, although in general terms the ability of the militia to conduct even limited operations was greatly in doubt.

During 1813 the American army launched three major offensives. In early January a force under Major-General William Harrison had invaded the north-western territories of British North America. Harrison was halted by the British and their native allies at Frenchtown and Fort Meigs, but the decisive battle took place on water: after the American victory on Lake Eire in September, the British were forced to abandon Detroit and the Michigan territory, since their line of communication was now severed. Harrison followed up on land, destroying the British force under Brigadier-General Henry Proctor at Moraviantown. The onset of winter and want of supplies prevented the exploitation of this success and the Americans withdrew to Detroit. Harrison, the only American general who had yet won any significant victory over the British, returned to Washington and was sent to a minor command in Cincinnati: he resigned in protest. In the northern, or central, front a second American army under Henry Dearborn attacked and burned York (now Toronto), the provincial capital of Upper Canada. Two weeks later he seized the main British base on the Niagara, at Fort George. A timely diversionary attack by the British on the American naval base of Sacketts Harbor caused the withdrawal of maritime support to Dearborn's force, depriving him of both mobility and firepower. Two British counter-attacks, at Stoney Creek on Burlington Heights and Beaver Dams – the latter essentially a victory for the native warriors – inflicted heavy casualties on the Americans and led to the evacuation of the occupied territories and of Fort George. The British completed their revenge by burning the small town of Buffalo on 29 December: the war thus took an ugly turn, for the torch and the scalping knife characterised operations in Upper Canada for the next year, leaving the frontier on both sides of the border in ruins. The third American invasion was led by the 61-year-old Major-General Wade Hampton and was aimed at Montreal and the St Lawrence. The invasion was left until very late in the year: it was not until 17 October that the force left its bases and it was 5 November before it was assembled close to Sackett's Harbor. Four days later the Americans began landing on the Canadian side of the St Lawrence but were stopped and defeated by a small force of British regulars, militia and native warriors at Crysler's Farm. The third American invasion, like the first two, withdrew back to its own territory. Days later, an agreement to enter into negotiations was reached and, although fighting continued well into 1814, these concluded with the treaty of Ghent and the end of the war largely on the basis of the *status quo ante bellum*.

Meanwhile, at sea, American privateers, backed up where possible by their small regular naval resources, continued with considerable success. The privateers interfered with the sea communications between Britain and the Peninsula, and Wellington's despatches are full of complaints about the inability of the Royal Navy to check their activities. They intercepted cargoes bound for Spain, their presence forced ships to sail in convoy, thus slowing down the supply rate, and they attacked the valuable Indiamen and Guineamen carrying rich cargoes from Asia and Africa. Privateering did, however, have disadvantages: it diverted the best seamen and resources from the US Navy, and because it was private enterprise, it was more likely to try to intercept the rich, profitable Indiaman than the less glamorous, but vital, supply brig loaded with weapons, ammunition or equipment. On the other side, the British blockade on American ports was highly effective, for US shipping losses were greater in volume – and therefore far greater in effect – than those of Britain, for the Royal Navy took 1,400 American ships and 20,000 seamen between 1812 and 1815, effectively stopping all American trade except for that needed by England, and bankrupting the US exchequer. US Gross Domestic Product rose dramatically between 1803 and 1814, from $0.5 billion to $1.1 billion, reflecting the fortunes being made from illicit wartime trade – it fell back rapidly once peace was signed. However, government revenues never rose above $20 million a year and the burden of paying for the war was therefore insupportable.

This was, perhaps, the great paradox of the world war in 1813. US trade continued with Spain and Portugal, and with England's continental allies like Russia and Sweden. Through their ports, transhipped American cotton could be brought to English mills, supplementing that which was smuggled out with the connivance of the blockading squadrons. Trade also continued with British North America: US beef and grain fed not only the British Peninsular and Mediterranean armies and the Royal Navy that was blockading its coasts, but also the British army in the Canadas and the Maritime provinces – and also to a large extent the allied civilian populations of Spain and Portugal thanks to English licences. It was a trade which had to be kept going, even when for

England to pay for the food in gold meant that allied troops in Europe fell six months in arrears of pay. So while American and British troops fought each other in the Canadas or on US soil, and while American privateers attacked British ships on the coast of Europe, and while the Royal Navy and the US Navy did battle at sea and on the lakes, it was American trade and American food, bought with English gold, that sustained the allied war effort against Napoleon.

Chapter 11

'*... upon the Sacred Territory*'
The Invasion of France,
November–December 1813

The wars of liberation in Spain and Germany may have been over in the late autumn of 1813, but the war against Napoleon was not. England, Russia, Austria, Prussia and Sweden had been bound together by the treaties signed at Reichenbach and Teplitz; Spain, Portugal and Hanover had been allies throughout the struggle in Iberia. Bavaria had acceded to the cause of the allies by the Treaty of Reid in October and therefore the Sixth Coalition, although not yet bound as Castlereagh wished by one single agreement, was now a very effective political, military and diplomatic unit. Under these various treaties, the allies had essentially agreed to fight for the dissolution of the Confederation of the Rhine and the freedom of the independent nations of Europe from French influence. Significantly, they had also agreed not to make any separate negotiations for peace. Once the allied armies reached the Rhine and the Pyrenees, the first major objectives were achieved: the Confederation was utterly ruined; Prussia had regained her old boundaries; the independent states of Germany were restored; and Spain was cleared except for Catalonia. But there was no general agreement on Napoleon's strength or capability for further mischief. This being so, it was Metternich's view that new negotiations must be opened, and he was determined to take up the proposals which Napoleon had offered through Merveldt in the middle of the battle of Leipzig. Lord Aberdeen, the English Ambassador to the Austrian court, agreed: England, having expended huge sums on subsidising the coalition and funding the Peninsular War, was not opposed to peace if the terms were right. The Tsar too agreed in principle. Frederick William concurred with Graf Yorck's view, that the army needed time to recover. Bernadotte had by this time been diverted by a campaign in Denmark, in order to annex its dependency Norway to the Swedish crown. His view was that a campaign in France now might lose all that had been won thus far.

A meeting between the Tsar, Aberdeen and Metternich took place in Meiningen on 29 October. Here it was agreed to lay down as the basis of peace the so-called 'natural frontiers' of France – the Rhine, the Alps and the Pyrenees

– while at the same time issuing a proclamation to the people of France laying out the allies' war aims. It was further agreed that the publication of this proclamation, or manifesto, as well as the despatch of envoys to state terms to Napoleon, should take place before the main allied armies entered France – Wellington was already there. Therefore, although the Rhine fortresses were to be besieged and plans developed, no further offensives would be launched until Napoleon answered the allies' demands. If he rejected peace, or tried to undermine allied unity by making separate treaties, this would be publicly announced and it would mean war to the end. Thus the French people would, it was hoped, blame Napoleon for any continuation of a ruinous and probably hopeless war.

Meanwhile further south, it was not until a month after the crossing of the Bidassoa, on 31 October, that Pamplona surrendered, thus releasing all British, Portuguese and German troops, as well as the best of the Spanish, for Wellington's offensive operations deeper into France. It had not, however, been solely the need to complete the reduction of Pamplona that had caused him to pause once more. The news of Dennewitz, Kulm and the Katzbach had trickled in, but Wellington was waiting for a greater sign. He got it after the Nivelle. On the night of the battle, Wellington had invited the captured commander of the French 88th Regiment to supper. A rather brusque interview with the staff had met with only morose silence from the Frenchman, but Wellington thought that a good meal and a bottle of Madeira might do the trick. After supper, Wellington casually asked after the location of Napoleon's headquarters. 'Monseigneur', replied the Frenchman, 'Il n'y a plus de quartier général.' He related the first news of the calamity at Leipzig, of which the news had just been received. 'Then,' wrote Wellington, 'I saw the way clearly to Bordeaux and Paris.' The German troops in Soult's army obviously felt the same way: at the Nive the whole brigade deserted to the allies except for one battalion, which was disarmed and interned. Wellington realised immediately that after Leipzig, the invasion of France from several directions was a strategic and operational inevitability: the only question was, when? Napoleon was known to have withdrawn behind the Rhine, but would the allies follow at once? If so, Wellington would be obliged to co-operate, but if the armies went into quarters, Napoleon might order the evacuation of Catalonia, reinforce Soult and make the drive on Bordeaux that much harder. Wellington therefore needed to know more of Metternich's and Tsar Alexander's intentions.

These intentions still needed time to develop, and to carry them forward a fuller allied council took place in Frankfurt am Main in early November, attended by the Emperor of Austria, Tsar Alexander, Metternich, Count Johann Stadion-Warthausen – the Austrian ambassador to the Tsar; the Tsar's advisers

Count Karl Nesselrode, General Duka von Kadar and Pyotr Wolkonski; the King of Prussia's ministers Chancellor Prince Karl von Hardenberg, Karl von Humbolt and General Karl-Friedrich von der Knesebeck; also present were Lord Cathcart, Lord Aberdeen and Major-General Stewart from England; and Count Carlo Pozzo di Borgo, a Corsican nobleman once closely allied with the Bonapartes but who had opposed the Revolution and the Consulate, sought service abroad when the British evacuated the island and had declared a *vendetta* against Napoleon: he was now in the pay of the Tsar. The final member of the council was the former *Tugenbund* leader Heinrich von und zum Stein, now also in Russian service and chief administrator of all conquered territories. The council agreed that the Comte de St Aignan, brother-in-law to Caulaincourt and ambassador at the Court of Saxe-Weimar, should be sent to Napoleon to propose that French territory should be limited by the natural frontiers. If Napoleon would accept this as a preliminary to a general peace, then England would compromise over free trade and shipping. It was further proposed that, while not stopping the war, a neutral area on the west bank of the Rhine would be declared as the venue for negotiation. The last point was considered to be important, especially by Metternich, who did not believe that Napoleon would ever accept terms unless forced to do so by military defeat. He wrote as much to Caulaincourt on 20 November: 'Napoleon will make no peace, of that I am convinced, though nothing would make me happier than to find I am mistaken.'

Metternich would chiefly have been happy to be mistaken because he still feared that the destruction of France would tilt the European balance of power too far in favour of Russia. So far, Russia had done well out of the Revolutionary and Napoleonic wars: Alexander had gained territory from Prussia in 1807, from Austria in 1809, Swedish Finland in 1809 and Turkish Bessarabia in 1811. The Tsar had now also re-conquered Poland and Metternich feared that Alexander might want even more, perhaps at the expense of Austria. The position of the Bourbons was also in question: was Napoleon now so much hated that the French people would return to the old allegiance? The messengers from London assured Wellington that this was so, but his own feeling was that although the French people – including many in government – might be tired of Napoleon, to the extent that they might not support him actively, rapacious behaviour by the invading allied armies might yet convince them that he was still their best prospect. Wellington's despatch of 21 November set this out:

> The Allies ought to agree on a Sovereign for France instead of Napoleon, if it is intended that Europe should ever enjoy peace . . . [but] Possibly all the Powers of Europe require peace even more than

the French. If Buonaparte became moderate he would probably be as good a sovereign as we could desire in France. If he did not ... he would find himself engaged single-handed against an insurgent France as well as all Europe.

All the signs were that Bonaparte would fight and thus continued allied solidarity was still the over-riding consideration. In parallel with diplomatic activity, therefore, an allied campaign plan for the invasion of France had to be drawn up. This was done principally at the Tsar's insistence, in spite of Metternich's suspicions of the Tsar's ambitions: the Russian armies were now larger, stronger and fresher than those of their allies; moreover, Russian losses at Leipzig had been comparatively light. If the Tsar decided to push on without his allies, the likelihood of Metternich achieving a general restitution of the old order would be slim. Metternich was therefore ready to approve only such military activities as would hold the coalition together and support his own objective. After much discussion, the plan agreed on was for Blücher's army, 107,000 strong, to cross the Rhine and engage the French field army, while the main allied army of 155,000 men under Schwarzenberg marched into Switzerland (then neutral but pro-French), and crossed the Rhine to link up with Wellington's army moving up from the south. This army would be reinforced as soon as possible by an additional 68,000 troops from the Austrian Army of Italy. The Netherlands would be conquered by Bernadotte's army. The Austro-Bavarian Army under Wrede, 100,000 men including the Prussian corps of Bülow, was to link Blücher and Schwarzenberg, protect Germany and guard the middle Rhine. Finally Bennigsen's Army of Poland would continue to reduce the remaining French fortresses east of the Rhine; once this task was accomplished, Bennigsen was to reinforce Bernadotte. It was a military strategy designed to avoid a major engagement, while pressuring Napoleon into negotiating seriously. On 9 November the main Austrian army began its move towards Switzerland, but on 13 November King Frederick William arrived at Frankfurt. He at once opposed crossing the Rhine unless all else failed, although Radetzky, Schwarzenberg and the majority of his own commanders – especially Blücher – were in favour of invasion. Frederick William also continued to hold to the view, perhaps rightly, that a period of rest was needed, for the armies were near exhaustion after the autumn campaign. He refused to move from this view and so operations were suspended pending an answer from St Aignan.

* * *

Wellington's moves, in concert with the main allied armies further north, had also begun. Soult's new defensive position on the line of the Nivelle river was forced on 10 November, but both it and the battle on the Nive, where Soult's terrible counter-attack almost shattered the allies, properly belong to the story of the invasion of France and will not be covered here. Wellington's knowledge of wider allied political intentions was, however, incomplete; moreover, he faced the task of trying to win over the southern French provinces with offering either freedom from Napoleon or any alternative, and of trying to adapt his military policy to an uncertain political direction. But even with this overall strategic and operational uncertainty, the invasion was a tactical certainty, for Wellington had shown that with Soult on the defensive, the allies could concentrate anywhere in the southern theatre, at a time of their own choosing, and break any position Soult took up. Surveying the Nivelle position, Wellington said as much to his subordinate commanders: 'Those fellows think themselves invulnerable, but I shall beat them out, and with great ease ... I can pour a greater force on certain points than they can concentrate to resist me.'

There was no matching confidence on the French side: 'The men are fighting badly. They are no good. At the head of such troops we shall certainly come to shameful grief,' wrote Soult. But even if the French army had no more stomach for the fight, Wellington was always afraid of the potential of the civilian population to turn guerrilla: '... in France every man is or has been a soldier. If we were five times stronger than we are, we ought not to enter France, if we cannot prevent the men from plundering.' For in order to maintain any kind of favourable force ratio against the French field army, as well as satisfy the needs of winning over the population, Wellington could spare no troops for internal security, lines of communication duties or garrisons. Thus before his next victories against Soult, he had first to win the battle for discipline in his own army, once it had 'infringed upon the Sacred Territory'. This would be no easy task with an allied army containing large numbers of Portuguese, Spanish and German troops who had seen their own homes pillaged and burned and their families driven out or murdered. Many were sworn to revenge. But pillage was also a necessity for the Spanish divisions, most of whose soldiers were literally starving because of their own government's continuing neglect. On the night after the Nivelle, Longa's Cantabrians indulged in an orgy of looting and burning in Ascain, which prompted an immediate riposte from Wellington:

> I despair of the Spaniards. They are in so miserable a state, that it is really hardly fair to expect that they will refrain from plundering a beautiful country, into which they enter as conquerors; particularly adverting to the misery which their own country has suffered from its invaders. I cannot therefore venture to bring them into France

unless I can pay and feed them ... If I could bring forward 20,000 good Spaniards, paid and fed, I should have Bayonne. If I could bring forward 40,000 I do not know where I should stop.

The upshot was that after the Nivelle, most of the Spanish divisions except for those of Morillo and Carlos d'España were left on the frontier investing the Catalonian fortresses. As Wellington wrote: 'I am not invading France to plunder; thousands of officers and men have not been killed and wounded in order that the survivors might rob the French.' Much to the relief of the inhabitants of the French borderlands, Longa's division was sent to Medina Pomar in Old Castile, Giron's corps to Elizondo and Freire's corps to San Sebastian and Vera. Here they were to gather supplies and recover the numbers of sick – up to a quarter of their fighting strength – from the hospitals. Thus Wellington made a conscious decision to reduce his own strength by 20,000 men who had fought with skill and bravery and deny himself another 20,000 who had not crossed the border. In the event, his determination to preserve discipline was greatly helped by the addiction of the French army to plunder, even in its own country, so that the invaders could be made to appear as liberators by comparison. Discipline amongst the allied troops was ferociously enforced, all forage was paid for, local mayors were invited to dinner by Wellington himself – no French general, child of the Revolution or not, would have done such a thing! This amazed and delighted the French people, who could scarcely believe such a manner of making war; soon they were coining money by selling foodstuffs to the commissariat, whose stores bulged with fodder, grain, meat and good drink. The allies, it was said, waged war not on honest men, but only on those who carried weapons. In vain Soult issued proclamations to the people to rise: the only guerrillas in France were those who took up arms against Soult's own recruiting parties. Thus Wellington, by this remarkable success, added at least an army corps to his strength.

As well as the problems with the Spanish field armies, other difficulties remained to be settled at government level before the invasion of France could be carried forward. In September Wellington had written to the Council of Regency, to the effect that as his recommendations for promotions and dismissals were continually overturned, he would offer his conditional resignation as *generalissimo*. The Regency, far from backing down, referred the matter to the *Cortés*, which was to meet for the first time on 1 October. This new *Cortés* was far more representative of the whole nation than it ever had been before but even so it declined to address the issue and in turn referred it to the Council of State, not the Regency, for a decision. On 8 October the Council issued a censure of the Regency and upheld Wellington's authority. But even with this satisfactory resolution, minor irritations continued. The Spanish press continued the accusation that Wellington had ordered the burning of San Sebastian and even that Castaños had offered to make Wellington King of Spain if he would but turn Catholic. Spanish customs officials too were found to be interfering with the supply of the armies through Bilbao and Passages. As Wellington said, in a comment which revealed the underlying Spanish political view of the alliance as a short-term necessity: 'The officers of the government would not dare to conduct themselves in this manner, if they did not know that their conduct was agreeable to their employers.'

Problems with the Portuguese government also rose to the surface. There was a clear feeling in Lisbon that the war was now far away from the national frontiers and that the burden of military spending was growing intolerable. The recruiting laws were allowed to lapse and recruits and convalescents were held back at the depots, so that many battalions in the Pyrenees were reduced to no more than 350 men of an establishment of up to 1,000. Beresford was sent back to Lisbon in September to try to resolve matters, but found the Regency in truculent mood. The real grievance seemed to be that with the transfer of the military line of communication to the ports of northern Spain, customs receipts at Lisbon – and thus the money to pay for the army – had dwindled. There were also worries about Spanish designs and hurt pride that recent dispatches had emphasised the role of Spanish troops while neglecting that of the Portuguese.

Spain was, after all, the ancient enemy of Portugal – it was only English and French intervention in the Restoration War between 1662 and 1668 that had allowed Portugal to wrest back her independence. Although differences had been buried for the greater good of the coalition, national priorities were once more beginning to surface as the unifying fear of the French receded – such is the way of coalitions. The Regency therefore proposed to Beresford that Wellington should form all ten Portuguese infantry brigades, with the support-ing cavalry and artillery, into a national corps under a Portuguese general. Wellington, in spite of the excellent conduct of the Portuguese units, was aghast at this proposal: 'Separated from ourselves they could not keep the field in a respectable state, even if the Portuguese government were to incur ten times the expense.' But Wellington took good care thereafter to be louder in his praise of the Portuguese in his dispatches. The underlying success of the integration of Portuguese and British troops could not, and was not, denied by anyone. If proof were needed, it came in 1815 when Wellington made an urgent, but fruitless, application for a Portuguese contingent to fight in the Netherlands.

* * *

Metternich, meanwhile, had been hard at work drawing up the allied proclamation to the French people, designed to undermine Bonaparte. Distributed by the thousand on the west bank of the Rhine, it was generally reckoned to be a masterpiece – even Napoleon praised it as appealing to the French character. The manifesto stated that the allies were united in the belief that French power must be confined within the natural frontiers; the allies did not make war on France herself, but against Napoleon's power projection outside these frontiers and the results it had had for the last ten years. The manifesto went on to say that the allied sovereigns wished to see France great, strong and happy, enjoying an extent of territory which she had not known even under her kings. Thus the first use which the allies made of the victory of Leipzig was to offer peace, not war.

Napoleon was certainly in a difficult position. St Aignan had warned him that the allies could not be divided and he was well aware of the psychological dimension of war which lay behind the manifesto. His position was not made any easier by divisions in the nation and the government. He himself still clung to the idea of making peace after a victory, thus keeping as much as possible of his empire. On the other hand his chief ministers, Maret and Caulaincourt, believed that no victory was possible; they were intent on peace as soon as possible. Next there was an influential group of men with fortunes founded on Napoleon's success: Charles de Talleyrand, Grand Chamberlain of the Empire; the Abbé Dominique de Pradt, Ambassador to Warsaw and Archbishop of Mechelen; and Karl von Dalberg, Archbishop of Mainz and Prince-Primate of the Confederation of the Rhine.These men knew quite well that Napoleon was doomed but believed that France, and they themselves, could be saved by making terms with the allies that laid every responsibility for Europe's sorrows on Napoleon alone. Last came the mass of the French people, willing to give up the empire but attached to the natural frontiers and the civic freedoms gained in the revolution. It was at the last two groups in particular that the manifesto was aimed.

Napoleon himself accepted nothing from the allies at once, but the allies' terms were no secret and they became so well known that, as the Duc de Pasquier reported in his later autobiography, 'there formed in the palace, in the city, in the council a sort of league to push Napoleon into that way of safety. M le Duc de Vicence [i.e. Caulaincourt] was the soul of it, and M de Talleyrand was not a stranger to it.' Eventually Napoleon wrote to Metternich, suggesting Chatillon as a venue for negotiation and saying that he would accept the Frankfurt proposals if England would make it possible to conclude a peace founded on what he termed 'the balance of power in Europe, on the integrity of Nations within their natural boundaries, and on the absolute independence of all states, without any form of supremacy by sea or land.' If he thought this letter would succeed, he was wrong. Suspicion grew that Napoleon did not mean business at all, but was only attempting to divide the allies. He was wrong, too, because he misjudged the effect of the letter on Metternich. Metternich had already sent Pozzo di Borgo to London to ask that either Wellington, or Canning or Castlereagh should join the allied headquarters. It was Castlereagh, the Secretary of State for Foreign Affairs, who came. Secondly, Metternich believed that Napoleon's letter showed him to be close to collapse: only a little more pressure might be required to finish the war on the allies' terms.

Napoleon's next mistake was to try to divide the allies by ending his war with Spain. To do this, he proposed to release King Ferdinand VII from prison and restore him to the Spanish throne (thrusting his own younger brother Joseph Bonaparte contemptuously aside), in exchange for a treaty favourable to France. The driving force behind the treaty was the need for the 100,000 veteran French troops still on the southern front, which Napoleon now believed the only force capable of stemming the main allied invasion across the Rhine: their obvious lack of enthusiasm for further battle, as reported by Soult, seems not to have registered with him at all. To release them, Napoleon was prepared not only to offer Ferdinand his freedom, but also to restore all the territory and the fortresses occupied in the annexed territories of Valencia and Catalonia. In return, Napoleon asked for no less than Spanish withdrawal from the coalition, free pardon for all collaborators – the *Afrancesados* – and the removal of all allied troops from Spanish territory. Thus Spain would cease to be a base for allied operations and Wellington's army would be confined to its small bridgehead in France between the Bidassoa and Ardour rivers, with the port of St Jean de Luz the only supply base.

On paper this was an excellent scheme, but Napoleon failed completely to understand that Ferdinand would agree to anything in order to gain his freedom, but, such was his hatred of Napoleon, he had no intention of keeping his word when it was given under duress. Napoleon gambled on traditional Spanish hostility towards the English, but entirely misunderstood the intense anti-French feeling that had followed his annexation and the five years of repression which had followed, even after the devastating effects of the Spanish guerrilla war. That he could have believed that such an agreement *was* possible shows just how far Napoleon's grasp of reality had slipped – both of the reality in Spain and in terms of its effects on the allies. Ferdinand, in prison, understood the true situation better than Napoleon. On 22 November 1813 a draft treaty was presented to Ferdinand which, after two weeks' discussion and much feigned reluctance, Ferdinand signed. Next day, 11 December, Ferdinand's envoy the Duke of San Carlos rode to Madrid with the treaty, but also with the

King's private instructions, which were that nothing was to be agreed that might be contrary to the requirements of the alliance. The British government was also to be fully informed that as soon as the King returned home the treaty would be declared void. Quite independently, the *Cortés* also presented to the Regency its determination that nothing signed by the King in captivity could be considered legal or valid, so that when the treaty was laid before the *Cortés* on 2 February 1814 it was thrown out.

But from December 1813 until the rejection of the Treaty of Valençay, Napoleon acted under the belief that it would be accepted. He considered it highly likely that the bulk of the Anglo-Portuguese Army would be shipped to the Netherlands to support a popular rising against his rule there, a plan which had certainly been suggested by Lord Liverpool but which Wellington had been firm in rejecting: 'I am now as a commander sitting on the most vulnerable frontier of France ... Does any man believe that Napoleon would not feel an army in such a position more than he would feel 30 or 40,000 British troops laying siege to one of his fortresses in Holland?' But in this firm, if misplaced, belief, Napoleon had begun to draw off troops from the armies of Soult and Suchet. Wellington could hardly have believed his good fortune: the loss of the Spanish divisions had reduced the main army to 76,000 men in France, not including the cavalry, which was yet to come up, only slightly greater than Soult's total, while the Anglo-Sicilian Army and the three Spanish corps in Catalonia, a total of 36,000 men, were again at rough parity with Suchet.

In spite of Frederick William's doubts, on 21 December 1813 the main allied armies began to march west of the Rhine. Faced with this imminent threat, three weeks after Christmas 1813, Napoleon summoned half of Soult's cavalry with its horse artillery, two infantry divisions with their artillery and a large number of individual officers and NCOs to form cadre battalions in and around Paris. These 14,000 troops and thirty-five guns were followed by an infantry division and a cavalry brigade (10,000 troops and twelve guns) from Suchet's army. With the commitment to garrisons, this reduced the Army of Catalonia almost to impotence. At the same time the Spanish brigade in the French service was disbanded and sent home, so that by the early spring of 1814 Soult was reduced to 60,000 men including cavalry, National Guard and garrison troops, with seventy-seven guns, and Suchet to 18,000 and twenty-four guns. Of these, at least 9,000 were fully employed on guarding the lines of communication. After that, it was only a matter of time: the war ended on 17 April 1814.

*   *   *

It was George Canning who had foretold that one day a British army would stand on the Pyrenees and look down into France. And so it was. One soldier described it thus: 'From these stupendous mountains we had a most command-ing view of an extent of highly cultivated French territory, innumerable villages and the port and town of St Jean de Luz. We could also see our cruisers sailing about near the French coast which gave an additional interest to the view before us.' In Spain Napoleon had made his first major strategic mistake, an act so insulting and so treacherous that it drove the Spanish into the arms of their ancient enemies, the English. As Napoleon himself later said on St Helena, 'the whole affair was too immoral.' His second was the Continental System and his third, the invasion of Russia. These last two had given birth directly to the Sixth Coalition, but even so, the course of the war in Central Europe could well have been substantially different with the addition of 200,000 extra French troops tied up in Spain by the British, Portuguese and Hanoverian armies and the ubiquitous Spanish insurgency. The Peninsular War also made both Wellington and Castlereagh important figures in the allied counsels: even taking into account financial subsidies, the British record of resistance to Napoleon and of success in the field could hardly be matched. Then the victory of Vitoria, stiffening the resolve of the allies at Pleiswitz, pointed the road to Leipzig. And thus was Pitt's prophecy after Trafalgar fulfilled, that 'England has saved herself by exertions, and will (as I trust) save Europe by her example.'

Select Bibliography

Primary Sources

Archives de la Ministère des Affaires Étrangères (Paris)

Bonaparte, Napoleon, *Commentaires de Napoleon Ier* (6 vols, Paris, 1867)

Bonaparte, Napoleon, *Correspondence de Napoleon Ier*. Publiée par ordre de l'Empereur Napoleon III (32 vols, Paris, 1858–1870)

Bonaparte, Napoleon, *Correspondence inédite de Napoleon Ier* (3 vols, Paris, 1912–1913)

Bonaparte, Napoleon, *Mémoires et Correspondence politiques et militaires du Roi Joseph* (10 vols, Paris, 1855)

Bonaparte, Napoleon, *Supplément à la Correspondence de Napoleon Ier*. Lettres curieuses omises par le comité de publication. Rectifications. Ed. Baron Du Casse (Paris, 1887)

Bonaparte, Napoleon, *Lettres inédite de Napoleon Ier*. Publiées par L. Lecestre (2 vols, Paris, 1897)

Bonaparte, Napoleon, *Le Registre de l'Isle d'Elba*. Lettres et ordres inédites de Napoléon Ier, 28 mai 1814–22 février 1815. Publiés par L.G. Pélissier (Paris, 1897)

Bonaparte, Napoleon, *Lettres, Ordres et Décrets de Napoléon Ier*, en 1812–3–4 non inserées dans la «Correspondence». Recueillis et publiées par L. de Brotonne (Paris, 1898)

Bonaparte, Napoleon, *Lettres Inédites de Napoléon Ier*, collationnées sur les textes et publiées par L. de Brotonne (Paris, 1898)

Bonaparte, Napoleon, *Dernières lettres inédites de Napoleon Ier*, collationnées sur les textes et publiées par L. de Brotonne (2 vols, Paris, 1903)

Bonaparte, Napoleon, *Supplément à la Correspondence de Napoleon Ier*. L'Empereur et la Pologne (Paris, 1908)

Bonaparte, Napoleon, *Lettres de l'Empereur Napoleon* du Ier août au 18 octobre 1813, non inserées dans la «Correspondence». Publiées par X … (Paris, Nancy, 1909)

Bonaparte, Napoleon, *En Marge de la Correspondence de Napoleon Ier*. Pièces inédites concernant la Pologne, 1801–1815. Ed. A. Skalkowski (Warsaw, Paris, Lvov, 1911)

Bonaparte, Napoleon, *Ordres et Apostilles de Napoléon*, 1799–1815. Ed. A. Chuquet (4 vols, Paris, 1911–1912)

Bonaparte, Napoleon, *Correspondence inédite de Napoleon Ier*, conservées aux Archives de la Guerre. Publiée par E. Picard et L. Tuety (4 vols, Paris, 1912)

Bonaparte, Napoleon, *Inédites Napoléoniens*. Ed. A. Chuquet (2 vols, Paris, 1913–1919)

Bonaparte, Napoleon, *Lettres de Napoléon à Joséphine*. Ed. L. Cerf (Paris, 1928)

Bonaparte, Napoleon, *Maximes* (Paris, 1874)

Bourienne, Louis de (ed. R.W. Phipps), *Memoirs of Napoleon Bonaparte* (4 vols, New York, 1891)
Bulletins de la Grande Armée, ed. Alexandre Goujon (2 vols, Paris, 1822)
Caulincourt Armand de, *Mémoires du Général de Caulincourt, Duc de Vincenza* (3 vols, English pocket edition, London, 1950)
Caulincourt, Armand de, *No Peace With Napoleon* (English edition, New York, 1936)
Jomini, Baron (tr. H.W. Halleck), *Life of Napoleon* (New York, edition undated)
Wellington, Field Marshal Lord, *The Dispatches of the Field Marshal the Duke of Wellington*, ed. J. Gurwood (12 vols, London, 1834–1839)

Secondary Sources
Beardsley, E.M., *Napoleon: The Fall* (London, 1918)
Blumensen, Martin and Stokesbury, James L., *Masters of the Art of Command* (New York, 1975)
Broers, Michael, *Europe Under Napoleon 1799–1815* (New York, 1996)
Browning, Oscar, *The Fall of Napoleon* (London, 1907)
Chandler, David, *The Campaigns of Napoleon* (London, 1966)
Chandler, David, *Napoleon's Marshals* (London, 1984)
Clausewitz, General Carl-Maria von (tr. and ed. Michael Howard and Peter Paret), *On War* (Princeton, 1986)
Connelly, Owen, *Blundering to Glory: Napoleon's Military Campaigns* (Wilmington, Delware, USA, 1987)
Connelly, Owen, *Napoleon's Satellite Kingdoms* (London, 1965)
Creveld, Martin van, *Command in War* (London, 1985)
Creveld, Martin van, *Supplying War. Logistics from Wallenstein to Patton* (CUP, 1977)
Danilewski, Lieutenant General Mikhailovski, *Military Operations of the Emperor Alexander against Napoleon from 1805* (St Petersburg, 1886)
Dunnigan, James F., *Leipzig* (Simultaneous Publications Wargame, 1971)
Ellis, Geoffrey, *The Napoleonic Empire* (London, 1990)
Elting, John R., *Swords Around a Throne: Napoleon's Grande Armée* (London, 1989)
Esdaile, Charles, *The Wars of Napoleon* (London, 1995)
Forrest, Alan, *Napoleon's Men. The Soldiers of the Revolution and Empire* (London, 2002)
Fortescue, Sir John, *History of the British Army* (13 vols, London, 1899–1930)
Fregosi, Paul, *Dreams of Empire. Napoleon and the First World War 1792–1815* (London, 1978)
Hall, Christopher D., *British Strategy in the Napoleonic Wars* (Manchester UP, 1992)
Herrold, Christopher J., *The Age of Napoleon* (London, 1970)
Kerchnawe, Hugo, *Feldmarschall Karl Fürst zu Schwarzenberg* (Vienna, 1913)
Kissinger, Henry, *A World Restored* (New York, 1964)
Kraehe, Enno E., *Metternich's German Policy : I. The Contest with Napoleon, 1799–1814* (Princeton, 1963)
Markham, Felix, *Napoleon* (London, 1963)

Marshall-Cornwall, James, *Napoleon as Military Commander* (London, 1967)

Mowat, R.B., *The Diplomacy of Napoleon* (London, 1924)

Muir, Rory, *Britain and the Defeat of Napoleon* (London, 1996)

Nicholson, Harold, *The Congress of Vienna 1812–1817: A Study in Allied Unity* (London, 1946)

Petre, F. Lorraine, *Napoleon's Last Campaign in Germany 1813* (London, 1974)

Riley, Jonathon, *Napoleon and the World War of 1813: Lessons in Coalition Warfighting* (London, 2000)

Riley, Jonathon, *Napoleon as a General* (London, 2007)

Smith, Digby, *The Decline and Fall of Napoleon's Empire* (London, 2005)

Wartenburg, Count Yorck von, *Napoleon as a General* (English Edition, 2 vols, London, 1902)

Webster, C.K., *The Foreign Policy of Castlereagh, 1812–1815* (London, 1931)

Wilkinson, Spenser, *The French Army before Napoleon* (OUP, 1915)

Woolf, Stuart, *Napoleon's Integration of Europe* (London, 1991)

Index of Persons

Abbé, General Louis Jean Nicolas, Baron (1764–1834) 107–9, 125–6, 134, 137

Adam, Colonel Frederick (later Major-General Sir) (1781–1853) 188–90

Alexander I, Tsar of all the Russias, King of Poland (1777–1825) 6, 11–13; role in forming the 6th Coalition 15–18, 20, 194–6; at Lutzen 45–9; at Bautzen 54–61; Congress of Prague 65; role in forming the Trachenberg-Reichenbach Plan 70–2; at Dresden 144–51; August–September 1813 154–5; at Leipzig 167–84; planning the invasion of France and victory 201–4

Alten, Lieutenant-General (later General) Sir Charles (Karl), Count von (1764–1840) 76, 128, 139–41

Arakchaiev, General Count Alexei Alexandreiev (1769–1834) 72

Arrighi, General Jean-Toussaint de Casanove (1778–1853) 167, 172–3, 179

Ashworth, Major-General Sir Charles (c1778–1832) 107

Augereau, Marshal Charles Pierre François, Duke of Castiglione (1757–1816) 21, 74, 160, 171, 181

Aylmer, Major-General Matthew Whitworth, 5th Baron (1775–1850) 140

Baille, General Louis-Paul, Baron Saint-Pol (1768–1821) 96

Barclay de Tolly, Field Marshal Prince Michail Bogdanovich (1761–1818) 12, 51, 53, 56–9, 61, 143, 146, 149, 151, 159, 168–9, 179, 181

Barnes, Major-General Edward (later Lieutenant-General Sir) (1776–1838) 109–10

Bathurst, Henry, 3rd Earl (1768–1834) 37

Beauharnais, Eugène de, Viceroy of Italy (1781–1824) 20–5

Bennigsen (Benigsen), General Count Leonty Leontovich (1745–1826) 69, 71, 162–3, 167–8, 176, 179, 181, 184, 204

Bentinck, Lieutenant-General William Cavendish, Viscount Portland (1781–1828) 37, 77, 103, 131, 188–90

Beresford, General William Carr Beresford, 1st Viscount Beresford, 1st Marquis of Campo Maior (1768–1856) 34, 207

Bernadotte, Marshal Jean-Baptiste, Prince of Ponte Corvo, Crown Prince (Charles) of Sweden 1810, King of Sweden 1818 (1763–1844), role in forming the 6th Coalition 19–20, 24; role in forming the Trachenberg-Reichenbach Plan 70–4; at Dennewitz 157–8; at Leipzig 167–84; planning the invasion of France and victory 201–4

Berthier, Marshal Louis-Alexandre, Prince of Wagram and Neuchâtel (1754–1814) 9–11, 68, 159

Bianchi, General (later Field-Marshal) Vicenzo Frederico, Duke of Casalanza (1768–1855) 168, 171

Blücher, Field Marshal Gebhard Leberecht von, Prince of Wahlstadt (1742–119), early moves in 1813 11–18; at Lutzen 45–9; at Bautzen 54–61; role in forming the Trachenberg-

Reichenbach Plan 65–72; at Dresden 144–51; August–September 1813 154–64; at Leipzig 167–84; planning the invasion of France and victory 201–4

Bonaparte, Joseph, King of Spain (1768–1844) 25–6, 28–30, 32, 38–9, 77, 79, 81–5, 87, 89–93, 95, 97, 100, 126, 188–9, 209

Bonaparte, Napoleon, Emperor of the French, King of Italy (1769–1821): plans the Spring campaign in Central Europe 20–5; at Lutzen 45–9; at Bautzen 54–61; agrees to the Austrian mediation 63–5; Congress of Prague 65–72; plans the autumn campaign in Central Europe 70–2; at Dresden 144–51; August–October 1813 154–64; at Leipzig 167–86; retreats into France and final months 201–10

Boyer, Pierre-François Joseph, Baron (1772–1851) 138, 140

Bradford, Major-General Sir Thomas (later General) (1777–1853) 140

Browne, Captain Thomas Henry (1787–1855) 101

Bubna-Littiz, General Baron Ferdinand (1768–1826) 19, 62, 182

Byng, Major-General Sir John (later Field-Marshal the Earl of Strafford) (1772–1864) 112–14, 120, 123–4

Cadogan, Charles Henry Sloane, 2nd Earl (1749–1832) 87

Cameron, Colonel John (later Lieutenant-General Sir) (1773–1844) 107–9

Casa Palacio, General Marques del Torres 89

Cassan, General Louis Pierre, Baron (1771–1852) 131–2

Cathcart, Lieutenant-General Charles Murray, Earl (1783–1859) 66, 203

Caulincourt, Armand de, Duke of Vicenza (1773–1827) 10

Charles, Archduke of Austria – Carl Ludwig, Erzherzog von Österreich (1771–1847) 70–2

Charles IV of Bourbon, King of Spain (1748–1819) 26

Chasteler, General Johann Gabriel du, Marquis de Courcelles (1763–1825) 146, 164

Chernikov, Ataman of Cossacks Alexander 160

Clausel, Marshal Count Bertrand (1772–1842) 29–30, 81–4, 94–6, 102, 110–11, 113–14, 116–17, 119–20, 122–7, 134, 136–8

Cole, Lieutenant-General Sir Galbraith Lowry (later General) (1772–1842) 102–3, 106, 110, 112–17, 119, 124

Collier, Captain Sir George, 1st Baronet (1774–1824) 98

Colloredo-Mansfeld, General Hieronymous, Count von (1775–1822) 146, 176, 179, 181

Compans, General Jean Dominique, Count (1765–1845) 56

Conroux, General Nicolas François, Baron (1770–1813) 120, 122–3, 125, 128, 134, 138

Constantin, General Peter, Grand Duke (1779–1831) 55, 172

Copons, General Francisco de Paula María Baso Copons y Navia (1764–1842) 32, 189

Dalberg, Karl Theodor Anton Maria, Archbishop Freiherr von (1744–1817) 208

Dalhousie, Lieutenant-General George Ramsay, 9th Earl of (1770–1838) 85, 88–90, 94, 103, 106, 120–1, 128, 137, 139

Danilevski, Major-General Alexander Josef Michailovski (1789–1848) 182

Daricau, General Augustin, Baron (1773–1819) 138

Darmagnac, General Jean Barthélemey Claude de Toussant, Baron (1766–1855) 95, 107–8, 125, 127, 134, 136, 138

Davout, General Louis Nicolas, Marshal, Prince of Eckmühl (1770–1823) 21–2, 62, 71, 74, 160, 167

Dearborn, Major-General Henry (1751–1859) 198

Decaen, General Charles Mathieu, Count (1769–1832) 189–90
Delmas, General Antoine Guillaume (1768–1813) 175
Del Parque, General Diego de Cañas y Portocarrero, Duke (1755–1823) 33, 131, 189
Dembinski, Captain (later General) Henryk (1791–1864) 185
D'Erlon, General Jean-Baptiste Drouet (later Marshal) (1765–1843) 29, 80, 82, 84, 91–2, 102,
    106–10, 115–16, 119, 121–8, 134–8, 140
Dombrowski, General Jan Henryk (Jean Henri) (1755–1818) 74, 173–4, 179
Doumerc, General Jean-Pierre (1767–1847) 172
Drouot, General Antoine, Count (1774–1847) 47, 171–2
Duroc, General Geraud Christophe Michel, Grand Marshal of the Palace (1772–1813) 62

Elio, General Francisco Javier de (1767–1822) 33, 188–9

Ferdinand VII of Bourbon, King of Spain (1784–1833) 26, 32, 100, 209
Fletcher, Lieutenant-Colonel Sir Richard (1768–1813) 217
Foy, General Count Maximilien Sébastien (1775–1825) 27, 82–4, 94–7, 114, 116, 119, 122–6,
    134–8
Francis I, Emperor of Austria (1768–1835) 72, 178, 184
Frederick Augustus I, King of Saxony and Grand Duke of Warsaw (1750–1827) 67, 145,
    184
Frederick William III, King of Prussia (1770–1840), role in forming the 6th Coalition 15–20; at
    Lutzen 45–9; at Bautzen 54–61; Congress of Prague 65; role in forming the Trachenberg-
    Reichenbach Plan 70–2; at Dresden 144–51; August–September 1813 154–5; at Leipzig
    167–84; planning the invasion of France and victory 201–4
Freire, General Don Manuel (1764–1834) 131, 135, 140, 142, 206

Gazan, General Théodore Maxime (1765–1845) 29, 81–2, 84, 87, 91–2
Girard, General Jean-Baptiste, Baron (1775–1815) 43, 74
Gortschakov, General Prince Andrei Ivanovich (1779–1855) 170
Gourgaud, General Gaspard, Baron (1783–1852) 144
Graham, Lieutenant-General Sir Thomas (later General Baron Lynedoch) (1748–1843) 77, 80,
    85–6, 88–9, 92–7, 103–7, 122, 130, 133
Guyot, General Claude-Etienne, Count (1768–1837) 10
Gyulai, General Count Ignatius (1763–1831) 146, 150, 168, 172–3, 176, 179, 182

Hamilton, Major-General John (later Lieutenant-General Sir) (1755–1835) 139
Hampton, Major-General Wade (1752–1835) 198
Harrison, Major-General William (later 9th President of the USA) (1773–1841) 198
Hessen-Homberg, General (later Field Marshal) Phillipp, Prince of (1779–1846) 173, 179
Hill, Lieutenant General Sir (later General Viscount) Rowland (1772–1842) 77, 79–80, 85, 87–8,
    90–1, 94, 103–7, 110, 113, 115, 119–25, 127, 131, 138

Inglis, Major-General William (later Lieutenant-General Sir) (1765–1835) 136

Jefferson, Thomas, 3rd President of the USA (1743–1826) 190, 195
Jomini, Antoine-Henri, Baron (1779–1869) 58, 61, 64, 72–3, 148, 151, 153, 157
Jourdan, Marshal Jean-Baptiste, Count (1762–1833) 79–84, 87, 91, 94, 100

Kadar, General Friedrich Peter Duka von (1756–1822) 72, 203
Kellermann, Marshal François-Etienne, Duke of Valmy (1735–1820) 74, 185
Kempt, Major-General James (later General Sir) (1764–1854) 140–2
Kennedy, Commissary-General Sir Robert Hugh (1772–1840) 36
Kirgener, General of Engineers François Josef (1766–1813) 61
Kleist, Field Marshal Freidrich Heinrich Ferdinand Emil, Graf von Nollendorf (1762–1823) 20,
    42, 45, 49, 56, 75, 146–51, 154–5, 169–71
Klenau, General Johann, Count von Janowitz (1758–1819) 150, 152–3, 170–1
Knesebeck, General Karl Friedrich von der (later Field-Marshal) (1768–1848) 16, 72, 203

Lamartinière, General Thomas Mignot, Baron (1768–1813) 120, 123–5, 134–5, 137
Langeron (Langerone), General Count Louis Alexander Fedorovich (1763–1831) 75, 174–6,
    179, 181
Larpent, Judge-Advocate Francis Seymour (1776–1845) 36
Latour-Maubourg, General Michel Fay, Marquis de (1768–1850) 23, 61, 144, 148, 158, 172,
    184
Lauriston, Marshal Jacques Alexandre Bernard Law, Marquis (1768–1828) 21, 41–2, 44, 49–50,
    53, 56–9, 61, 170–1, 184
Lebrun, General Charles-François, Duke of Plaisance (1739–1824) 9
Lefebvre, Marshal Pierre François Joseph, Duke of Danzig (1755–1820) 160
Leith, Lieutenant-General Sir James (1763–1816) 132–3
L'Estrange, Lieutenant-Colonel George Guy Carleton (1780–1848) 113
Leval, General Jean-François, Baron (1762–1824) 89
L'héritier, General Samuel François de Chézelle, Baron (1772–1829) 144
Liverpool, Robert Banks Jenkinson, Second Earl of (1770–1828) 66, 76, 210
Long, Major-General Robert (later Lieutenant-General) (1771–1825) 117
Louise Auguste Wilhelmine Amalie, Queen of Prussia (1776–1810) 14

Macdonald, Jacques Etienne Joseph, Duke of Tarentum (1765–1840) 15, 21, 40, 42, 44–7, 50,
    53, 55–6, 61, 143–4, 156–9, 161, 167–8, 170–2, 179, 183–4
McGrigor, Sir James, 1st Baronet (1771–1858) 35–6
Madison, James, 4th President of the USA (1751–1836) 186, 195
Maison, General Nicolas Joseph, later Marshal (1771–1840) 57–8
Maransin, General Jean Pierre (1770–1828) 108–9, 125–6, 134, 136, 138
Maret, Hughes Bernard, Count of Bassano (1769–1839) 64, 68, 115, 208
Marmont, Marshal August Frédéric Louis, Duke of Ragusa (1774–1852) 12, 23, 27, 29, 41–9, 53,
    55–6, 59, 61, 73–4, 144, 149–50, 152–3, 158, 160, 167, 170–1
Martin, Rear Admiral Byam (later Admiral of the Fleet Sir) (1773–1854) 98
Maucune, General Antoine Louis Popon, Baron (1772–1824) 96, 114, 122–4, 135, 138, 140
Mendizabel, General Gabriel Iraeta de (1765–1838) 104
Merveldt (Meerfeld) General Count Maximilien von (1766–1814) 168, 170–2, 176, 178, 201
Metternich, Prince Clement Wenceslaus Lothar (1773–1859) 12, 18–9; Mediation and Congress
    of Prague 64–9, 71–2; role in the downfall of Napoleon 98, 201–4, 208–9
Miller, Colonel James (later Major-General) (1775–1855) 136
Miloradovich, General Michail Andreevich (1771–1831) 13, 42, 45, 50, 52, 55, 59, 146, 151
Montfort, Colonel of Engineers 183
Moore, General Sir John (1761–1809) 26

Moreau, General Jean-Victor-Marie (1763–1813), as adviser to the Tsar 13, 72; death at Dresden 151–3

Morillo, General Pablo, Count of Cartagena (1777–1838) 85, 87, 91, 112–13, 117, 124, 130, 139, 206

Mortier, Marshal Adolphe Edouard Casimir Joseph, Duke of Treviso (1768–1835) 74, 148–51, 153–4, 156, 170–1, 179

Müffling, General Friedrich Karl Ferdinand, Freiherr von (1775–1851) 59

Murat, Marshal Joachim, Grand Duke of Berg and Kleve, King of Naples (1767–1815) 1, 21, 149–53, 158, 160, 163, 166–7, 178

Murray, Major-General Sir George (1772–1846) 37, 95, 106, 112, 118

Murray, Lieutenant-General Sir John (1768–1827) 37, 71, 188–9

Ney, Marshal Michel, Duke of Elchingen, Prince of the Moscowa (1769–1815) 9, 23, 34; early moves in 1813 41–4; at Lutzen 45–50; move to and battle of Bautzen 51–61; autumn campaign 72–3, 143; Dresden and after 148–50, 157–9, 161–3; at Leipzig 167–84

Normann-Ehrenfels, General Karl Friedrich Lebrecht, Count von (1784–1822) 179

Odeleben, Ernst Freiherr von (1777–1833) 11

O'Donnell, General Joseph Henry, Count of La Bispal (1769–1834) 103, 106, 116–17, 124, 130–1

Ostermann-Tolstoy, General Count Alexander Ivanovich (1770–1837) 154, 167

Oswald, Lieutenant-General Sir John (1771–1840) 132–3

Oudinot, Marshal Nicolas Charles, Duke of Reggio (1767–1847) 9, 23–4, 41, 50, 53, 55–6, 61–2, 73–4, 144, 156–60, 170–1

Pack, Major-General (later Sir) Denis (1772–1823) 121

Pahlen, General Carl Ernst Wilhelm Phillip von der (1775–1834) 170

Pakenham, Lieutenant-General Edward, 2nd Baron Longford (1778–1815) 95

Palombini, General Giuseppe (1774–1850) 29

Paris, General Marie-Auguste, Baron (1771–1824) 138

Picton, Lieutenant-General Sir Thomas (1758–1815) 88–91, 112, 114–19, 124–5, 139

Poniatowski, Marshal Prince Josef Anton (1763–1813) 18, 21, 143–4, 158, 171, 181, 183–4

Pozzo di Borgo, Count Carlo Andrea (1764–1842) 203, 209

Pradt, Abbé Dominique G.F. de Rion de Prolhiac Dufour or de Fourt de Pradt (1759–1837) 208

Pringle, Major-General Sir William Henry (1771–1840) 107–8

Proctor, Brigadier-General (later Major-General) Henry (1763–1822) 198

Reille, General Honoré Charles Michel Joseph, Count (later Marshal) (1775–1860) 78–9, 82, 85–7, 89, 93, 97, 102, 110–11, 116–17, 119–20, 122, 124, 126–8, 134–8, 140

Rey, General Antoine Gabriel Venance (1763–1836) 97, 102, 105, 132–3, 135

Reynier, General Jean Louis Ébenézer (1771–1814) 18, 21–2, 53, 61–2, 157–8, 167, 176, 179, 184

Robinson, Major-General Frederick Philipse (later General Sir) (1769–1852) 132

Roche, General Philip 188

Ross, Major-General Robert (1766–1814) 114

St Aignan, Charles Paul François de Beauvilliers, Comte de (1745-1828) 203–4, 208

St Cyr, General Laurent Gouvion, Count (later Marquis and Marshal of the Empire) (1764–1830) 23, 74–5, 144, 146, 150–1, 153–4, 156, 159, 163, 167, 185

St-Pol, *see* Baille

St Priest, General Guillaume Emmanuel (1776–1814) 75, 174–5, 179, 181

Sacken, General Fabien Gottlieb von der Osten, Count (1752–1837) 75, 156, 174–5

Sarsfield, General Patrick 189–90

Scharnhorst, General Gerhard Johann David von (1755–1813) 14–15, 45, 70

Sébastiani, General Horace François Bastien de la Porte (later Marshal) (1772–1851) 23, 158, 184

Severoli, General Filippo (1767–1822) 29

Silveira, General Francisco, Count of Amarante (1763–1821) 85, 107, 117, 121, 124, 130

Skerret, Major-General John Byrne (1778–1814) 136–7

Somerset, Lieutenant-Colonel Fitzroy (later Field Marshal Baron Raglan) (1788–1855) 118

Souham, General Count Joseph (1760–1837) 29, 43, 170–1, 173–4, 184

Soult, Marshal General Nicolas Jean de Dieu, Duke of Dalmatia (1769–1851) in Central Europe 27, 29, 45, 53, 57–8, 67; in Spain 74, 100–7, 110, 115–17, 119–31, 134–9, 142, 189–90, 202, 204–6, 209–10

Soult, General Pierre Benoit (1770–1843) 84

Stadion-Warthausen, Count Johann Philipp Karl Josef (1768–1824) 19, 67, 202

Stein, Karl von und zu (1757–1831) 14, 16, 18, 203

Stewart, Major-General Sir Charles (later Lieutenant-General, Marquis of Londonderry) (1778–1854) 66, 174, 203

Stewart, Major-General Sir William (1774–1827) 107–9

Suchet, Marshal Louis Gabriel, Duke of Albufera (1770–1826) 29, 77, 79, 97, 101–3, 131, 137, 188–90, 210

Talleyrand-Périgord, Charles Maurice de, Prince of Benevente (1754–1838) 208

Tauenzien von Wittenberg, General der Infanterie Bolslas Friedrich Emanuel, Graf (1760–1824) 157–8

Taupin, General Eloi Charlemagne (1767–1814) 116, 134, 136, 138, 141

Thielmann, General Johann Adolf, Freiherr von (1765–1824) 160

Toll, General Count Karl Fedorovich von (1777–1842) 13, 70

Tormassov, General Count Alexander Petrovich (1752–1819) 13, 45–6

Torrens, Major-General Sir Henry (1779 –1828) 37

Tovey, Captain George (later Lieutenant-Colonel) (1787–1858) 114

Vandamme, General Dominique Joseph René, Count of Unsebourg (1770–1830) 144, 149, 153–7, 159

Victor, Marshal Claude Perrin, Duke of Belluno (1764–1841) 22, 53, 143–4, 149–52, 160, 171–2

Villatte, General Eugène Casimir, Count (1770–1834) 79, 87, 90–1, 102, 134–6, 138, 142

Wellesley, Field Marshal Sir Arthur, 1st Duke of Wellington and Viscount Douro (1769–1852), campaign in Spain in 1812 11–12, 26–7; use of guerrillas 28, 32, 78; coalition/alliance command 31–4, 98–9, 131, 205–7, 211; plans campaign of 1813 35, 37–40, 77–8; relations with Bentinck 37, 186–90; march to and battle of Vitoria 67, 76–98; on the Pyrenees 97, 100–16; sieges of San Sebastian and Pamplona 98, 104, 106, 131–4, 202; concentration at and battle of Sorauren 117–27; battles on the frontier, August–October 1813 130–42; crossing the Bidassoa 140–2; invasion of France 202–8, 210

Wessenberg-Ampringen, Baron Johann Philipp von (1773–1858) 19

Winzingerode, General Ferdinand Ferdinandovich (1770–1818) 21, 157
Wittgenstein, Field Marshal Ludwig Adolf Petr von, Prince of Sayn-Wittgenstein-Ludwigsberg
    (1769–1843) 13, 20–1, 23, 41–3, 45–6, 48, 51, 57, 59, 61, 65, 143–4, 146, 149–51, 169
Wolkonsky, Prince Pyotr Mikhailovich (1776–1852) 72, 146, 149
Wrede, Karl Phillipp, Field Marshal Prince von (1767–1838) 6–7, 73, 185, 204
Württemberg, Eugen Friedrich Karl Paul Louis, Duke of (1788–1857) 62, 146, 149, 154–5,
    169–72
Württemberg, Frederick I, (1754–1816), Duke of 1803–1806, King of 1806–1816 24

Yorck, Field Marshal Johann (Hans) David Ludwig, Graf von Wartenburg (1759–1830) 14–16,
    18, 20–1, 45, 53, 56, 58–9, 162, 174–6, 182, 201
York, Prince Frederick Augustus, Duke of York and Albany (1763 –1827) 37